Left of the Dial
Conversations with Punk Icons

David Ensminger

Left of the Dial: Conversations with Punk Icons
David Ensminger
© PM Press 2013
All rights reserved. No part of this book may be transmitted by any means without permission in writing from the publisher.

ISBN: 978-1-60486-641-4
Library of Congress Control Number: 2012913628

Cover by John Yates/Stealworks
Interior design by briandesign

10 9 8 7 6 5 4 3 2 1

PM Press
PO Box 23912
Oakland, CA 94623
www.pmpress.org

Printed in the USA on recycled paper, by the Employee Owners of Thomson-Shore in Dexter, Michigan. www.thomsonshore.com

Contents

Introduction

Over the last few decades, punk has become a Culture Industry replete with jargon, history, and identikits. My own small journalism-meets-folklore attempts don't try to undo the myths, tear down the walls, and provide a portrait that is any more authentic than has been delivered via ratty fanzines and box store biographies. I simply try to recreate punk on a human scale, person-to-person, and ask questions that flow like ticker tape in the back of my mind. My mother taught me this.

Armed with a proclivity for retracing events, she asks questions effortlessly. She is curious and open-armed, while my father is much more reserved and probing, unsatisfied with glib conversation and sometimes testy in his demeanor. I straddle both personalities, unevenly. When interviewing, I am drawn instinctively to the biopic curves of people, their charisma (or lack of), but I also desire to unearth some kind of incisive truth about them, however complex or faulty.

Punk, imported by my scrawny older brother, hit me when I reached ten years old and affected the full spectrum of my life. It corralled me into its aggravated aggression (not just a rhetorical stance), its fetish for a code of individualism, and its tenuous relationship with ethics. Sometimes punk seemed to offer scalpel-like observations, or offer refuge, a black hole in the middle of "normal" youth cognition, a zone or rabbit hole in which I could disappear. Looking back, punk seemed to de-monopolize culture. All the shaggy hair and Peter Frampton images burned away, as did *Hee Haw* and *Soul Train*, for better or worse. My "mind-forged manacles" fell off and dropped down on my dirty sneakers, or so it seemed, right as teachers began to enforce culture-at-large.

In middle school, when I was instructed to put my Circle Jerks shirt on inside out (the same shirt I wore to Black Flag, my first large punk concert, in 1986), my usually grin-and-bear-it mother took to the phone line, condemning the moral police, whom she considered onerous. Parent culture was not always on the side of hegemony, I understood.

Shawn Kerri's image of the skanker on that shirt later melded into my book *Visual Vitriol*, in which I was able to reprint her flyers and discuss her work to a new generation—those skankers to be. Touching her flyers, pathetic as it may seem to some readers, is my way of getting inside the skin of the times that were a few years beyond my reach due to the timing of my birth. Still, punk rock came to me like a secret language, a bold tonic, a soothsayer in tangled three chords, a golden oldie tune dynamited, a bold endless rush of saccharine, a feisty political gambit, and a creed I figured out on-the-fly.

Even when utterly moronic, punk felt like reportage. Sometimes it invoked a careening left-wing manifesto, replete with sweat-drenched drama. Other times it dripped with vile images, a compiled list of terrors, including skulking and monstrous figures, figurative and literal, that inhabited Misfits and early Dead Kennedys tunes. It was also a sonic tattoo, a signature of angst worn on the body. It offered predatory-like declarations of autonomy—"leave me alone"—that sometimes clearheadedly stared capitalism down, too, especially when soaked in Crass sentiments.

To critics, though, especially upon viewing films like *The Decline of Western Civilization*, punk seemed more or less akin to artless entanglements. Entrenched in ennui, punk become the calling card of germ boys and poison girls. Ensconced in its own destructive mythmaking, punk offered a study in psychosis. I saw punk's sheer audacious change-stirring revelation; they saw recast antiauthoritarian slogans shorn of context, a movement missing sober reflections, and logic that evaporated in millisecond guitar patterns. Punk was the trope of living wreckage, born of ill repute. I saw punk packed with conscience, from Better Youth Organization to Dischord, not mere discord. Punk was a genealogy of disgust, sure, and embodied enduring disagreements over its own aims. In punk dwelled a bent and unruly fanzine nation, a rough and ready van plowing down the road with Government Issue or Swiz.

Punk offered a bonus round of carelessness and overhastiness, unfazed determinism . . . The list goes on.

This book represents my stabs at recovering punk in words, from the bottom up, directly from the participants, the pursuers of dreams, the folk of punk, the informants, and the living actors. Conversations become a kind of litmus test—"this is what mattered, that opinion is bullshit, this is what happened, man"—in which the telling of stories, anecdotes, half-dim recollections, and off-the-cuff phrases becomes a landscape of memory. Each portion unlocks a satori, a glimpse.

Readers like me crave to touch the elusive identity of performers, though writers tend to understand that any identity is fictive, as Roland Barthes told us, no more than fragments of a multiple, like slices stolen from the locomotion of life. These fragmented identities, we don't realize until later, were made up on the spot, defined by double standards, or often reimagined. MDC never really had a steadfast plan, TSOL signed contracts in blood or flushed them down toilets, and the Dils hit the studio, aiming for compressed fury, not a diatribe that would box them in when they turned forty years old.

I am wary of canned Q&As, but I am also guilty of shaping and asking leading questions. Readers, I still hope, will feel immersed anyway, as if eavesdropping. In my own way, I tried to understand the essential selfhood of Mike Watt and others, and perhaps I did come close at times, while other times I spun around the subjects, ejected by them, experiencing no more than their piecemeal input. Sometimes I felt deluged in fieldwork, sometimes I felt immobilized by the speaker, spellbound, without tactics, groping, as if a voyeur. Sometimes I felt kinship and became close friends and cohorts, such as my experience with Peter Case.

I interviewed the punks on front humid porches next to hair salons; I interviewed them on tour buses between sips of spilled beer and off-color jokes; I interviewed them in dressing rooms dark and shabby; I interviewed them in vans reeking of mileage, petrol, and old clothes; I interviewed them on the phone, straining to hear every cell phone–bled vowel; I interviewed them using e-mail as clickety-clackety keyboards rattled through the weird silent night; and I interviewed them on the sidewalks and curbs, feeling the last heat emitted from concrete soaked in Texas sunrays.

These pieces, albeit in differently edited forms, found a shelf-life in *Maximumrocknroll, Houston Press, Thirsty Ear, Trust,* and *Artcore.* Many of them became the backbone of my magazine *Left of the Dial,* which ran for eight issues from 2000 to 2005, maintained by a network of volunteers, especially lead designers Russell Etchen and Ellen Dukeman. I later moved it online for a few years before I shifted gears and wrote for other sites. Many interviews became the research trove for *Visual Vitriol,* my book examining punk flyers and graffiti as urban folk art. The same book also detailed myriad subcultures, like gays and lesbians and people of color, which tested the democracy and pluralism of the movement. They all hark back to my zine *No Deposit No Return,* which my father spun out in small batches on a Xerox machine at his factory after-hours. I was a teenager trying to emulate the basics of DIY culture, mirroring the cut-and-paste aesthetic bible *Sniffin' Glue.* He was the patient and helpful father who probably still doesn't quite understand me.

Thank you, PM Press, especially Ramsey and Craig, for seeing the worth in this project. I thank the entire editorial staff at PM Press for their patience while sifting through hundreds of pages of transcripts—the whole barrage of my career, thus far. Though this digital era of print may not be the same as the early 1980s, when my brother returned from Chicago with stained punk rock singles and fanzines that smelled like used cigarettes, I still believe print sits in a reader's palm with purpose. These are the words of punk participants centered on the legacy of punk's sometimes fuzzy political ideology, long-term legacy, rupture of cultural norms, media ecology, networking and outreach aims, sexual identity and race relations, and musical nuances.

But don't forget to pause in the clamor, and see yourself as well, glimpsed in traces, between the lines, which sometime speak louder than words.

PART ONE

Tales from
the Zero Hour

Peter Case
(Nerves, Plimsouls)

"I was always sort of not interested in what my generation was doing," former Plimsouls and Nerves member Peter Case told me the first time I met him. He was flipping through Louvin Bros. reissues at a suburban bookstore in Sugar Land, Texas, surrounded by car dealerships, business parks, and seamless lawns. The skinny, five-o'clock-shadowed, gumption-filled rocker had a poise that reminded me of a cinema of solitude. "Yeah, I liked that one Velvet Underground record, the one with 'Heroin' on it," he murmured before venting about rock'n'roll's infantile, cream puff, lackluster edge. His bluntness was indelible. After he sang "Space Monkey" by John Prine, striking chords like he was chipping away at heaven, to a confused, grassy-haired five-year-old, I gave him a tape of Texas yodeler Don Walser's broken-down drive-in, Indian Country tear-jerkers.

"Thanks" fell from his lips, and over the last decade we have continued to trade music, play a rare gig together, and even write a book together. I still stand by a line of prose I first scribbled in ode to him: "Case knows you have to unhinge memories and know where to fall down. You have to die a little to remember anything at all."

In the early 1970s, you were actually going against the grain of popular music. I had this girlfriend, and she really liked me and started taking me to concerts all the time. Every weekend, she'd take me to a different one. I wasn't going to many myself, but she started carrying me to those things. She'd win tickets in a contest, or this, that, and everything. I was the only guy at the Led

Zeppelin show in 1969 in Buffalo who wasn't digging it. I just thought it sucked. It was so fucking boring. Ten Years After was not good.

Because it was all so bombastic?
No, it was just really boring. It was like really long, drawn out, and excessive. Even the singing wasn't right.

So, in a sense, you were already in the punk vein, which you pursued with the stripped-down Nerves style?
I was already a fan of things that were really good, but I was a real choosy fan. I was really into Lennon's first solo record, but I knew when *Imagine* came out that it wasn't as good. I knew "Crippled Inside" was not really a great song, just a piece of humor. Or Randy Newman's third record, too. People think I'm nuts. I knew by that record that he was no longer cutting edge. You could just hear it in there. It had become a formula already, and I quit listening to him. I love Arlo Guthrie for *Alice's Restaurant.*

But everything following was a disappointment?
I wouldn't say it disappointed me; I just never listened to the records. He was a complete genius in my pantheon, but that was it. He never let me down because I never got into the other records. Other people too would win your attention, and just lose it. Like the Doors, whose first two records were great, but I knew by the time *Waiting for the Sun* came out that it was bullshit. So, I didn't go for Grand Funk Railroad.

You told me once that Creedence Clearwater Revival was bubblegum.
People put me down and called it bubblegum. I liked "Born on the Bayou." That thing killed me. It was a really great brand of bubblegum, the great American bubblegum that Elvis made too.

Jack Lee from the Nerves found you playing on the street?
I had been playing on the street in San Francisco for about two years. The whole period of playing on the street was very exciting because it was almost the last gasp of the 1960s. Patti Smith has referred to 1974 as a huge energy year, and it was. There was an explosion in the folk clubs and poetry places. During 1973–74, I was on the street corner every night, from about 9:00 p.m. to 3:00 a.m. on Broadway and Columbus, right across from City Lights Bookstore.

Did you both decide to make the Nerves a different kind of pop band?
The original concept was that we were going to write these songs and play them on the street and be the first band that blew up right off the street. We were

going to do what the Beatles did, but our strip bar was going to be the street. We were fashioning a whole new approach to music. It was punk for us. Jack was the real prolific writer. I was a performer and wrote some of the lyrics, but I didn't have it together. I was recreating myself and learning a lot about music. I was low man on the totem pole, driving the car, and playing rhythm guitar. I was not a leader. I could have been, but Jack was way ahead of me. He had a mad vision and was kind of on the run, and Paul Collins was an enthusiast. We were going to use amps that had batteries and rock right on the street, go to jail, and get really famous. But the problem was that the streets dried up after the winter of 1974. The energy dissipated over that winter and never came back. That vibe was gone, and we entered into a period of attrition and went into the clubs. It was like, "Where is my generation?"

Did the generation of 1975 supplant the one you were already familiar with?
For a while, there was no generation.

A real Generation X?
It was lonely, and we were just busking around doing our own thing. It felt really bad. But we started crossing paths with bands like Crime, who were really raga-muffins. A lot of the punk rock people from San Francisco I knew from being on the street. We moved down to LA even before the Mabuhay started having shows and put on the first punk rock shows there with the Weirdos and the Germs. We had seven hundred bucks and rented a hall and invited everyone to play. Then we became the opening act for the Ramones on their tour.

By van?
No, by station wagon, actually, my first car ever in my life because I left home before I could drive Dad's car.

Did you know you were on the cusp of something, or do you see it as an accident?
We were disappointed because we were there, fostering this whole new thing, then watched it take off in commercial terms, but we were left standing in the station with a suitcase in our hands. The thing that we started and had a vision for didn't include us commercially.

Like Blondie covering "Hanging on the Telephone"?
There's something about Blondie, something they got, maybe their frontper-son. The whole period with the Nerves was like being in the Merchant Marine for me, like going around from city to city meeting people. It was very excit-ing meeting people like Pere Ubu and Devo. Yet, I still have never felt like I've

been a part of any of the waves that have gone out. It hasn't been my experience, for some reason. Perhaps because of my restlessness, which pulls me out before things pop.

The Plimsouls had the hit "A Million Miles Away."
We probably broke up before we had major success. At the time, I did what I had to do, and decided either the Plimsouls were going to do it with me, or I was going to leave them and go do it myself.

At after-hours parties at hotels, you often ended up playing acoustic guitar and blues songs you grew up with?
I was doing this jug band, with the Plimsouls roadies. I was doing it after the gigs, and it soon became more important than the gigs themselves. It was crazy, but that's what was happening with me.

On stage at your own shows, did you feel like saying, "This sucks"?
It was actually in Lubbock during the 1981 Plimsouls tour. I just suddenly woke up and said, "I can't keep on doing this. I've got to take it to another place." It was just a command.

You've never told me how you met Paul Collins.
Well, he met Jack. Jack was trying to audition drummers, and I was off on some adventure, so Jack comes up and says, yeah, I got this guy, he's really good. Paul just showed up at the door, and that's how he got in it. I think Jack put an ad in Don Weir's *Music City* over in North Beach. I think he auditioned fifty guys, and Paul was one of them. He auditioned by playing a beat on a phonebook.

How did you, a guitar player, end up playing bass, and Paul playing drums?
Well, Paul was already a drummer. He'd never really sung before. He wasn't originally a singer. Me and Jack were. Jack is a really good bass player, and I'm a better guitar player than Jack, so why I ended up on bass and Jack on guitar, I can't really remember [laughs]. Jack just wanted to be the guitar player, and he was ahead of me, so if I wanted to be in the band, I had to pick up the bass. Jack's a really good bass player, though. I had played in a few bands. Much later, Jack said, "We really fucked up; you should have been the guitar player, man." I was like, "Well, it's a little too late for that." But I just got into the bass. I love playing bass.

Tell me about the Hollywood Punk Palace gigs.
We got to LA in January of 1977 on January 1. We drove down on New Year's Eve and got into Hollywood and just got off on the first exit, like Vine Street, and

checked into the first hotel, called the Vine St. Lodge, basically a brothel. We
checked into that place, a horrible hotel. We started going around town. The
first thing we did, on January 2, 1977, we went to the Whisky to see what was
happening, and fucking Van Halen is playing. There were like sixty people there.
I was like, "What the fuck, they're still playing this kind of crap? This is ridiculous, how could you still be into this dinosaur music? What the fuck, man, this
is horrible." So, we leave. The next night, I saw Tom Petty and the Heartbreakers,
and we liked them a little bit more, and there were like fifty people digging the
show. It was empty at the Whisky, pretty much, for all these bands. We tried
to get a gig at the Whisky, and they'd go, "Nah, we don't really want your type
of band here, forget it." They wouldn't book us at the Whisky. We said, "Fuck
it, man." The first thing we did was rent out this place called the Punk Palace,
and we asked the Screamers to play. We met them, but they didn't want to play
because they weren't ready yet, and we just tried to get people to play. The first
gig was weird.

This glam rock band from outer space called Zolar X all lived in an apartment, and they all wore space suits around town, like to the grocery store. They
were a pretty famous band in LA, like Rodney and everybody knew who they
were back in 1977. We were driving down the street and we saw Rodney and Kim
Fowley walking down the street by Denny's on Sunset Strip, and we were like,
"Fuck, that's Rodney Bingenheimer," so we just hopped out of the car. We pulled
over and I go running over to him and say, "Hey, man, we're running a punk rock
show down on Sunset Blvd. Would you guys host it?" They were like, "Yeah, sure"
[laughs]. They started hosting the show, and the fire marshal came, too, and we
got into some trouble. That week right before the show we met the Weirdos.
They were using rehearsal rooms in what used to be the Columbia Pictures lot,
right off Sunset Blvd. at Beechwood, an old movie lot converted into a bunch
of small rooms where a few bands rehearsed. We just thought they were great,
and Cliff Roman still has this tape of our first meeting with them when we told
them, "Man, the Whisky is never going to book you guys. If you guys wait for
that, you are going to be old men and still never have played anywhere. You just
got to go for it. We've been doing these punk rock invasion shows. Just do the
show with us." They finally said, "Okay, but we don't have a drummer." And I go,
"Just play the show, and you will have a drummer." And that's what happened.

They played the show, and Nicky Beat was there. The first bill was the Dils'
first gig in LA, the Weirdos, and some weird criminals from New York City called
Short Ice. But they just disappeared. The Zippers, too. They were sort of power
pop. They were good and worked a long time in LA, too. They were hooked in
with *Backdoor Man* magazine people. We played that night, too, but the big hit
of the night was the Weirdos. People just went crazy. Our next show, I believe,
was the Nerves, the Weirdos, and the Zeros, and we moved up the strip to this

place called the Orpheum Theater, right across from Tower Records, and we put our last money on it, that's all I remember. We had like $700 or something from the band fund. We just put everything in. Though a lot of people came out that night, we were basically losing money on the whole thing, and we wanted to go on the road. Before this had all happened, we had booked our tour. So, we left, but right before we left, we turned the thing over to, I think, the Weirdos, and then the last one of this series of shows was the Germs' first gig. I used to talk to Bobby Pyn (Darby Crash) on the telephone in the middle of the night a bunch.

You were the first local Frisco band to tour nationally without a major label deal?
We were the first band in the United States to tour without a record label to support us. No one had done that before. We were the first fucking ones.

Ironically, later on, bands like Black Flag got all the credit for forging such ground in 1980s.
We were out there and played everywhere in 1977. We bought a car for 750 bucks. It was a black '69 Ford LTD, and we put twenty-eight thousand miles on it the spring/summer of '77. At times, we had all our equipment in it, and for a while, we were pulling a trailer. We just went everywhere—three people and our road manager.

Tell me about some of the bands you met.
We met Cheap Trick in Rockford, then we went over to Cleveland and met David Thomas of Pere Ubu right when we came to town, outside of Brown Stadium. He took me over to his mom's house or something, and we hung out there for a day. We met Devo, Pere Ubu, and then we went to Boston and met DMZ, and a couple of guys who were in the Modern Lovers. It just went on and on. We met the Ramones. We went to NYC and played Max's Kansas City, which we played for nearly a week at one point. We met Miriam Linna of the Cramps. In Cleveland, we met the Dead Boys, Stiv and all them. We also got fired from a few gigs, too. To fill in the spaces, we had these regular club gigs that Paul had booked at these big rock clubs. We'd go out to these places, and they'd tell us to get the fuck out. We got fired from a few, like Washington, DC. In East St. Louis, we were supposed to play for a week at this biker bar, and we got fired after the first night down there. That was a rough one. We didn't have any money. We were always broke and shit. We'd go out and do these scams with cigarette machines, like pretend we'd lost our change, to get money. The whole thing was one big hustle, trying to get from town to town. We were doing scams of different sorts to get gas and just barely made it around out there, but we were on the road for a long time.

You gotta realize when we went across the country in 1977, some cities had like one band, some had no band, that were doing original material. Chicago had like no scene. There was a band up there called the Hounds. They weren't any good. Then there was like the Boys from Illinois, or some shit like that. That was about as close as you got to something that was sorta hip up there in Chicago. There was nothing up there. Cleveland was Devo and Pere Ubu. Devo was from Akron, and so was Rubber City Rebels. New York had about ten bands or something, but everywhere else they had like zero or none. Two maybe, something, it was very weird going across the country at that point. There are more bands right now on *South Kalamazoo Vol. III* than there were in the whole United States back then. Most apartment buildings have more bands than there were in the entire United States back then.

When you played shows, how did you get the word out?
There was like a network. Greg Shaw was our mentor and friend, in certain ways, and he gave us a bunch of phone numbers of people who would be into it that he knew. Those people included Cary Baker in Chicago, Ralph Alfonso in Detroit, David Thomas in Cleveland, Oedipus in Boston, who was a DJ. Then he gave us Jim Nash of Wax Trax records, which was in Denver at that time. That was like the first stop on the tour, so we pulled up into Denver, and the gig was, of course, associated with the Wax Trax record store, and they had a whole realm of people that frequented that store, like maybe fifty people, or hundred, that were really into it. It was more like fifty, I think. The gig was right upstairs from the record store, and then they bought a keg and stuck in front of the record store. It was just like a three-day party going on there, then the gig was around that, and we were just hanging out, played in Boulder and there. It was all under the auspices of Jim Nash and his buddies from Wax Trax. There was a following for it in Denver, and we got to Chicago and they didn't even have a local band in Chicago. So, I met Patrick Goldstein who was a rock writer up there, and Cary Baker. They would publicize the gigs a little bit. A few people would come out, but really Chicago was a dead zone until we hooked up with the Ramones, and at the Ramones gig there was only like hundred people. Or maybe 150 at their best gigs, but it was that kind of thing. Cincinnati, the same thing with the Ramones, and they were on their third album. So, a lot of places it wasn't really happening. When we got to Cleveland, the place was called Hideo's Discodrome and it was up on Cleveland Heights. It was a great little record store. The guy who ran it, Johnny, had a band too. And he was friends with Destroy All Monsters in Detroit. It was a network of people. Then there were the friends of Devo and Pere Ubu and Rubber City Rebels. Once again, that was a party of the Discodrome and everybody came out and went to the gig.

Did the guys from the Pagans come out?

That I don't recall. I think there was a guy from the Pagans there, but he wasn't playing. I think he was a friend of Rod Firestone's. Rod was like a roadie for Pere Ubu. That's what it seemed like, and David Thomas was yelling at Rod Firestone, and I didn't realize yet that Rod Firestone was like a super-rocker at that point. He was just this guy taking a lot of shit from somebody. He looked like he was going to kill him. Finally, I think he told him off. Then we went up to David Thomas's mother's house and stayed there. That lyric by Pere Ubu, "My mother tells me my pants are too tight" is funny because she was standing there yelling at him about shit like that. Really funny man. We went to Boston and played with DMZ. It was, Conolly from . . .

From the Lyres.

Yeah, Jeff Conolly. They called him "Monoman." Our gig up there, the guys that were going to be the Cars showed up. Actually, at the time they were in the Modern Lovers. It was David Robinson, the drummer. They weren't the Cars yet, but a couple of those guys were there, and "Monoman" and his band. When we got to New York, Greg Shaw flew in, Phast Phreddie was there, and Miriam Linna. We played for about a week at Max's Kansas City, maybe four nights, with different bands on the bill every night.

One funny story is when we were in LA playing at the Punk Rock Invasion Show that was over at the Orpheum Theatre. Some guy says, "I paint the billboards on the side of Tower Records, and I'll paint one for you guys for fifty bucks." So, we give the guy fifty bucks, and he goes and he makes one of those album art paintings of the Nerves EP and he puts it up on the side of Tower. He was the guy who did that for them, right. All of a sudden one morning you go down there, and it's like, the new record by Boz Scaggs, *Saturday Night Fever*, whatever the crap was, and there's the Nerves record. The record companies freaked out and they called Tower and ordered them to take it down. They did. They took it down, because the companies were like, "Who are these fucking guys? This bullshit. We don't pay you all this money to have some upstarts come out and get their billboard up there for fifty bucks!" So, they took it down, and it's this beautiful billboard. So we're on our way out of town going on tour, and they gave us the billboard, and we're like, "What the fuck are we going to do with this?" We went, "Ah, fuck it." We just tied it to the roof of the car. So we took it all the way across the country. Everywhere we went we had this big fucking billboard.

Would you place it behind you on stage?

Sometimes we did. We'd stick it somewhere. We really didn't have it behind us on stage. We did different thing with it. Finally, we got to Max's Kansas City and we're like, "We're sick of this fucking billboard." At Max's, they go, "That's cool.

We'll just put it up here." And it was in Max's for quite a while. I think it ended up in somebody's apartment, I don't know where it went. Somebody told me they went into some girl's apartment, and it was in her apartment, so that's how it went, you know what I mean? Then down into Texas with the Ramones. It was continually the same thing. Word of mouth. The joke was that we booked the whole tour with one dime, because we'd go to the operator, "I lost my money in the phone. I just put two dollars in, and I lost money," and then they'd put the call through. That was before they'd been fucked eight million times. So, we booked the whole tour and made all the publicity phone calls without paying. We didn't have any money to pay for phone calls, so that's how we did it. On the way back at the end of the tour, we were broke. We had a bunch of Ramones T-shirts and we pulled into Wax Trax on the way back to LA, Jack and me, Collins stayed back in New York, but we went back to hang out for a week and we sold the Ramones T-shirts right off our backs for cash money.

How did you end up hooking up with the Ramones?

I was handling a lot of press contacts and trying to get some publicity for the gigs. We did it all ourselves, and then Paul was booking stuff. He started booking all these gigs. At one point, I don't know if he started talking to Danny Fields, who knew our tour route. He wanted to play Texas, so we booked the Ramones into Texas for the first time. You'd have to ask Paul, but we played Randy's Rodeo in San Antonio, and we played Waco, which was fucking crazy, with the Ramones. Those are the two Texas shows I remember. This is six months before the Sex Pistols played Randy's. It was a crazy, violent, and weird gig. A fun gig, too, but there was an element there that just wanted to whomp some punks. It seems like they got brooms from out of the broom closet and gave them to people and they were trying to hit us on stage with these brooms, like some guy was like, "Hey, let's go fuck 'em up. Here, get your broom." There were people with brooms in the front row swinging them at the stage, but whatever [laughs].

Tommy was real quiet. He was not street thuggish at all. He was a record producer. When he was like sixteen, he was working at Electric Lady with Jimi Hendrix. People don't know that, but he worked on those sessions. That's when he started. He was recording the Ramones, and they kept bringing these drummers in, this is all documented, and no one knew how to play, and Tommy was showing them how to play, and finally it was like, "Why don't you just do it? You know what to do." So, he did it. Then he was on the road with the Ramones. Now I mention to him, "You were really quiet on that tour." He goes, "I was depressed. I just didn't like being on the road. It was hard being on the road with the Ramones. A lot of problems." He was a real nice guy. The guy I hung out with and talked to was Dee Dee. He was the easiest guy for me to get along with. Joey seemed like he was on a whole other level, and Johnny was just a tough guy.

Dee Dee and I hung out one night and we were down in Houston in this all-night restaurant, like a Denny's or something. We were like real drunk, or something, and he's going, "I named the band. And I wrote like all of the best songs." He goes down this list of songs. I wasn't sure. Maybe he was bullshitting, because he was like the low man on the totem pole of the group, but he was telling me basically he was the main contributor. Then years later you find out he was. That he had named the group, but they didn't treat him like that. In fact, Johnny was really kind of dismissive of him. They seemed like they treated him with little respect. I walked into the club one night, and Johnny was yelling at Dee Dee, going off, and Dee Dee is just sitting there listening to him. Johnny is going, "Look, man, Dee Dee, you were just standing there last night, man. I don't care what happens tonight. I don't care if you just jump up and down, I wanna see you moving on stage tonight." I walk into the club later that night for the gig, and I look up on stage and Dee Dee is just standing there in one place bouncing up and down. Another time I remember we're all sitting there, and the club owner comes in, and he said, "Why don't the Ramones and the Nerves jam?" The room was quiet, and Dee Dee goes, "We don't know how to jam" [laughs].

You never really liked the term "power pop" and instead preferred the term "punk."

I guess it also related to all the 1960s garage bands, which were considered punk at that time, you know, that Standells '60s garage punk. So, I was really into all that stuff. That was the whole connection.

Did the Nerves spread graffiti and self-made media?

We used to do that but I can't remember much about it. Everybody did that. We'd write on walls. Yeah, absolutely. Everywhere we went. We'd write "Nerves," this or that. That was a big thing for a long time. That was sorta the start of it. The walls were still pretty fresh at that point. We did a lot of posters.

How did you relate to other bands in the San Francisco scene that weren't necessarily part of the punk fabric, like Psychotic Pineapple and Pearl Harbor and the Explosions?

Well that was a lot later, both of those bands. That's way later. That was during the Plimsouls. I gotta tell you, when the Nerves started up, there were no bands in San Francisco. There was Crime, and that was it. There were no Nuns, no Readymades, there was no any of that. No Sleepers. Those guys all hung out on like Polk Street. You'd see them around town, in North Beach. I knew those people by sight. But there was no movement yet. We did a residency on 6th Street, which went on and on and on. People didn't come to it. Like complete outlaws came to it. There was no punk rock movement. One night the Meters came in. They must have been down on Sixth Street scoring. They were like in town with the Stones. So we did this residency on Sixth Street, right up between Mission and Market, you know. A few people came. It was like complete outlaw. It wasn't like a youth movement; it was like a freak movement. And then slowly it started, and by the time we came back up in April, there was a scene at Mabuhay just kicking off. It was born right between January and March or May. The first time we got on the radio, they weren't playing any other local bands. The Nerves got on the radio. I think it was New Years Eve, 1976–1977. None of these groups were around. They were probably doing shit, but I don't know what they were doing. Pearl Harbor, they were actually a great band. They were really good. They were an incredible show, and had a big following. She was going with the guy from the Clash. The Stench Brothers were an incredible bass and drums combo, you know, but I didn't feel like it had anything to do with what we were doing. Psychotic Pineapple was like garage band shit. They were cool.

In 1977, Greg Shaw wrote that black music had no connections to punk rock, which struck me as weird, because obviously the Clash, Jam, and Chelsea were highly influenced by black music.

The Talking Heads were, who weren't really punk rock. But like Iggy and the Stooges, man, that's the connection that came up through the Ramones. Like Iggy is all about fucking black music. The Stooges were. They're about the blues man. Like Iggy ran away and went to Chicago and got into music from watching blues guys in blues clubs. That's where Iggy is coming from, from a really soulful place. Same with the MC5. Those were his heroes. The MC5, those guys were totally into black music. I mean they were like into James Brown and Sun Ra. Stuff like that. So that's the influence on the Ramones, for one. On the other hand, the other influence on the Ramones is New York girl groups, and the start of that whole thing was black, too. So the whole idea that there is no connection between punk rock and black music is a joke. There is no great music in the United States that doesn't have a connection to black music, including country. So, is that a slightly racist statement, I'm not sure. I think it is. It's at least deluded. Why they were so intent on there being no connection to black music, I can't get, but I dug disco. And nobody dug disco back then, but I thought disco was fuckin' rockin'.

Why did you like it so much?

Because it was soul music. There were some great fucking records. Shirley & Company, come on man. That was a rockin' little groove, man. I didn't like all that ballroom shit, but I liked when it was a funky group playing some shit.

When I was living on the street in San Francisco, I'd go down to the first discos. It was the only thing to go to all night. It was like the gay places up by Castro where you could stay out all night and sit in a club. You'd hear Al Green and all that shit. That was the start of disco music. So, I always dug that. So if you listen to the Nerves, like the track "Working Too Hard," the influence on a bass line like that is coming right out of Ike and Tina Turner. It's a fucking rock groove. It's a black groove. But you know, people didn't want to think about that at the time. But I was always into it.

And you used to play reggae songs on the streets in the early 1970s as well, right?

I wanted to be a reggae singer. I was nuts over reggae. I was at the very first Bob Marley gig in North America, which was at the Matrix ballroom in San Francisco. Me and my other guy from my street band ran in the side door. It was one of the best gigs I have ever seen in my life. Loud, fucking rockin'. Peter Tosh and Bob Marley, just a great gig. So, I was super into that. The other Nerves weren't really into it. Jack wasn't really into soul music, but Paul was. Paul was into black music. I mean Jack appreciated it but only through a filter of . . . he liked songwriting. He liked certain things about it, but Paul and me were really into it. I was always really into it.

Tell me about the Breakaways.

The Nerves fell apart. We had another guitar player, then we said fuck it, why don't we play guitar. Paul wasn't such a great drummer at the time, and he couldn't play guitar, so I said, "Man, look, we'll put you on electric guitar and turn you down until you learn how to play. As you get better, we'll just turn you up." Then we got a real drummer, Michael Ruiz from Milk and Cookies, so we were going to move to NYC and wanted to be something like the Heartbreakers. That was my vision of it, something like a real rockin' band.

But . . .

Eddie Money was an old friend of ours from San Francisco, okay. He used to have us open shows for him, I think, because everybody would boo us. He really loved the Nerves, and we'd play, and sometimes the audience would be really hostile to us, but he kept on having us play, right? He was playing packed clubs, but he wasn't signed yet, either. We were kind of friends. Eddie was a big drug addict, alcoholic kind of guy, and he was doing an in-store for a record and there were a thousand people lined up on Hollywood Blvd., and we went down to see him. We walked up to him from the end of the line, and he's sitting there, signing autographs, and he's like, "Paul, pull up a car to the back door, man. I got to get out of here, I'm going fucking crazy." So, we go get our fucking

car, pull up behind the place, and he comes running out and jumps in the car, and says, "Let's get the fuck out of here," and we go driving away. He says, "Man, you guys, my manager is driving me crazy, he won't give me any money, he won't let me go drink or anything. Let's go to the liquor store."

So, we go to the liquor store, buy a bunch of booze and shit, then we go, I don't know, just drove up to Paul's apartment or something, and we just all started drinking. He calls up his manager and goes, "I'm out here, man. I'm not going to tell you where I am at, man, fuck you," and all this shit. So, that was pretty weird. We spent the night with Eddie, then I had to split to take care of something. I got back about an hour or two later, and they had been drinking. I knock on the door to get into the apartment, and Paul comes out and says, "Look, man, this is really weird. Eddie wants to get us a record deal, but you have to go along with this. I told him that I wrote all the songs. He thinks I wrote all the songs, and I am doing the whole thing. You just got to go along with that. I don't want to fuck it all up." That's my buddy Paul, right? [laughs]. So, we go in there, and Eddie's all fucked up, going, "Fucking Paul, man, you are so fucking talented. Peter, I am going to get Paul a record deal, man. You can be in the band, man. We'll let you be in the band." I was like, what the fuck is this? He's talking about songs I wrote, you know, about how Paul is so fucking great, parts of songs that I wrote for Paul, like, "It's brilliant, man, fucking Paul, I'm going to get you a record deal." I said, fuck this, man. So I split. I just told Paul, "You can take your band and shove it. Fuck you," and I split, and that started a year of painting houses and other labor. That was the first time I had been without a band for a few years. Paul's like, "Ah, man, come back. Eddie's getting us a deal with Columbia and Sony." I was like, "No fucking way, man, I quit." I just couldn't deal with it anymore.

That began the downtime between Paul and Plimsouls?

That was 1978, so I had already put the whole band together for Paul, and then they immediately got signed. That band beat me out the door, but I went back and started working labor in LA. The Nerves' road manager, Ron, was going around doing all these painting gigs, so I just started painting and writing songs at night and just hanging out, and I did that basically through 1978. Then, on the very first day of 1979, I met this guy, Lou Ramirez, and he was playing this nightclub gig in El Monte, California, a country-rockabilly-rock'n'roll kind of five-sets-a-night, five-nights-a-week gig. They drafted me into that. The bass player and the drummer of that band ended up being in the Plimsouls, so we just started playing out there, but that's a whole other series of things. I finally got fired from that gig. The boss said, "Pete's on acid. He's fired."

Were you?

Nah, I was just drunk. I had taken a lot of acid at that point, so I really didn't need to be *on* it. What was going on is that we were working on our Plimsouls material. As the night went on, we'd get louder and louder, and by the end, we would be totally rocking. There were people coming and digging it, but then one night, the club owner came in. He had quit drinking. Usually they were carrying the guy out of the place, but when he came in one night straight and saw what I was doing, he fired me. Then the band quit, and the next thing you know, we started playing in Chinatown.

Those bars?

They started happening, so we played Madam Wong's. Some other time we played the Hong Kong. We played Club 88. It was the whole start of that scene. It was really weird because the Nerves played, played, and played, and people didn't really get it, but the first time the Plimsouls played, all of a sudden we had a huge following. Sometimes things just happen. When that band started playing, the whole thing just kicked in. There were people at shows, the shows were packed, and then we made a record for Beat records down in Redondo Beach at Spot's studio down there. The group in there before us was Red Cross. They were like twelve or something. We were pretty fucking young ourselves.

Why does it sound so subdued?

The *Zero Hour*? Oh, I don't know. I don't think it is subdued. We just didn't know how to get together any kind of sound. "Great Big World" starts off with acoustic guitar, then we got really drunk and put an Otis Redding track on there. But "How Long Will It Take" is not subdued; it's pretty rockin', if you go back and listen to it. That was the best thing on there. I don't know. We were a brand new band. We didn't know what the fuck we were doing. It doesn't feel subdued to me, but it just feels fucking trashy or something.

Did the EP or the intense live following attract Planet?

I think because KROQ was playing "Zero Hour," which became a bit of a LA hit. Then the shows were packed, and we had all these record companies chasing us around and shit. I don't like the Plimsouls records. The live stuff is the best stuff we did. Some of that's coming out on Alive. "A Million Miles Away" and that stuff are really good, and I like "How Long Will It Take" on that first record.

Do you think the attention from the Nerves releases and tour overlap into your solo career?

I've actually gone out and played that stuff at my solo gigs sometimes. You never know what's going to happen. It's so weird. When you've been putting stuff out into the world for twenty-five or thirty years or whatever the fuck it is, it's out there and it's doing its work, and people come up with it, whether or not there is any popularity for it. It's like a cult or something. People lock into it, and you hear from people who are way into it, hidden in these way out of the way places, and they got all the stuff. You never know what's going to happen. The stuff I am writing now in certain ways is really different, but in other ways, the ABCs of the songwriting are still the same. It's all one path, as far as I am concerned. But basically it's all in a line there, the different styles being developed. You see this thing from 1973 with me playing on the street, in a really weird way, is the proto-Plimsouls. I'm doing reggae and all that stuff back in 1973. The music on the street was a form of punk rock, which was a form of rock'n'roll, which was a form of Woody Guthrie.

But you have become more blatantly political with your songs.

On *The Man with the Blue . . .* record we had "Poor Old Tom." I was singing songs about homeless people and people on the street, and then I guess we got into it on that one song on *Six-Pack of Love* about Neil Bush, that me and John Prine wrote. Not too many people picked up on that. It's about the Denver savings and loan fiasco, called "Wonderful 99." Which, if you check out the lyrics to that, people are going to suffer because of the Denver savings and loan fiasco. I was really pissed off about that. These people ripped off the American public for so much money, and no one ever talks about that because it was like a bipartisan rip-off. One guy told me that the figures worked out so that they could have bought every man, woman, and child a Mercedes Benz. A total fucking rip-off. That was in 1991, the time of the first Bush.

And for you that goes back to Woody Guthrie?

I guess so. I mean, my first band was called Pig Nation in 1969 with Jim Whitford and Mark Winsick. They're still back there playing—and Mike Bannister, who is still out there from time to time, and now he's in a band called Burning Sky, a Native American band. And Whitford just made a record with Gurf Morlix, so we are still around. Our very first gig we got into the newspaper. We were part of the whole Yippie thing, the Youth International Party, antiwar, antigovernment.

Captain Sensible
(The Damned)

For many British punk "critics," the
Damned were no darlings: they were
the goofballs and hell-raisers—flash-
in-the-pan yobs that actually turned
out to be compelling, long lasting,
and genuinely inventive. On American
shores, they were adored for their
furious pop-slanted tunes in which listeners could easily discern traces of
the MC5 and 1950s rock'n'roll. As the
first foreign punk band to set foot in
LA, they became a fave, even as they
mutated into goth territory in the mid-
1980s. Upon their reinvention in the
1990s, they have continued to woo new
and old fans with their old world mirth,
their satisfying meld of rock'n'roll genres,
and their tireless working-class kind of
poetry that avoids being obtuse and
unwieldy.

Captain Sensible was not a dumb guitar behemoth. He evoked the persona
of a court jester/drag queen/rock'n'roll misfit that made Dave Vanian's monster
movie motifs pale in comparison. Maybe you like the so-called street politics of
the Clash or the FM radio sheen of the Offspring, but the Damned offer up equal
parts punk fantasy and savvy social critique in one fell swoop. So dig out and
dust off *Machine Gun Etiquette*, dance half-naked in your hole-strewn socks,
and pray that Phil Collins does not end up on your doorstep one night with a
pack of Budweiser.

You were the first punk band to put out a single, and the first punk band to tour America, but you don't consider yourself a punk band?

I do, I do. I love what punk stands for, but punk became something different . . . around 1978, when the Exploited and UK Subs became a kind of standard sound. Real shouty, loud, tuneless kind of thing. The original bands like the Clash, Pistols, the Stranglers, and the Damned all had some melodies, but punk became a nonmelodic thing. I love Charlie and the UK Subs, but I couldn't actually play one of their records.

Did Nick Lowe seek you out for the first record?

No, he was managed by the same bloke as us, Jake Riviera. Nick's just a country twanger, a country artist. He was always in pub rock bands playing crappy easy listening country shit. He was chosen as our producer, which I think was inspired because he didn't know a thing about production. The Damned's first album, which is supposedly a classic, sounds obviously more dulled and lo-fi obviously because of the lack of production compared to the Pistols' *Never Mind*, which sounds classy. The drums and guitar are perfectly produced, and the Damned album sounds like we just went in and recorded it in a day and a half, which is, in fact, what happened.

You came from the tradition of the early 1970s prog rock.

Yes, I still like that stuff. It's still what I listen to all the time. I was in a record shop the other day, it's all a blur, in Tampa. There's a record store next to the State Theatre, and they were playing this record, and I was like, fucking hell, that sounds like Soft Machine, with a little bit of the Groundhogs thrown in. I said to the bloke behind the counter, what's that, and he says, it's a new American band called Zero Zero and the album is called *AM Gold*, and it's just a great, new, fresh-sounding album. You know, I would like to speak to the band and ask them if they have any Soft Machine records, and I bet they bloody say no, we haven't. But they've discovered it the same way, just by putting Farfisa organs through fuzz boxes and things like that. Yeah, I love progressive rock, but the five or ten percent that is good, not like Yes and Genesis, who were absolute dog shit. They gave the whole genre a bad name really.

What led you from that prog sound into the rather straight-ahead ideas of punk?

I knew something was going to happen, because in the mid-1970s, the music at the time was just so turgid, it really was really Yes, Genesis, and Emerson, Lake, and Palmer, or it was disco, or the Osmonds, it was really bad and there was hardly anything good about it. Glam rock had kind of run its course and something had to happen, and when I met Brian James through an advertisement I

could see he had the vision to put something spectacular together, something I had never considered. He had this wild kind of gang mentality, a kick-ass, blitz-krieg kind of noise that he had in his mind. I slept on his floor with Rat Scabies, we both slept on his floor, and he just played us nonstop New York Dolls. He taught us these manic songs and the whole thing I could see because he was doing stuff that no one else was doing. And he just had these great ideas, so that's how I got involved with it.

When you met him were you playing guitar or bass?
I was playing guitar in two bands. One was the Johnny Moped group, who put out a reasonably good punk album themselves, called *Psychodelic.* Is that an awful pun or what? And the other band I was in was actually a band called Oasis, and we'd go out and playing working man's clubs doing Elvis Presley covers and things like that. I remember telling them, you've got to change this name because you'll never get anywhere with a name like that. I thought it was absolute shit, but it shows how wrong I was.

Were you listening to pub rock bands like Dr. Feelgood and Eddie and the Hot Rods?
Yeah, it was the only thing worth seeing, really.

Like with the Clash and Buzzcocks, was the idea of punk crystallized by the Ramones show in 1976, or did you already know what you wanted by then?
We all turned up at the Ramones gig as we did at an Eddie and the Hot Rods gig, although it was never said, because the P word, punk, was never spoken. None of the bands said, we are forming punk bands, it's going to be a massive movement. We didn't know that any of us was doing anything similar, but then again, we all turned up at the Ramones gig. And I kept seeing the same faces, the Steve Jones, the Joe Strummers, the Tony James. There was a little underground scene, but it was always underground. It was just that we were at the right place and the right time, and it did actually gel into a mainstream thing, whether people wanted it to or not.

Did it surprise you when it jumped from small clubs like the Roxy, 100 Club, the Nashville, and others to really big venues like the Rainbow?
Yeah, because I always thought, and I still think, that people are going to realize that real music is made by genius musicians who can play a flurry of wonderful, perfectly formed notes like Eric Clapton or wankers like that. I honestly didn't think it would last much more than three or four weeks, so much so that when our first album came out, it had a picture on the front . . . Well, we turned out for the session for *Damned Damned Damned* and they had all these custard pies and cakes and shaving foam and shit like that, and they smeared it all over our faces. But I didn't know it was going to happen. Now, when I turned up, you got to understand, I thought this was the only album I was ever going to make. I didn't want my picture on that fucking album cover to be covered with shit, so my Auntie and Uncle in bloody Glasgow couldn't recognize me. I was absolutely furious. When I saw the picture they had chosen for the cover, I said no, right, so let's see what you got on the back then. On the back there's a picture of the band live on stage with my back turned to the camera. I couldn't believe it, so I

got a little passport photograph and they stuck it on to where the monitor was on the stage so you could actually see a picture of my face.

Why did they put a picture of Eddie and the Hot Rods on the first thousand copies?

Well, that's typical Stiff records, instant collector's items. I think they fetched up a fair few for themselves and put them under their beds for their retirement. I think that's what it was, just a cheap scam.

Did they have the consent of the band?

I have no idea.

How did you get to America without even having your records released here?

Who knows? I have no idea. It was all done on a very low budget, and we played CBGBs. I remember that cunt Patti Smith telling us to get the fuck out of her dressing room. They had two shows on that night. We were supposed to clear our equipment out as quickly as we possibly could, behave ourselves, get out of there quickly, so the next show could come in. Patti Smith and that guitarist bloke came in and said, you limey assholes, get out of our dressing room. I thought, thank you very much, New York punk welcomes us. Then we went across to Los Angeles.

Where you played two shows?

Yeah. With Television. But Television pulled out of the gig, so we had to sleep on someone's floor in Los Angeles.

That was covered in the first issue of _Slash_. You guys were the big spread.

That's right. It was at this guy's house who was in a band called the Weirdos. We put together a hastily put together, mocked-up small show and we had to have a collection box at the door saying, if you want to help the Damned go back home, put some money in here because we didn't even have the airfare home.

Why weren't the first three records released in America?
That's business chitchat. I'm just a guitarist.

Why do you think *Music for Pleasure* is the most overlooked Damned record?
Well, the mistake was that there was always an experimental streak running through this band. I don't think we have ever repeated ourselves. There's a theme running through, but I do think we try to do something different each time. So with the second album we though, all right, we'd done the punk record with *Damned Damned Damned*, so let's get Syd Barrett in, the crazy psychedelic genius, to produce it. The Pink Floyd people, of course, were embarrassed by the way they treated Syd Barrett, you know they had thrown him out of the band. He turned up at their gigs, but they wouldn't let him up on stage. So, of course, they thought, if we could get Syd back in the studio, it might spark his creativity to be the great musician that he is. So, they donated the Pink Floyd studio to the Damned with Syd Barrett producing, but we were sitting in there waiting for him. He's my fucking hero, you know. I couldn't wait to meet him, and it was really going to happen. In through the door about five to six hours late walks the fucking drummer, Nick Mason. Nobody could believe it. We were like, what are you doing here? Because the current line up of Floyd was not exactly very popular in punk circles because they were part of the dinosaur shit we were trying to get rid of. He was like, I'm your producer. Syd couldn't make it. Needless to say, the whole thing was a disaster. The whole band was splitting up, Nick Mason didn't know what the fuck he was doing with us, let alone mix it. We had a jam with him one day, and he couldn't even bloody drum. He couldn't even play "Johnny B. Goode." We asked him, and he said, "Johnny B. Goode, what's that?" It was a disaster.

How did you feel when Robert Plant and Marc Bolan would come by and see shows?
We absolutely loved Marc Bolan. We thought he was marvelous. Some people from the old guard understood that punk was just different, a little dangerous, compared to the idea that it was kicking them out of a job maybe. But some of them liked it, some didn't. Both of them thought it was fantastic. Bolan would come out to our shows, and in fact he asked us on tour with him. We went

out and played twenty dates supporting T. Rex. It was fantastic, what a great bloke he was. He was getting fit and healthy and wearing a tracksuit. While we were all eating greasy fry-ups, he was jogging around the café. We'd have another slice of cholesterol-ridden junk food, and Marc Bolan would jog past. He was off the drink, off the drugs, and he had a car crash! Nice man. But Phil Collins said, "I've looked at this so-called punk phenomenon and I see nothing of any worth." What a wanker, so I never miss an opportunity to dis that scab.

Being Scottish, do you agree that punks in Scotland were a bit more tough and hardcore because "that's all they had"?
Maybe. It was much more of a fashion in London. You'd get people like the Bromley sect, who were just little rich kids. Bromley is a rich area of South London. All their parents had money, so they could afford to go down to Malcolm's shop and buy the two-hundred-pound bondage suits. Two hundred pounds in those days . . . Imagine how much that is now. They are the only people who walk around wearing this punk fashion, while the rest of the country was going to thrift stores, buying shitty clothes, and tearing the sleeves off of 'em, sticking safety pins in and wearing bin liners and things like that. I identified with the working-class side of it, being of that persuasion myself. There is a debate going on between the two sides of the historic aspect of punk, whether it was the bands themselves that invented these phenomena, or whether it was Malcolm, Jamie Reid, and Bernie Rhodes, the kind of university types who were pulling the strings, which is led by Jon Savage's *England's Dreaming*, which is a ripe load of shit if you ask me. I much prefer Johnny Rotten's *No Irish, No Blacks, No Dogs*.

Do think the Damned were unfairly characterized as jokers, especially early on? If so, did it anger you?
Oh yeah. It did actually. Because I think there's a much serious comment in this band as in any of the others really, although we are reasonably theatrical on stage [laughs]. You know, Johnny Rotten is as theatrical as they come. A very nice bloke, but it was a great act he put on. Really terrific. When the Clash were going on about "No Elvis, Beatles, and Rolling Stones," it didn't stop them from buying their records.

Did you see them as hypocrites when they sang "1977" and were flipping through record stalls buying those records?
Yeah, at the time. Especially when you consider as well this punk thing that said, we ain't gonna become a part of this stinking industry. We're going to turn it all upside down, all the horrible rock'n'roll lifestyle, all the cocaine, the groupies, and the big fat record company cigar bastards, we're going to tell all those people to fuck off. Then, of course, when the Damned signed to a small label,

Stiff Records, believing in what we were saying, what were the others doing? Signing to the biggest fucking fat cat labels they could possibly get their hands on. So, that was another bit of hypocrisy. I thought, bloody hell. That said, small labels can rip you off in a way that big labels never can.

Could you explain to an American audience the difference between the Labour government of the 1970s in England and the current Labour government?
The Labour government of the 1970s was more socialist, now I think all the political parties in the Western countries have realized that there's only one option for them, unfortunately, which is market capitalism, which is like groveling and scraping to the World Bank and the IMF and people like that. This is why our song "Democracy?" has a question mark after it, because there's isn't really much choice between the Labour Party and the conservative wing. Somebody in the Conservative Party said that Tony Blair is the best conservative prime minister we've ever had. I mean really, that sums things up, doesn't it? And with Gore and Bush, there was not much choice between them really.

Has it surprised people in England how gung-ho Blair has been with the war on terrorism?
It doesn't surprise me in the slightest because whatever this country says, England is your faithful loyal poodle. You say "Jump," we say, "How high?" I think there is a kind of Anglo Saxon, English-speaking people's conspiracy, and once people are in the British government they realize their jobs as part of America and Britain is to go around bullying the rest of the world. Britain is a loyal ally that does whatever you say. To be honest, if you want an honest, decent world, you got to treat people good. You shouldn't shit on whole countries the way the West is doing. The Palestinians should have a homeland, shouldn't they?

It's unfair that the Israelis have one, but not the Palestinians?
I wrote this song one time "A Holiday in My Heart." The phrase came from this Israeli film director who said that every time a British squady is killed in Palestine, there's a holiday in my heart. The song actually doesn't reflect that, but that's actually where I got the title from.

Is the Damned it for now, or will you be pursuing solo projects?
It's the only thing I can do. Well, I was a fairly good toilet cleaner, so the council said when I handed in my resignation. They said, we'll hold the job open for you! So, if this doesn't work out, that was very nice of them. But the only other thing I can do is goof around on stage, but if anyone ever has a wacky film project and wanted some incidental music, then I'm the man. Dave is into that

as well. Dave's really into films, totally. I mean, I don't dig the films, but I like the music.

When you think of good incidental music, whom do you think of?
Ennio Morricone (the spaghetti westerns), John Barry (James Bond), and people like that. Then there's . . . What's that wanker's name . . . John Williams, who does terrible, bombastic overblown crap and gets away with it time after time. He did *Superman*, *Star Wars*, and shit like that. Disgusting. So, I think they should get more interested in getting bands to do that sort of stuff, but unfortunately, I think you have to talk the talk, kind of walk around wearing a suit and stuff, and I can't do that. But if there's any weirdoes out there making a film, we don't wear suits, but we produce atmospheric, meandering ambient music.

Would you guys consider putting out a record of ambient music?
If a film happened, then yeah it would happen, because Dave would be so interested.

But even without a film?
I'd do it anyway. I have an album called *Meathead*, which is full of ambient, ten or fifteen-minute excursions into the unknown. That didn't sell very many [laughs]. It was a double album; I filled both CDs full of music. Stuff that had been sitting on my shelf. It would have never seen the light of day, but it's out there sitting in the cheapy racks, if anyone is into that sort of thing.

Who's someone you'd like to play with that you haven't so far?
I'd like to work with the guys from Talk Talk. They did a fantastic album this last time. It got them thrown off their label because it's so experimental, but it's the most beautiful album. Who else? I'm still into Terry Riley.

Who are you listening to now that's inspiring?
That Zero Zero record. It's the best record I've had for years. Stereolab I like a lot, and Ladytron, and Spiritualized.

Mike Scott from the Waterboys mentioned how powerful the Spiritualized record was for him.
Brilliant music can move you to tears; it can change your entire mood for the day. I remember when I was going to school, and if I had a particularly grueling day ahead, I'd throw something terribly aggressive on the record player, and run off to school with a spring in my step. Music has immense power. Listen to Rachmaninoff's Second Symphony. That's the most amazing piece of music. It takes you on a journey.

Or the middle movement in Ravel's Piano Concerto is outrageous, one of the best bits of music I have ever heard. It's sandwiched between these jazzy kinds of things because Ravel had this thing going on with Gershwin. They were trying to match each other for the swing jazz orchestral. The middle part of the piano is so outrageous because it's such a melancholic piece. My girlfriend and I listen to it and call it the twitch notes because of the out-of-tune notes he plays on the piano, but they are strategically placed and make you shudder.

Do you feel your generation was driven and invested in music more than the MTV generation?
I would imagine that the people in these bands are sort of driven. I mean, Noel Gallagher knows his stuff. Mind you, he's no spring chicken.

Do you command a different audience in England than the States?
An English audience is a bit different than an American audience. It's kind of a mixed bag out here: there's the punk moshers, the oldsters, the youngsters, and down in front there's always three or four rows of pretty goth girls, which we don't get in England. All you get in Britain is straight in your face, ugly bastards with the "Fuck Off and Die" T-shirts and their fists up going, "You wankers, ah! Play faster." So, yes, the toilet tour is beckoning. On the tour this far at almost every show the crowd has got involved with shouting back and forth stupid, inane comments, and requests for goth songs. I fell off the stage in Salt Lake City and done my knee in. I was reaching out to grab a blue wig off a transvestite.

Were you going to wear it?
Oh yeah. I think Johnny Rotten was right. I'm not here to entertain you, you're here to entertain me. That's the way I see it. If the audience doesn't give something back, then the show doesn't take off.

Tony Kinman
(The Dils)

Left-wing agitators in the Me Generation era of consumption, the Dils made two-minute tirades that feel inchoate, and pitch-perfect political manifestos, including the much-lauded "Class War," which is still sung in Occupy rallies across the world. Tony and brother Chip also helped stir the cowpunk Americana revival of the 1980s, shifted gears into post-punk drum machine art rocker Blackbird, and returned to dusty balladry with their stripped-down Western combo Cowboy Nation.

One of you said that if the whole point of playing rock music was to keep it simple and pure as possible in the sense of Little Richard, Bo Diddley, and early Elvis, then what is the spirit or point of playing cowboy roots music? I think it's the same thing, basically. To me, that's a matter of personal taste. Well, I think the weight of popular art tends to collapse under the weight of complexity. Not necessarily the eight of intelligence, because intelligence is always a welcomed asset to anything its brought to, but under the weight of complexity . . . Well, let's use rock music as an example. To me, Little Richard is—if you are going to talk to an alien, and he says, what is this rock music you are talking about, and you had Little Richard (imagine a *Twilight Zone*) and he's in a plastic booth playing "Lucille." Then in another Plexiglas booth you have Rick Wakeman doing "The Six Wives of Henry VIII." Which one are you going to point to and say, that's rock music? You are going to point to Little Richard, at least in my mind.

I think it's the same in cowboy-type music, or cowboy music. To me, the truest and most beautiful forms of that are the actual recording, like those two volumes (I don't remember what label) of actual old recordings of people singing traditional cowboy songs and some they had written, mostly unaccompanied, very crude recordings, something that Peter Case would probably know all about, because I don't know that much about the nuts-and-bolts details of old stuff like that. It's very simple, very simply delivered and you actually get to the core of the music without hearing a lot of other stuff. Of course, you can take that sort of thing to the extreme, but I think that all things being equal, simplicity allows you to get to the elements of popular music that actually communicate something, that might have some meaning or some worth to it rather than chops or production or whatever else gets layered on top of it time after time after time.

A good example of that is when people later in certain points of their careers start rerecording versions of their songs to "update" them. I know country performers did this a lot. It's rarely an improvement on the original thing, because it's rarely in the form of simplifying something. It's usually in the form of gussying it up, putting more fins or chrome on the car or lights on that, but you're saying, the car was best when it had a good engine in it and a fender and a stick shift and you could go fast and it didn't matter what kind of paint it had on it or how much chrome it had on it. To me, it seems the same in popular music. I think in so-called higher art forms of music, that's not necessarily true, but I think popular art once meant "appeal to a popular audience." I think simplicity is good, especially in popular art forms that are not so distanced from their actual folk sources or root sources.

Do you think that people often confuse simplicity with being pedestrian? For example, I might use the example of the poet Langston Hughes, who used a simple, direct language, but it does not mean he was a simple man. No, because actually in some ways once you reach a certain point, especially knowing he was an educated man, simplicity actually becomes a discipline, almost an intellectual discipline you impose on yourself. I mean, I can listen to Robert Johnson—well, that's a bad example because his music is actually complex. But I can listen to music played by, well, an old recording by somebody who obviously had never been educated, probably an illiterate—very crude performance but honest delivery, unschooled—and I can hear and know the context of that. You know that's one of the reasons it will have a primal flavor to it because it is, in fact, primal. There's not a whole lot affectation, it's very close to the source, and it's very close to the roots. On one of my favorite albums of all the times, the first Ramones album, the music is very simple, but to me it's an artistic simplicity. That record was cut in the contemporary world of *The Six Wives of Henry VIII*. It was cut in the world of Steely Dan, cut in the world of Jethro Tull, in the world of pop music getting ever and ever more complex, and that album was a brilliant intellectual reaction to that. There is the studied simplicity. It takes a lot of discipline. I'm a bass player, and I know that.

I go into Guitar Center to buy some strings or something, and I'll hear these kids on a Saturday all sitting there trying all the gear, and all this stuff is coming out of the amps. Tony and I were in there the other day buying some record-ing tape, and there was a guy in there with a fretless, five-string bass just doing all kinds of stuff, and here in LA we have the Bass Institute of Technology, the school which a lot of these people come out of, and I often wonder . . . Well, if I was a bass teacher . . . I would tell a student, hey, you are going to sit down and for an hour, here's the D, here's the fifth fret on the A string. You are going to play an eighth note for an hour and nothing else.

Do you think it would be the first time they've actually ever heard that note?
Well, you know, yeah. It would teach them this is important to know, it's impor-tant to know that, it's important to know how to play like Dee Dee Ramone, or it's important to know why Dee Dee Ramone played the way he did, and why that is sometimes the right thing to play. That sort of simplicity. To get back to the point of Langston Hughes: sometimes simplicity is discipline . . . and com-municating whatever it is you want to communicate in a direct and effective way. Once you reach a point of knowing, let's assume that you are not an illit-erate sharecropper, that you were born and lived within a space of five miles somewhere, in the days back before rural electrification, but once you reached an age of awareness in the modern world simplicity does require discipline because there is so much information out there. To pull back and find simplic-ity is a matter of discipline, temperament, and creativity—everything that goes into something worth making. It all has to do with that.

Would you include Nirvana in the larger arc of punk rock?
Yea, Nirvana is what I'm talking about in the sense . . . Well, I think Nirvana and bands like that . . . No, I think Nirvana and the whole grunge thing was a con-tinuum of white stadium rock, basically, with punk rock references. I am not saying there wasn't a lot of talent and quality in that stuff. I'm not saying this was shit. There wasn't a significant change. Its commercial success was, but the music wasn't. In the sense that Elvis was, or the Beatles were, or the Sex Pistols or Ramones were. Those things were qualitative changes in the midst of the status quo, or compared to the status quo of the time. Obviously, the Sex Pistols and Ramones didn't enjoy the same commercial success that the grunge bands did, but not counting the commercial aspect of it, the creative aspect of it, the actual shake up of the ambience of the genre or the standards. The standards changed because of that. I think in white popular music there hasn't been any change. The last gasp of real was the original punk rock era, and black music. Nothing has really changed since the early days of hip-hop.

But people might ask, why aren't Chip and Tony making it change?
Well, I think it takes more than an individual. It takes a *Weltanschauung* . . .

One of those German words!

Yeah, one of those German words, but the time has to be ready for it. I think that the social conditions being right and people coming together is what actually create that moment. You know, rock'n'roll would not have existed without the electric guitar. The electric guitar had been around for a long time, and Elvis was not an electric guitar player, but it was an integral part of his sound, then you had people who were guitar players like Chuck Berry, Buddy Holly, and Bo Diddley. They couldn't have done what they did with an acoustic guitar. The same goes with hip-hop and rap. Drum machines, there you go, that's what did it.

Or turntables.

Turntables had been around for a long time, and scratching and stuff like that had been around for a while, but programmed music, the real computerized age of music combined with the social ambience of the inner city, and people ready to hear something new, wasn't there. Punk rock was a qualitative change at the beginning, but the reason why I don't think it made any quantitative change at first was because the audience was simply not there for it, at least here in states. It definitely wasn't here for it. It took like a whole new generation of people entering the record buying demographic in order to create grunge or stadium punk. Because those people simply did not exist back in the early days. They hadn't been born yet.

But three thousand people did show up for the Sex Pistols show in San Francisco.

But you know the Sex Pistols' *Never Mind* just went gold a few years ago? That's a mind-blowing thing to realize. That one album, which is one of the two great albums created from the original punk rock era, that and the Ramones' first album, only just now went gold. I don't even know if the Ramones' first album had gone gold yet. Compare that to however much *Nevermind* sold, like ten, fifteen million?

And both had major labels behind them pushing the records.

The sad fact of show business is, when you are talking show business, you are talking numbers. You know, five million Elvis fans can't be wrong. I'm sorry. It's numbers that count. I love some great, little, obscure records, but when I go shopping or walking down the street, I don't see these records on somebody's T-shirt or somebody with a tattoo of this obscure band name. It's the other stuff. I don't walk into a house and see somebody with a wall of pictures of these people. That's showbiz. That's the way it is. It's a cold, hard fact, but it's true.

In terms of the Dils, you've stated, "We were not a popular band, we were an unpopular band. People did not like the Dils. We were the enemy." Why?
The Dils would have ebbs and flows in popularity. Of course, this was within a very short amount of time. The Dils were only around two years. A lot of it was very scene-oriented in the sense that if we said something in a *Slash* interview or *Flipside* and it pissed somebody off that week, them and fifty of their friends and buddies wouldn't come out because the word would get out, and they would say, fuck those assholes, I'm not going to go to the show. I think the Weirdos live were a better band than we were. We tended to be more hit and miss. The Weirdos were like a great punk rock machine. They put on great shows. The Dils did have good shows, but we also, for some reason, I don't know . . . Chip and I have always been turds in the punch bowl or something [laughs]. Or shit disturbers. We stir up shit. When you are working within a scene type thing among your peers, let's says there's three or four hundred punk rockers up and down the West Coast of California, and you do something or say something in an interview or play something that ripples the water a little bit, people react against that. People, especially at a certain stage when they feel like their identity is at stake, and they feel like they have invested heavily in this character they have become, they don't necessarily want to get thrown a wild card. They don't want somebody monkeying with the works, in the sense that I just went out and bought my bondage clothes, and now you are wearing a plaid shirt. Stuff like that. It could have been just little things like that. The Dils were a good band, and when we would play we'd definitely have some good evenings, but back at the time, we didn't hit the consistent level of a band like the Weirdos, who were consistently good night after night. I mean, the Weirdos shows were something to see. Soon after the original bunch of punk rock bands, that's when you started getting the machine-type bands that were consistently hard-hitting night after night after night.

Like Fear and X or something?
No, not so much X, because they were never a real machine band, I mean bands like the Dead Kennedys, or a lot of the bands from Orange County . . .

TSOL?
And a lot of the SST-type bands. Black Flag is a good example, or the Minutemen. It was like there was an almost physical discipline to their shows. I always liked things on stage that were a little bit loose or fuzzy around the edge, in the sense that there was room for things to happen musically or performance-wise. So when the machine bands really started happening it wasn't really my taste, compared to a band like the Sleepers, one of the original bands back then. The Sleepers were not a punk rock band, but they were in the punk rock

scene, because they fit nowhere else. They were an awesome band to watch live because you literally never knew what was going to happen. It wasn't like performance art; in fact, it was hardly performance at all. It was real. They were mesmerizing to watch because their music was fantastic, and you knew every time you saw them play, something was unfolding from the moment they stepped on stage to the moment they left, not in a conscious way, but in an unconscious way . . . Kim, the drummer, I don't think he was loaded, but I think most of the guys in the band were, and it definitely contributed to their performance.

Another difference between the first and second waves of punk is the sheer number of records the second bands produced and the current availability. If you go to a record store, most likely it's impossible to find records by the Bags, Mutants, Crime, but you'll always find some Dead Kennedy or Black Flag records.

SST is a good example of that. The guys at SST, they wanted to create a market. That was their point: to create a label identity and make records and sell them. I remember those guys joking about creating a Black Flag franchise, like creating other Black Flag bands, like here's your set, this is the Black Flag of Cleveland or whatever, which is a fascinating idea. That was their point. I'll speak for myself as far as an old-school punk . . . The point of the Dils was never to make records and never to have a career. It was never like, "the Dils twentieth anniversary, the Dils reunion tour, the Dils greatest hits." It was never ever about that.

Making a record to us was like, some guy walks up to you and says, hey, man, I want to make a 45, and you're like, all right. And you pick out the two best songs in your set at the time and go in for a day or couple of hours and make a record and walk away. It comes out a month or so later, and there's your record. We never even once thought of making an album. Every several months, someone would come up, like the guys from Dangerhouse, or the guy up in Canada, and say hey, you guys want to do another record? And we were like, sure, let's go in. We took our strongest songs from then and put them out. It was never to do an SST-type thing.

But are you saying that even a label like Dangerhouse was fundamentally different than SST?

Yeah, I think so. The guys at Dangerhouse were serious about what they were doing, but those guys at SST wanted to make a label and were serious about it. Dangerhouse might have been serious, but it wasn't at the same level of intensity. Those guys at SST were driven to do what they do. All of those bands on there saw what they were doing as, this is something we can make some money at, not in the sense that it was the only reason they were doing it, but they saw that as part of what was going on. The Dils did not care about that at all. Not in the sense that it was radical or revolutionary, but we just didn't because it wasn't part of our temperament. We were enjoying what we were doing at the time in the moment, and we weren't thinking about that.

There's a guy writing a book here about punk rock, and he's been doing extensive interviews with the "original five," which is what he calls the Zeros, the Screamers, the Weirdos, the Dils, and the Germs. He was asking me about things because he had done all this research and talked to other people obviously about what the Dils had done or were done to the Dils, just Dils stuff, and I simply did not remember half of it because it was not important. If somebody is writing a story twenty years later about it, it might make a nice part of the story, but I was absolutely unhelpful. Our manager at the time was Peter Irving. Back in those days, you used your friends and they became either your drummer or your manager because no one wanted to be in a punk rock band back in those days. Peter became a manager, and a year to year and a half later, we split from each other. This interviewer was like, "Do you remember why you and Peter parted company?" I said, "No, I'm sure it was something stupid and silly." He said, "Why can't you remember?" I said, "I'm sure it was something stupid and silly." There was absolutely nothing at stake. I said, there was no money, no career opportunity. It wasn't like our movie deal with HBO folded. We were friends, and probably had some sort of friend fight, and if your friend is your manager, at the end of the friend fight you just go, that's it, man, you're not our manager anymore. It was totally unimportant.

I was a very dedicated punk rocker, but not like what you would call a dedicated musician or songwriter. It was just not important. To me, songs back then were like, you put together a cool chord change, a cool drum beat, and something you call a verse and something you can a chorus, and half of the times we wouldn't even write lyrics for these songs. You would just be up there yelling stuff during it, and then when the chorus came, you yelled something a little more coherent. Later on, of course, we started writing songs, and we always did have song songs, but a lot of our stuff was us getting up there and writing these song things, playing them for two or three sets, and then never playing them again. I'll hear cassettes now of live stuff we did back then, and a third of the set is songs that I know were only around for two to three weeks that we wrote, played awhile, and discarded not because they crappy or anything, but because they weren't meant to last. It wasn't like I'm going to write a classic, or I'm going to write a song that is going to make the world sing. That's not what it was about.

The early bands like the Screamers and the Crime either didn't put out records at all, or put out limited-release records . . .
I know Crime put out some records, but you cannot find them now. I think the Screamers, well, Chip and I are working on a new record and we were

just talking about the Screamers, but the Screamers were waiting for the deal that never came. While bands like the Dils, the Zeros, and the Weirdos, who later released an album or two more or less after the fact, but all those bands had singles out, so there's still stuff out there from the original days, but the Screamers don't have any of that stuff because they were convinced that they were going to get a deal. That just was not the way to go in terms of any recorded legacy such as it is. In rock journalism cliché, people say that the Dils were criminally underrecorded. The thing to me is, no, it was just about right. It just wasn't meant to be. That's not what it was about.

As Ian MacKaye mentioned, things tend to be overdocumented now, like Pearl Jam releasing a huge catalog of live recordings [ed. note: which Fugazi has now done online].
Frankly, "overdocumented" is actually a critical assessment of something, because there are some things that can withstand that sort of documentation and scrutiny. If it's there, if there's a lot to look at. It starts getting thin indeed for some people. I would say that Pearl Jam probably shouldn't be releasing a tremendous amount of live stuff, but if you look at the Ramones' world tour video, stuff like that is valuable and interesting. It all depends on what it is you're looking at. If there's a lot worth looking at, it's worth looking at, but if there's not a lot there to look at in the first place, it just doesn't need it. He's right.

The last Dils show was with Black Flag at Blackie's, with Dez singing, I believe. At that point, did you realize machine bands were supplanting your generation?
I knew that when bands like the Dead Kennedys came on strong in San Francisco . . . Here it starts getting intertwined in the personal. I had gotten really sick to death and bored with punk rock and the state of punk rock. I was an avid buyer at the time of import singles from England, like Eater and all this stuff. Then I started noticing that the quality was falling off really bad. I remember the last punk rock record I went out and bought and got excited about was Sham 69. After that, the songs that I wanted to play during the Dils were punk rock only in the sense that we were a punk rock band doing them. We were starting to write different kinds of songs. A style that would later go on to fit Rank and File.

Some of them would even be transformed into the Rank and File sets.
By that time, there was becoming a self-identified punk rock audience in cities like San Francisco and down in Los Angeles that basically wanted to see their punk rock. Damn it, we came to see punk rock, you're not punk rock, you're wearing a flannel shirt. You're not punk rock, you're playing a Buddy Holly song.

You're not punk rock, you're playing a Johnny Cash song. You're not punk rock, that song you just played is midtempo. You're not punk rock, that song had a harmony in it. We actually had people start telling us, you're not punk rock. I knew the Dils' place in punk rock was gone because of the sense of what was happening. Al Escovedo had already bailed on the Nuns for similar reasons because the music just wasn't interesting to him anymore. The notes were still going, but Al wasn't in them anymore. A lot of the original bands were fading and petering out. I know in fact that the Avengers were on the verge of breaking, though I am not saying for the same reason I did, although it could be. I know that Penelope and Jimmy from the Avengers definitely went on to do something different than punk rock.

Jello Biafra has said that the Dils broke up . . . over a Dirk Dirksen incident. See, Biafra was a suck-ass. The original bands were all very independent-minded and had a very independent spirit. Dirk Dirksen was not important to us. Rodney Bingenheimer was not important to us. The Mabuhay was not important to us. What was important to us was what we were doing and the music. I remember when we were getting together to do a show at the Gay Community Center. I don't remember if it was going to be a benefit or a regular show. What had happened was that it was going to be the Dils and the Avengers. At the time, the Dils were coming on strong, but the big bands in town were the Nuns and Crime. The Nuns could pack Mabuhay ten nights in a row. They were what kept Mabuhay going. They were the moneymakers for that club, and that's what clubs care about. When Dirksen got wind that we were going to be doing shows in different places, he said, anybody who plays someplace else will never play here again. The Nuns were our buddies. When we told them that, basically Alejandro went to Dirksen and said, you ban these guys, we'll never play here again. Dirksen backed down. Biafra was one of the ones who walked around saying to the bands, "You're going to wreck the scene, and you've got to work with Dirk Dirksen." He was a complete suck-ass. And then later Dirk returned the favor by promoting Jello's run for mayor, which is what made him a celebrity and made the Dead Kennedys a big band. It made him a celebrity in San Francisco because it got him in all the papers and on TV: "Punk rock musician Jello Biafra and his band the Dead Kennedys, who are outrageous, are playing Mabuhay this weekend." Jello, like the Dickies down in LA, was the mainstream media's idea of what punk rock was. This guy's name is Jello Biafra, his band is named the Dead Kennedys, and he takes his pants off on stage, wow.

So, regardless of what you think of his records . . . Well, I always thought Jello was a stupid performer. I think his performances were stupid and I think his lyrics are stupid, but I always thought his band was good and made good-sounding records. What Jello is and what he wanted to become, was like a fifth-level celebrity nationally, who gets on a talk show occasionally, does a lecture here and there, and is a San Francisco character, like Emperor Norton or Wavy Gravy or one of those guys. He's a San Francisco character, he'll get in the gossip columns, he'll do that silly suing thing with his band, and he's the First Amendment guy. Yeah, he's a First Amendment guy, but what was one of his first pivotal moments as a public personality? Trying to get bands not to play somewhere. To me—I'm sorry, I read your piece in your magazine with him—he's just a phony. I've always thought that guy was a phony, and I'll believe it until the day I die.

He was very clever. This has a lot do with, well, I'm going to use a vague amorphous term loaded with potentially pompous sounding shit, but the "artistic community," and you can look at the punk rock community as an artistic community. To try to find comfort in conformity among your peers and among your old neighborhood is always a really strong human tendency. For true rebels and independent thinkers, that's not something that is important to them. They're always looking for something else out of life or out of art or anything, any human endeavor. Something more than comfort, something more than, okay, here's my four walls, everything is groovy inside these walls, so I never want to change. He's an example of example of somebody, and Tim Yohannon of *Maximumrocknroll* was an example of this too, because he was part of this whole thing, of what happened in San Francisco. The guys needed to have punk rock become something that had a finite beginning, a finite end. "You will go this far and no further, here's a list of what is punk rock, here's a list of what isn't. Please read the list, you are responsible, and ignorance is no excuse. We will actually decide who among us are and are not punk rock." That's what they were waiting for, and by the time 1980–81 rolled around, because by 1979 that whole thing was coming on strong, but by the time 1980–81 came around, it was there. The Yohannons and Biafras of the world had it.

That's why punk rock started to . . . sound like it did, you know? That's why a lot of the color was gone, a lot of the flamboyance was gone. A lot of the creativity was gone. With the first wave of punk rock, not one band sounded alike. They all sounded different, and a year to a year and a half later when you'd go see a punk rock show, every band would sound the same. Maybe the one that was a bit better would be the one that got bigger or more popular than the other ones. Every band sounded the same. I remember there being these stupid debates when the first PIL record came out among these kind of people. Is this punk rock, man? I don't know. I don't think so. What's that? Because it didn't sound like some stupid SST record? There was just unbelievable fear and conformity, like shut it down, shut it down, we cannot handle this. Johnny Rotten used to be a punk rocker, but he's not anymore. The whole mentality just got in there. That's why I just walked, even ran away from it as fast as I could. It was an ugly scene.

I found out how much you liked Bob Marley, I thought, maybe Tony and Chip were getting their protest politics from Bob Marley records more than _The Communist Manifesto_.
One thing that I have always loved about reggae music is that I love music . . . Well, whatever the ins and outs of Rastafarians, it's their thing, not mine, but . . . it's a heartfelt emotion and it's real. That always came across to me in a lot of my favorite reggae bands or performers. It's like getting back to the thing about simple, direct communication. That kind of music has always appealed to me, like the way that real original blues appealed to me. I like directness and honesty in music. I mean, I like other things in music, but that's like an attractive thing to me. I loved those Bob Marley and the Wailers records, and I saw them play down in San Diego. Nowadays, I feel privileged to have done that because he died way too early and his legend has only grown since then. It always amazes me when I talk to people and tell them that when I saw him, they're like, what, you saw Bob Marley, because there was like 2,500 people, and Little Anthony opened up for him, from Little Anthony and the Imperials, a Vegas act. They opened with "Philadelphia Freedom." And you could tell his whole band were totally professional Vegas black musician dudes just doing their thing, and you could tell, the idea of them opening for Bob Marley was like, this is a drag. There was pot smoke everywhere, and that's uncool. You could tell that they were not thrilled with the idea. I don't even know if Little Anthony knew who Bob Marley was. But that's an idea of where Bob Marley was at during that point of his career in America, that he could play San Diego, a several-thousand-seater, and get some Vegas act to open for him. I actually take that back, because for all I know, Little Anthony could have been one of Bob Marley's favorites when he was younger because he loved American R&B. You listen to Bob Marley, and you're hearing Curtis Mayfield. So, I take that back about them being foisted on Marley. Marley might have said, "Get me Little Anthony, man."

The political thing came about because when I was in college almost all my professors were Maoists. I was already leaning their way before I got to college, and when I got there it was pretty straight-forward . . . Well, you're young and your mind is absorbing stuff, so by the time I got out of school, that's what I wanted to write about. That stuff was important to me. Of course, there was the whole protest vibe and stuff like that. That combined with the sheer radicalism of punk rock, because my thing back then, and thinking about it now I would regard it as something an ignorant nineteen or twenty-year-old would say, because that's what I think now, but then I would go around and say, man, you guys go around wearing swastikas, that's not going to scare anybody.

Why don't you wear a hammer and sickle, because that's what scares people. That's who this country is at war with. The red revolution and all that, so if you want to scare them, wear something that will scare them.

Did you know that the New York Dolls had used the communist flag as their backdrop for a while?

Yeah, because of the whole red leather period. That was also one of the inspirations for it because we had seen a picture of them in *Rock Scene* performing in their outfits with the big hammer and sickle and thought, that's cool. It was all mixed up. Nowadays, I don't find much time to write songs or sing songs about hating people and wanting wars, like "Hate the Rich" or "Class War." But back then, that was what I was totally into, so it wasn't just that, it was stuff like that New York Dolls thing. Just the whole flamboyance of it, the sort of in-your-face thing. We had some shows booked up and down the West Coast, and they said, do you have any pictures we can put on the fliers like at colleges, and we sent them one with Chip jumping up in the air with a hammer and sickle T-shirt, and they cancelled the shows when they got the picture. They were like, nope, we can't have this.

But serious-minded punk rock revolution aside, how did you end up in the Cheech and Chong film *Up in Smoke*?

We were done in Carlsbad at the time. Chip and I were still living down there. Peter Irving, our manager, was living up in LA, and at the time, you could not play the big nightclubs in LA because they were not booking punk rock bands. That film was shot at the Whisky or the Roxy, I can't remember, but it was filmed at one of those places. One of the big goals of all these bands was that we had to get into these nightclubs. We got to play some places with stages and PAs and stuff. All the bands wanted to do that. Peter heard, I think maybe Rodney on the radio or something, that punk rock bands were playing at some Cheech and Chong filming. There was a casting call for all the punk rock bands. If you look at the audience in the film, it's all like John Doe and Exene, and the whole punk rock scene from the time were in the audience. The Germs and all these other bands had signed up to be in the movie. We weren't there. Peter called up and said, get up here right now and see if we can't bust into this. What we did, we got my best friend from high school, Andre, to be our drummer because we couldn't find our drummer, and we bought him like a fifty-dollar drum kit. He's the one that played on "I Hate the Rich." We came up to LA, picked up Peter at his place, and he lived about five minutes from the club they were filming it at. We pulled up to the side door where there was a line of bands waiting to get in. We pulled up to the door right when the assistant director or something leaned out the door and said, "Who's next?" and Peter jumped out of the car and said, "We are." We walked in there with our stuff, set up, played, and left, because we wanted to play a nightclub. Later we found out that out of all the bands, we were the ones they picked.

For the final cut?
Yeah, we weren't signed up for that or anything. It's truly a wild punk rock story, but that's exactly the way it happened.

You and your brother are army brats. How did your military veteran father take to all this radicalism?
My dad was very tolerant. He didn't mind. Of course, we weren't living at home at the time.

But I'm sure he saw the picture of you guys with a hammer and sickle!
The way he looked at it was that we were a band, and that's just what bands do. We could talk about anything; we could talk about politics. He was very tolerant and understanding. He was a very smart man and we could talk about all sorts of stuff. He never demanded that we be like him, and he never encouraged us to go in the military. There was none of that stuff. My dad went to Vietnam, and when he came back, he hated it there, and he thought it was awful. He had been in World War II and Korea too. He wasn't a young guy. He had been a Marine his whole life. When he came back from Vietnam, he said it was the worst thing he had ever seen. Absolutely awful. So he was not a, like, gung-ho charley.

An eighteen-year-old kid who had been brainwashed.
Yeah. It was nothing like that, my point being that he didn't see anything wrong with what we were doing. He was supportive and thought it was great. He was thrilled. He always said it was the first member of his family that had ever gotten into the newspaper for something other than dying or getting married. We'd get write-ups and send them the press and they'd be thrilled. They thought it was great.

Speaking or radicalism and promotion, what was your impression of the Clash when you opened for them?

At the time, I really liked the Clash, I thought they were good, although I also thought they were a bit showbizzy, but that's my problem, not theirs. Let me put it this way, if I had been five years younger, if I had been like a freshman in high school that loved the Clash and was going to smoke some pot and drink some beer before going to the show, I would have thought it was an incredible rock show, but I wasn't. I was a punk rocker. I wanted to blow up the world with punk rock revolution, and I saw the Clash and thought they were really kind of showbizzy. Plus the show the Dils played with them was at the Santa Monica Civic. It was a real rock show with real security, real backstage, real this, that, and the other. I didn't like that at all. We were used to playing punk rock clubs or rented halls or stuff like that, and I was thinking, isn't this what we are supposed to destroy sort of thing? I wasn't in-your-face then, because I understood. This is what they were doing. They come to America, they come on a tour, and they don't want to play rehearsal spaces. They don't want to play some dude's storage unit in Salt Lake City, and I'll put up a PA, and we'll have a party.

Funny enough, when the Damned did get to the West Coast, they had no money to get home. They ended up crashing at some guy's pad.

That was different. I saw the Damned when they first played out here, and they did play nightclubs. They played the Starwood, and it was an incredible show. Actually, I happen to think it was the show, and I know in a lot of histories of LA punk, that show really gets mentioned. I think that show really ignited things. There were punk rocks bands in LA kind of around forming and doing stuff, but I think that show actually created the LA punk rock sensibility, to tell you the truth. The Damned were not like the Clash or the Sex Pistols. The Pistols were like the anarchist fringe of it, the Clash were the socialist fringe of it, but the Damned did not give a shit about any of that stuff. Captain Sensible comes on stage naked, and Dave Vanian came on stage with road flares, shaking them over the audience catching people's hair on fire. Them and the Ramones at the time were the most exciting shows I had ever seen in my life as far as sheer over-the-top, primal Little Richard–style energy, but a literal energy, not a machine energy, like what we were talking about earlier. I think that their sense of, well, not who gives a shit, but the fact that they did not have "socially conscious" lyrics or an approach to things, unlike the Pistols and Clash at different ends of the spectrum, helped create the Los Angeles punk rock sensibilities. That was an incredible show, but their first tour was at a very different level than the Clash. By the time the Clash came here, they were on the verge of being rock stars. The Damned were not; they were an English band on tour. I never thought of it before, but the Sex Pistols' first tour, the Clash's first tour, and the Damned's first tour were all very different, but in ways that reflected who the bands really were and what stages they were in their career.

When the Jam first toured America, they opened for Blue Öyster Cult. The first wave of bands to hit the states came and toured under very different circumstances.

Another thing about the Clash: a friend of ours at the time, Claude Bessy, who wrote for *Slash*, got the shit kicked out of him by security backstage at the Clash show. At the time, the show created so many repercussions, but I remember at the time thinking, people expected too much of the Clash when they came out here. They thought they were like the deliverance; this is it, not the second coming, but the first coming. This is the incarnation, "The only band that matters." Remember the quote? And when they played, the people that were like in the scene and on the fringes, kept thinking, oh, I can't get backstage at the Clash show because I write for *Slash* and stuff like that. People that were more close to that, compared to people who just happened to buy the record and said, oh, I like this . . . Is this what punk rock is? But fair enough, you need those people to fill the Santa Monica Civic. People in the scene and on the fringes of being the inner circle expected way too much from those guys. They expected the world to be turned upside down by the Clash being there. They expected the Santa Monica Civic to be cool. They expected the Clash to be cool, they expected no security. So, Claude got the shit kicked out of him, not by the Clash's security but by the Santa Monica Civic security, and I'm sure he was drunk. He was probably acting "punk" backstage, and they had probably never seen anything like that before. They probably said, you know what we do to drunk assholes backstage at the Santa Monica Civic, we kick their ass and throw them out, which is exactly what they did to him. "Claude got beat up at the Clash show and they didn't do anything about it!" people were saying, but the Clash didn't even know! But all of a sudden, it was their fault, and it became our fault too, because the ticket prices were like ten dollars for the show. We had big fights with promoters and even turned into little magazine *Slash* and *Flipside* wars over ticket prices. Our shows, we're talking about. With the Clash did this. It was the Clash's show, not ours, but we got blamed for the ticket prices, believe it or not. People were saying, "The Dils, man, c'mon, man, it's ten dollars." But whatever [laughs]. We just thought, we can't win, we just can't win. Bo Diddley opened the show.

Do you think it was an act of courage to bring Bo Diddley in front of that audience?

You know something, I have quite a different take on that. There's a long, historical tradition now for British bands to come over here and hire black opening acts. The Who had Toots and the Maytals open up for them and stuff like that. And I love Bo Diddley. To me, Bo Diddley is one of the gods. He is one of the untouchable icons of rock music. I didn't expect the Clash to have ten punk rock bands open up for them, but when they had Bo Diddley open up for them, that was a failure of the imagination. It's just like U2 having B.B. King open for them at Dodger Stadium. Now, I know U2 might be thinking, we want to introduce this great classic legend to our young stupid audience, there's seventy thousand of them out there. This gives B.B. a chance to stretch his legs, but when Bono came on stage to introduce B.B. King to his audience as somebody that we (U2) just recently discovered. Now, I know he didn't mean "we discovered this man"; what he meant to say is that B.B. was a man U2 just recently got into. But you know the way it just sounded, right? I can imagine that B.B. was thinking, you know, "I remember when Eric Clapton or Jeff Beck gave me the exact same intro at the Fillmore in 1968. You know what, get me back to Vegas." To me, it was a similar thing to the Clash having Bo Diddley open up for them. I can dig it if Joe and Mick and the dudes just dug Bo, he happened to be their favorite performer, and they were just thrilled to have him play with them. Fair enough.

Or was it a stab at roots and legitimacy?
I actually think . . . it's what English bands do because the Clash always wanted to be a classic English band. In fact, the Clash, of all the original punk bands, when I listen to their records, have worn the least well to me. It's a total surprise. That first record of theirs—I worshipped that record. I wore two copies of that record out. I loved the sound of that record. When I listen to it now, I don't like the sound of it. There's phoniness to it that I don't hear in *Never Mind the Bollocks*, the early Ramones records or even the first Damned record, *Damned Damned Damned*. Those records still sound as great to me as they ever did. I put the Clash on now, it's like, this is rock music. I think the Clash were the band of stature. I'm sure there were other bands, but none we are talking about twenty-five years later, that started the rock values coming back into punk rock, which is fair enough. The Clash weren't the saviors of anything, and they never claimed to be. A lot of people put that weight on them. That was my impression. I loved the show. I thought they were great, but it was a rock show.

So, in a way, it was the Who or Rolling Stones coming to America, redux?
That was exactly what it was. When I went to see the Who at Anaheim Stadium, I knew I was going to get a big rock show. The several times I went and saw the Stones I knew I was going to get a state of the art, stadium rock, god rock show. When I went to see the Clash, I didn't want that from them. I wanted my punk rock! I didn't get it twice. I got a great band, because they were a great band, but as far as a great punk rock band, maybe they were better than that. Maybe let's put it that way.

The liner notes and interviews included on some the Dils reissues show that you loved David Bowie too, because he bucked trends and made atmospheric Brian Eno albums like *Low* when he could have been a disco superstar. Do those records, all the way up to *Scary Monsters*, hold up?

Yeah. I think the whole *Low* period. To me, Eno yes, Bowie less so. I like Bowie, like Ziggy Stardust and all that stuff. I still think that "Rebel Rebel" is one of the best rock songs ever recorded, the sound of it and the sheer nonsensical passion of it. It's passion about nothing, but it sounds good. It's just a good record. It's hard for me to talk in any comprehensible way about it. Yeah, those records hold up largely because of Eno, not in the sense that those are great Eno records, because obviously it was a collaboration. Those Eno/Bowie records are an example of somebody working creatively to come up with something of real quality, at least to my ears. When I hear those records, they still sound as fresh and interesting as the time when I first heard them. In fact, startlingly so sometimes. Of all the records of those days, the records that look larger even than they did when I first heard them is the *Bollocks* record by the Pistols, and the first Ramones record. I loved both of those records when they came out, and when I hear them now they just seem even better to me.

But you disliked the second Ramones album, *Leave Home*, because of the keyboards.

I always dug the Ramones, but to me that first album is the thing because it is such a complete piece. They made other good records. I'm not a rock critic who says, "well, after this . . ." That's not what I am talking about. But that first album has sheer brilliance. That is the closest thing since rock became self-aware and

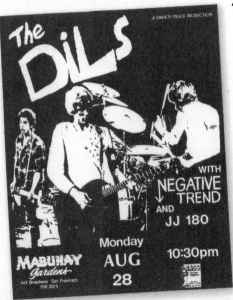

"this is rock'n'roll music" happened in 1963 or 1958, when rock music became self-aware of itself as rock music. I'm not talking about the Louis Prima days or even Little Richard, because that was back in the days when the foundations were being laid, the form-givers were working and actually making it. They didn't have time to sit around and think about what it is. They were making it. After it got made, and became what it is, at whatever point that is, 1961 or whatever, the self-aware era of rock'n'roll, we are rock'n'rollers, we are rock'n'roll musicians, we play rock'n'roll. We're a band, what we do is rock'n'roll, in that era the first Ramones album stands as if not the top, then close to the top, of the supreme artistic achievement. I think that album is that great.

"Beat on the Brat" is the equivalent of "Great Balls of Fire"?
Well, no, it is a different kind of thing. People like Jerry Lee, people like that are in another complete category. They are untouchable. Have you seen the *Shindig!* videos that Rhino puts out? They have one that is Jerry Lee on *Shindig!* which is a show from 1964–66, definitely the British invasion period of the Byrds, Lovin' Spoonful, and stuff, the mid-1960s era of rock'n'roll. But they had Jerry Lee on a lot, enough to put together a half-hour video of just his appearances. What's weird about it is that it's obviously after his marriage, the whole scandal went down, and if you know anything about him, you know this is the beginning of a real low point for him in his career. It's right before he recorded his country records and had his comeback. He's basically playing little clubs for no money, but he still was on TV, and his performances are incredible, but you can tell that it's not his era, not his scene. He is driving the audience crazy, but it's not his scene. He's got his hair slicked back, and he's not like some cute boy with bangs singing, "All Day and All the Night." He's like a nasty, sleazy-looking dresser. He looks like he's clean, but he has that southern, back seat of the car in a club parking lot in Louisiana look going on. He cannot wash that off. No matter what clothes he wears, he can't change that. He's always looked that way, and he's awesome, but you can tell, this is not his time, and his country thing has yet to come. He's delivering great rock music, but his world is over, that world is gone, that world of him on stage with Chuck Berry, and they both have hits in the top ten and Elvis and all that stuff. It's simply not there. See, I put Jerry Lee in a different era. I would not compare the Ramones album to what I consider the single greatest recorded moment of rock music history. Do you want me to tell you what it is?

Sure.
It's in Little Richard's recording of "Lucille." You can still hear it on oldies stations. Little Richard is screaming so loud that he overdrives his mic. On the hit version, there's actually distortion recorded on that. That is one thing that no engineer these days would let anyone get away with, I don't care if you are even recording for a shitty indie punk rock label. Punk rockers would not let that happen, nowadays. Two, that was a major hit song by a major hit performer of the time. I am speechless just thinking about it. To me, that is the single greatest moment because of what it is, which is incredible, how it sounds is great, and because of the context. He's overdriving the mic, but the way things were back then was, "C'mon, Richard, that sounds good enough. We're done here."

We've already done eight takes of it, let's go . . .

Yeah, let's go, man, I'm thirsty, or whatever, or we better get to the gig. The era, the primitive rock era and the way those guys worked back then . . . And to this day, that song still has more truly astonishing passion and emotion in it, real terrible energy in it, than anything that has come since.

Just this last week he announced his retirement. He talked a little bit about his sexuality and told everyone, "We're going to stop touring."

He never went away. He was there in the Fillmore era, he was always around. I had friends who would go to Vegas to see him. The advertising slogan for him three of four years ago was something like "Tutius Fruitius at the Circus Maximus." It was really kind of neat. Those guys are like the ones in Greek Mythology that the Olympian gods had to fight, the ones that created the world. That is where those guys are to me, that whole generation of Chuck Berry, Bo Diddley, and Little Richard.

Would you include the modern-day country founders like Buck Owens in that generation?

I think of these people like Buck Owens and Johnny Cash, and of course, Hank Williams, who seems that he never went away because his songs were always there. He died before I was born, but he was always there. There was always a version of those songs on the radio somewhere, even if it was B.J. Thomas singing them. His stuff never went away.

The same man who brought us "The Ballad of the Green Beret"!

Those guys were on TV when I was a kid.

In Carlsbad, CA?

Anywhere. I remember when we lived in North and South Carolina . . . Porter Wagoner had a show. I used to watch him all the time. I knew all of his songs, and I ended up knowing a lot of his songs that he ended up never actually putting on his records. Every once in a while, I'll go through a Porter Wagoner collection for a song that I remember singing, and I won't find it. Of course, Johnny Cash had his own TV show too, and Buck Owens had *Hee Haw*. This music was good on *Hee Haw*, even though the humor was corny. It seemed like Merle Haggard was on TV every week in the late 1960s because he had a lot of hits back then. A lot of that music was just around. Of course, it was their heyday because they had a lot of hits.

The current marketing campaign for Johnny Cash, the Rick Rubin stuff with him flipping off, like this is what Johnny is saying to all the DJs and stuff. The whole "Johnny Cash was the original punk rocker." You read all these articles obviously generated by the American Records press approach, Johnny Cash as seventy-year-old punk rocker. I've always found that kind of stuff distasteful. I suppose it's trying to create an audience for him. That's why he does a Danzig song or a Jello Biafra song or all this stuff. To me, it's tasteless and I don't like it. There are a lot of other songs I'd love to hear Johnny Cash sing, and that sort of advertising campaign seems to dishonor him in a way. He is the man in black. I'm quite familiar with the persona of Johnny Cash, I've read the biographies and know all about the pills and the violence and infidelity and his general wild-ass lifestyle.

Actually, it wasn't any wilder than other country performers back then. If you read any of their stories, they were all wild back then because they worked a lot harder than rock bands did. They made less money, they didn't sell as many records, and didn't play places as big as rock bands did. That means you have to make more records and play more places. It means you're always working. In fact, when you talk to the old country guys who are still around and you ask them, they don't talk about gigs, they talk about work and job, meaning playing. It never stops. They don't retire and do those spectacular reunion show, twelve dates only at Dodger Stadium. They can't, they never have. That's why country music has always revolved around package shows too. For Merle Haggard to fill a place that holds five thousand people, he has to have four other top-notch country bands on the bill with him. Hopefully ones that have had a hit on the country charts within the last year or two, otherwise he's not going to get any people in there.

So, that's the thing about country performers, and the whole thing about Johnny Cash now . . . It just seems sort of tasteless, but also I think it's funny. Living in LA, you get your belly full of showbiz. This was really interesting. Johnny has a new American Records release coming out and the prerelease publicity if starting on it. The latest thing I saw, obviously straight from Rubin's thing, is, well I'm paraphrasing here, "Although most Johnny Cash fans are familiar with his wild-ass rebel image, very few of them of familiar with the gospel side of him." Now I read that and said, that is a classic case of showbiz having its cake and eating it too. I'm quite familiar with his gospel side, and any true Johnny Cash fan is familiar with that. Punk rock and alternative dorks that have only bought the last three Johnny Cash albums because they had a Danzig song on them . . .

Or Tom Petty's band on them.
Yeah, and they saw a blurry picture taken forty years ago of him backstage flipping somebody off, man he's radical, check him out, man. They may not be familiar with the gospel side, but I am walking into my little room here I got on the wall, my LP copy of Johnny Cash's *The Holy Land* which I display because it's got a cool 3-D cover, like *Their Satanic Majesties Request*. You look at the titles,

"Land of Israel," "This Is Nazareth," "He Turned the Water into Wine," and the last one is "God Is Not Dead." The thing, you might only be familiar with the image American records has been pushing the last five years, but now here's the new image! It's just so showbiz. It's really funny.

I detest show business. When it's not funny, it's revolting. I was talking to Javier Escovedo, Alejandro's brother, and he was in the Zeros. Chip and I are doing some work with Javier because he's getting ready to play out again and he asked us to play bass and guitar and sing with him and stuff. We were talking old days, and were joking and exchanging old war stories. It's funny, we all had the same types of stories, and what's interesting is that coming of age during the punk rock era, Javier and I have exactly the same approach to showbiz stuff. There's certain stuff we cannot sit and listen to as far as showbiz bullshit. There's certain stuff that makes us laugh when we hear it, whether it's a showbiz person saying it or a person in a band saying it. You just have to roll your eyes. My bullshit detector is so finely attuned to showbiz stuff, and that is nothing but pure punk rock. I've never been able to sit down and do the things that other bands do, or say things other bands say.

I remember L7, a couple of the girls in the band started their own label. This is when they were flirting on the edge of success several years ago, and that deal fell through I think, and they started their own record label. We were reading an interview with them, Chip was there too, and we almost fell on the floor laughing. You know their image? Nasty rock girl. In this interview with one of them, she was talking about, yeah, we left the label because we didn't want to deal with major label bullshit. We're going to start our own label now, but we don't want a bunch of bands to send demo tapes. Our label is for L7 product only. We read that and just started cracking up going, you know, girl, even if you think that, don't say it, because you sound like an asshole. For our product only, we don't want your demos [laughs]. It was the thing about "this is our latest product." It was so showbiz. In some ways, it doesn't help to have my sort of attitude— however you describe what I have—because it actually hurts you in the actual, real showbiz world because playing the game is such an important part of it.

How did you end up going from the land of punk rock revolution to the land of the cosmic cowboy, meaning from San Francisco to Austin?
Actually, we went to Austin because we thought of the outlaw music of Waylon and Willie. It was long gone by the time we got there! We just thought, let's go. Okay, here's a quick chronological step through. When the Dils broke up, I quit playing for a year and moved to Portland, Oregon. Chip moved to New York because he wanted to play with Alejandro, who was already living there. Chip said, I want to play with you, and Al said, come on out. They started playing out there, and the year I was living in Portland they put together Rank and File,

with Kevin Foley on drums, who became the original True Believers drummer, and this English guy named Barry on bass. They were some tours around, one of which came through Portland, at which time a year later I was ready to get back in music. They picked me up, and I went back with them to New York and started playing with the band and stuff like that. It was Rank and File, but really hadn't developed. The sound was still in its formative stage. We came back and started playing around New York with Barry on bass and me on guitar and singing a little bit with Chip and Al. We were getting more serious about the band and the idea behind it. We all loved that kind of music.

At the time, the career trajectory for ex-punk rockers was that you either went into rock music, or rockabilly was coming on strong, and a lot of ex-punk rockers were getting into it, some reggae-type stuff, like jack-off punk reggae-type stuff. I call it jack-off not because it wasn't a good idea, it just wasn't very good. The people didn't know what they were doing, or James White and the punky-type jazz. That or art stuff, real art-type stuff. It wasn't a career move in the sense of, let's do something different. It was a personal dare to say, I bet we can do this. We actually spent a lot of time working on our sound, putting it together, because when punk rockers play country music they sound like Mike Ness. It's thrashy: it's basically punk rock with alternating beats played real fast. That's easy to do, but we wanted to take a completely different approach and actually try and make music that was good, that we would have wanted to hear. None of us were listening to thrash music, we weren't playing it, and we weren't listening to it. In New York, we did a couple of shows, and it was regarded as a real novelty. Oh, you guys are such a cool idea. We kind of realized that we had to go somewhere where we could play and get our shit together, get the ideas happening. We went to the place of Waylon and Willie, man! It was like someone moving to San Francisco in 1986 wanting to hang out with the Dils.

Like, "Where are the outlaw cowboys?!"
Yeah, where are they, man! So, we moved to Austin, Chip, me, and Al. By that time, Barry had left the band. He didn't want to go.

Barry was once a DJ for the Clash, right?
Yes, but he wasn't interested in moving to Austin. Kevin didn't want to move to Austin at the time either, though he later moved to Austin to join the True Believers. So, we moved there and auditioned drummers and everybody thought we were absolutely crazy. Slim was literally the only drummer in Austin that wanted to play with us. A lot of people wanted to audition for us, because the Dils and the Nuns were sort of pseudo-famous punk rock bands. We had a lot of people audition, but everybody said, you're crazy, I don't want to do this. Slim was the only drummer who wanted to play with us. We got this gig at a place

called Club Foot, a new wave club there. We played there, I think we got a good review from it, but the club said no thank you. We never want to see you again.

Did you play Raul's?
We ended up playing this club called the Short Horn, a little honky tonk on the north side of town, which isn't there anymore. We did every Wednesday there for several months, and that's actually where we started to put things together. There would be some lone bands that would come out to see us, and a bar full of drunks that would yell at us the whole time. A literal quote I remember is, "You boys can't play country music, your hair is too short." When we started doing it, people thought we were crazy. Slowly but surely, it started coming around. We started doing Alamo Lounge shows that were acoustic downtown and started getting a following, and then there were our regular shows too. It slowly built up from there. But even then, it was totally unexpected. We heard a lot from alternative rocker, punkers, or new-wavers, that, "I don't want to hear this shit. This is what my parents listen to." This was way before the *No Depression* country-is-cool days. This was regarded as treason by the hipsters. If Chip, Al, and me put together a Nuns/Dils greatest hits show, we could have automatically been packing clubs.

How did the elders feel about it, like John Dee Graham, who started the Skunks, one of the first Austin punk bands, and currently a singer/songwriter?
The only bands that really sort of liked us were like the Dicks, the punk rock bands. For one thing, we became friends with them and knew them, so they liked us. It seemed like guys like Gary Floyd and Randy Turner from the Dicks and Big Boys know who Gary and Randy are. They always have. You know, Gary is a large, gay, weird-looking punk rock dude who is a great guy. He has no problem being who is he and what he looks like. Those are the best people in the world. Gary was able to look at something like Rank and File and not feel it was threatening his punk rock identity. It wasn't treason. He had a great band, he was a great performer, and he's a great person. He didn't need to have some other punk rock guys validate who he was because he didn't give a shit. If you liked you, he liked you, if he didn't, he didn't. And he liked it, but he didn't dislike it because this was the enemy. The same with Randy. They were two of the friendliest guys when we moved there. But it was the new-wavers . . . You know what one of the biggest things in Austin was? "We've got to get MTV in Austin" [laughs].

When we moved there, we really started blowing people's minds. Sooner or later, people started coming around, and the band actually did do something, But to be honest with you, if David Kahne, who ended up producing the first record, had not seen us one night in San Francisco, the band would have played around Austin and broken up in a year or so because nothing would have happened. Everybody thought we were crazy, and although a lot of people liked the band, we really didn't have any future because there was no audience for that kind of music. Our first two albums sold well for the kind of albums they were. People were always surprised by how well we were doing, surprised we were able to pack places, surprised by how good the stuff was. When they're always being surprised, it means they're never ready to capitalize on any kind opportunity that's going to come their way, record companies, or management, or any of that record biz kind of stuff. Nirvana's *Nevermind* happens, an album that sold millions, when people aren't surprised anymore, when they are expecting that to happen it doesn't catch anybody by surprise. If he had not accidentally seen us that night, we would have gone back to Austin, played around for a couple more years, and broken up.

But what about the 1987 self-titled record? That seems to have a more polished rock sound, as if you were abandoning the roots rock sound you had been perfecting and the audience you had been working to build.
A lot of this gets into personal stuff. We actually got caught in a contractual problem with Slash. That third album came out on Rhino. When we got done with *Long Gone Dead*, we went out and toured a lot. If you're a band on an independent label, you basically have to keep working. We wanted to get in and make our other record fairly soon. What happened was, one of the guys at Slash had developed a very serious cocaine problem, and we had the material to make that third record, and we wanted to make it. We had a producer and everything. But the guys who ran Slash would not make the decision to let us back in the studio. It was worse than that. He never came out and said, in six months you will be recording. It was always like next week, next week, next week. It was a cocaine thing. For months and months, a year, we thought we were going to be in the studio next week, which means, we're not booking any shows, we're not booking any tours, we're always getting ready to go in the studio next week. It was a nightmare. You've heard stories about drugs and bands, imagine when the band is not on drugs, but the record company is. That's what exactly what happened. If I knew then what I knew now . . . or if anybody in my situation came to me now and just described it exactly as it was, I would say, look, fuck it. You want to record something, go in the studio and record it. In the meantime, get your ass out on the road and keep working.

Did you almost end up in the position of the Screamers, but instead of waiting for the next big thing, you kept waiting for the next studio session.
We were contractually obligated. We couldn't go record somewhere else. We couldn't go record for another label. If he would have said, look, you are not

ready to record, you're not ready to record because you haven't written a good song or something like that, we would have booked the tour and kept the name of the band out there. By the time that third album came out, people thought the band had broken up because we hadn't been out playing for two years.

At the same time, a new influx of roots rock bands surfaced, like Long Ryders and Del Fuegos.

I actually don't like that third album because by that time I was so burned out on the whole thing that I didn't care anymore, and I'm going to blame Chip for that. Chip was totally into hard rock. That's all he wanted to do. I didn't. I really wasn't into that, but I stopped caring. I was like, well, whatever, if you want to, it's okay. I basically reached a point where I had in the Dils where I was sitting there going, I don't really like this. So, the third record, I can't say that I disown it, but it's probably the record I was least involved or interested in making. I just simply wasn't interested in it at the time. I felt sort of lost and helpless, not in the sense of poor pitiful helpless me, but just that I didn't even know what I wanted to do with music and that's why after the record came out we toured for a while and broke up. I just didn't care anymore, and that's why we formed Blackbird.

Had you already been working on Blackbird material?

Actually, well, I'll speak for myself. When I make a real artistic decision like, this is done, like Rank and File is done, I just set the book down, close the back cover, and put it back on the library shelf. Now, I want to write a new book. Let's have some fun. That was the whole idea behind Blackbird for Chip and me. We had unfortunately gotten into that whole Slash thing. Also, we had fired our manager, and she sued us, so when we are on the road with Rank and File, we were sending her back thousands of dollars. It was an ugly showbiz thing that I thought would never happen. If we missed a day, our road manager at the time would have to collect money from the club that night, and we were still making good money at the time, and get up early in the morning and get a cashier's check at Western Union and fire it off to her, and if she hadn't received it by that afternoon she would be screaming on the phone. Her lawyer would be calling us, saying, we are going to sue you. Alejandro had a lawyer threatening to sue, saying he owed the name Rank and File. It was just really, really lame. It was not want I wanted to do at all. Lawyers and shit. It was like, forget it, and to this day, when Chip and I get into any contractual agreement with any company, and I actually urge this to bands, I say, if the contract is not simple enough for you to understand without a lawyer, have them rewrite it until you can understand it. If you like what you read then, then sign it.

Some people might wonder why you left a label like Slash, but then with Blackbird got on a label like Scotti Bros. Did they ask you to do a new version of "Class War," or did you both choose to do that?

No, that was actually an old buddy of ours who recorded some earlier Blackbird stuff. That was kind of a wank, a jerk off. That was ridiculous even for Blackbird, but as far as the Scotti Bros things was, yeah, we'll make a record. The company also makes movies. This is a joke, a real laugh. So, these guys had come by the studio and heard Chip and I doing vocal tracks, and they liked our singing. They were making a movie called *Jersey Girl*. Is that a Springsteen song sung by Tom Waits, or vice versa? The version I am familiar with is the Tom Waits version, right? So they say, we need a version of the song for the movie because they hadn't gotten clearance to use Tom Waits's version, would you guys like to try it . . . for $5,000? We said sure. They were kind of surprised that we hadn't heard it, but we said give us a tape and we'll go home and listen to it over the weekend. We went in, did a version of it in like an hour, which they hated, and we got our money. That was Blackbird . . . It was strictly just for fun. We stopped Blackbird because we were just running out of ideas for that band. This is going to sound strange, but we couldn't get un-poppy enough to get the sound we actually wanted. No matter what songs we wrote and recorded, they always ended up sounding like us. They also sounded like, well, if you sat down with an acoustic guitar, it would sound like Cowboy Nation, or if you sat down on a Telecaster, it would sound like Rank and File. That's how we ended up doing the Scotti Bros. record.

Do you think the early 1970s were as bad (overproduced schlock) for country music as it was for rock music?

I remember being a kid in the 1970s and driving around, and the only guitar songs on the radio at the time was when Steve Miller had his hits like "Take the Money and Run" and "Rock'n Me" and the middle part of "Saturday Night's Alright for Fighting" by Elton John. That was the only guitar you heard on radio because there wasn't any oldies radio then. That was the only stuff you heard. You heard all sorts of John Lennon, and saxophones on everything, and just that really cocaine-flavored jazz rock music that was big at the time, as well as the art music like Utopia, then those horrible stadium bands like Journey and stuff like that. I remember that was the only guitar you could hear, but at the time I wasn't thinking, wow, we are in a really bad era for rock music, because I didn't know when it began or if it was going to end, it just was. It's the same thing with country music. We can look back and say that there was a lot of garbage there, but there was a lot of good stuff too. You know, Don Williams was happening, who I like. Waylon and Willie were cutting good stuff.

There was a lot of garbage, but there's always a lot of garbage. There's a lot of garbage now. My basic rule of thumb when it comes to anything, whether it's movies, music, or books is at least 90 percent is going to be shit. At least, and sometimes it will get up to 99 percent shit. Only a tiny fraction of anything at any one time is going to be really good. I think when popular art forms tend to enter a period of lassitude in the short or absolute decadence in the long run, when you can basically tell it is over, I think there are other signs of it other than overproduction or stuff like that. One of the real signs, one of the reasons now why rock music itself is in a period of terminal decadence as far as any creativity goes is because it's becoming completely self-referential. There is no real change in it anymore. If you look back on the eras of rock music from, say from Chuck Berry to the Beatles breaking up, which is a span of maybe . . . Well, Chuck Berry was still having hits in the late 1950s and early 1960s, but you've got a span of like thirteen years. Thirteen years ago it was 1989. There hasn't been any significant earthquake time change in at least white popular music. Well, that last real change in white popular music was punk rock.

El Vez
(The Zeros)

El Vez (Robert Lopez) is one of the most intriguing figures in punk history. With roots in bands such as the Zeros and Nervous Gender, by the 1990s he spun a new identity that mixed class consciousness, identity politics, Hispanic pride, and pop culture appropriation and disruption. Part performance artist, part rabble-rouser, part swooning singer, his panache and irony, plus limitless gusto and charm, are unmatched.

This interview was originally published in *Left of the Dial*.

While in Europe, you met Joe Strummer from the Clash. Was it special?
Sure, meeting your punk rock hero over regular dinner, drinks, and fun. I think he's a great guy. I've always loved his music. It's the first time I ever met him. We have mutual friends, but we had never met. It was a full night as opposed to, oh, it's nice to meet you, on to next person. We became friends enough that we could tease each other at the end of the night.

In the Zeros during the late 1970s, the Clash were an important band to you?
Oh yeah. I left the Zeros in the later half of 1978, and they played with the Clash not long afterwards. I was very jealous.

The Zeros single "Wild Weekend" is in the music museum in Seattle?
Actually, it's the first one. "Wild Weekend" is actually the second single. "Don't Push Me Around" and "Wimp" are the first single, and it is at the Seattle museum. I saw it last time I was there behind Plexiglas. You push a little button and you can hear it.

Do they have any El Vez stuff there?
No, not yet. They'll have to enlarge their Elvis impersonator section.

Did punk mean something different to young Chicanos in the late 1970s in bands like the Plugz, Nuns, and Zeros than it did for the people in the Dils or the Weirdos?

That was the nice thing about being in that period because it didn't break down into girl bands, guy bands, and Chicano bands. We felt a part of the scene, the music scene, punk rock in whatever forms it was, like the Deadbeats, Weirdos, or nonguitar bands like the Screamers. You just felt part of a movement of the scene, rather than saying we're Chicanos and we feel this way, or those are girls, and they feel this way. You felt like, yeah, this is all music that we like, this is all music that is different than what we hear on the radio or see on TV. So, it wasn't broken down into . . . Well, being Chicano wasn't even a focal point or focus of the band. It was like, we're another band. I think people maybe pointed at the fact that we were younger than anyone else. It was a kind of nice thing because it didn't matter that we were Latinos. It was just that we were a band. It gave us a whole part of the scene rather than us having to feel we're "this."

What led you to the political perspective that comes out on *Graciasland*?

Um, when you are young you are moving on the energy of youth, and as you develop more ideas, you have more things you want to say in certain ways. I think that getting the agenda out is more my call now with El Vez. Just to get issues across or keep people more aware, especially in these times when things are in a conservative cycle back again. Ideas like border issues and other things are swept under the table unless you are the thorn in the side, or the thorn underneath the rose, or whatever you want to be. You have to be the agitator and bring it up again. I choose to verbalize it in songs.

Can you see yourself making music without those messages?

Oh yeah. Definitely. I have a country and western band called Trailer Park Casanovas. We're working on our third album, and we toured Finland last year. It's all original material, but it's bluegrass and roots kind of stuff. There are no real issues that are brought up at all.

How did you end up in Finland?

There's a big rockabilly convention that they have there. We're kind of blown-out bluegrass, which kind of fits under the alternative country rockabilly scene. They had this great three-day festival that is on the longest day. I forget what it is. The summer solstice, I believe. It's held way up north, a couple of hours north of Helsinki even. Some bands liked us, so they had us flown out there and paid our way. It was a nice experience. It was really weird being there because Finland is nice, they have a socialized medical system, and people are pretty much set, and there's not really any people of color at all there. But at this rockabilly fest, when I first got there I saw the rebel flags and stuff like that, and usually you say, okay, they are young rockabilly kids. When they think of rebel flags they think of the South, and when they think of the South they think of Memphis, and when they think of Memphis they think of Elvis, so it just goes with that territory. But then slowly I began to notice things.

There was one kid who had come like five hours from the Lapland area who was helping us out. He was a fan and all that stuff. He was wearing little bib overalls, and I saw a little peek of the top of the T-shirt, then later when he bent down I could see it was a Ku Klux Klan T-shirt. Then later I saw kids with these terrible T-shirts that said things like, "Watch Out Nigger, Finland Klan Is Getting Bigger," and then another kid had one with a picture of Hitler's sidemen. I was really put off by all this and ended up staying at the hotel most of the time. The other band members were hanging around the big field where all the kids parked their 1950s cars and stayed in tents. They said the kids were doing the equivalent of "We Are the Mods," but only as white supremacist versions of the song. It was really sad and disturbing. When we played, I addressed it a little bit. I didn't want to turn this band into something political, but when things happen you need to address them and make comments, even slip them under the table. So, maybe I will always say what's on my mind, but I can write a love song too, or a song about dancing, or a song about the stupidity of racism.

How did the Audi car company decide they wanted El Vez to play?

They had a commercial on that season with a Nastassja Kinski type of woman in a car. In it, an Elvis impersonator's car breaks down, and he had this wiggly Elvis car stick on the windshield mirror. Every time he would switch his gears, the Elvis would jiggle. He was having a good time, but then his car broke down. When he's picked up by the woman in the brand new Audi S42, shifting gears is so smooth that Elvis doesn't jiggle. You know, the little toy Elvis. So, she had to push it with her fingers. It was a big, popular commercial, so they had to have an Elvis impersonator. One of the organizers said, "I know a great Elvis impersonator in Los Angeles named El Vez." One of the head Audi people said, "You mean El Vez, the Mexican Elvis? Bring him over, we love him." We do pretty well in Germany, so we have a pretty big fanbase there. They paid for a nice trip to France again, and we got to see the races. It was good.

Tell me about "Around the World in Eighty Minutes," your stand-up show.

It's based around *Around the World in Eighty Days*, only I couldn't do it that long, so I did eighty minutes. It's monologues and a little bit of music, but it's like my travels and my tours. It's like tour memoirs almost, and my view of the world through El Vez, with political, spiritual, and sexual commentary. In each area I make comments and tell stories or sing songs. It went over really well . . . kind of like an El Vez show with less music, more talking, and fuller ideas. We have slide projections and movies behind me and all that kind of stuff. It's very nice.

Do you find labels like "revolutionary chic" and "king of camp" demeaning?

I think they're fun. I mean, I am not an impersonator, but I like the term because I'm more like a translator, so it's not like a full-on impersonation of Elvis. Names are just a way of helping you get a grip on something, but when you see the show, or listen to it, people say, this is completely not what I thought it would be like. I don't mind labels because I always think I break them. So, it doesn't bother me.

You've said, "I superimpose my culture and heritage over American icons because that's what America is about."

Well, it's the Statue of Liberty, bring me your homeless, your tired and weary, melting-pot kind of idea. What is America? Is it apple pie? It can be tamale pie too. The idea is that America is sauerkraut, America is sopapillas, America is chop suey, America is all these different things because America is based on the idea of immigration and people from other lands coming to this land to mix it all up together and establish themselves with other cultures, so to be of a different culture is an American thing. The whole thing of Elvis as an icon is pretty American, and I superimpose on it and put a moustache on it, but it could be easily become a black one, or a pan-Asian idea of what it could be. Like taking those cultural ideas and applying them to this American pie Elvis and saying, this is what America is about too.

Like the playwright Luis Valdez ("Los Vendidos"), who exaggerates stereotypes of pachucos, Americanized Mexican-American college students, and hardworking immigrant laborers, are you doing the same thing by deflating and exposing such stereotypes for what they are?

El Vez is an extreme of how Mexican I can be. It's overblown, and it's also an idea of an Elvis. No one really takes an Elvis impersonator very seriously. They're almost American court jesters. The idea of making it a Mexican one with charro, style, and flash is to gild that lily even more. But to have words of truth—revolution, safe sex, and Latino heroes—coming through that messenger is to completely confuse and enhance the issues at the same time. I think there are stereotypes of every culture, and I think that's fine. When I see the Chihuahua commercial for Taco Bell or Speedy Gonzalez, I don't think that's how people view me. Because sure, there's Mexicans with accents, and sure there might be lazy Mexicans, but there's lazy white people, there's lazy black people, there's lazy everybody. There's fast-talking Mexicans, there's fast-talking Japanese, there's fast-talking black people. Every culture can be stereotyped, but

it does not mean that every person is that way. I, for one, don't think that way, and think it includes all the people. Stereotypes can be used for humor sometimes, and I blow them up and then empower them with knowledge, strength, and issues that can be addressed.

When you've questioned the use of brown shirts by the Brown Berets or the stylized black eagle for the UTW, has it gotten you some flak in the Hispanic community?

No, but I wouldn't mind it. I think debating ideas, even things you might hold near and dear, is a good thing. You shouldn't take anything just on face value. Things can be questioned, analyzed, and changed or stay the same. You can look at things many different ways. When I had different shows, like the Gospel Show, or the Rock and Revolution, or El Vez for Prez, I'm not really running for president or trying to be a spiritual leader. I don't have a political manifesto, but I'm trying to open the door for debate or trying to get you to think about it or say here's a possibility. I'm not saying this is the end all, be all, and this is the way you should see God. Or this is the end all, be all, the correct political way things should go. I just want people to think. I want people to laugh because when you are smiling or laughing you are more open to different views and ideas. The idea of taking something you know, like Elvis, and saying, how about looking at things this way? It's like turning it upside down and putting a moustache on it. It's still that Elvis idea, but here's a new point of view of it. Here's someone else's point of view. I think the music can make them think, but at the same time it is entertainment and can make them happy.

What is it about the Strokes and the White Stripes that you like?

Well, sorry to say, but it's nostalgic because they remind me of good stuff. The Strokes remind me of New York, 1978, Blondie, Television, some Iggy in there. And the White Stripes remind me of everything from 1974, Jimmy Page to Howlin' Wolf to the Cramps to the Jon Spencer Blues Explosion. I like nostalgia a lot. It's a kind of comfort. I like when it's thrown around and out into a new way.

You are totally responsible for the total sound collage of your music?

All the live albums, all the shows, all the arrangements are all done by me. It's all my musical history, and the little things that meant something to me, or sounds that I like. It's like DJs now who use little bits of everything they like, but we did it with live musicians, so it's sad to say, very nostalgic, but I'm not closed to new things. Sometimes it becomes new. We got some new songs in this show. Using bits of other pieces can turn into something new. Even Picasso took bits from African masks or other things that he saw. That's part of the creative process I think. Take things from the past and make them totally new, but the ideas come from other bits.

You were the first person in California to be presented the Elvis stamp?

Yes, I was. I had made an El Vez stamp. This company had made a 1-800 number where you could call El Vez and get the information. It was one of those recorded messages, one of those 976s when they first started. They made these great El Vez stamps that looked just like the young Elvis stamps except they put the Mexican flag behind me. It was the same pose in the photograph. They were really great. I was at the Hollywood Library Post Office in downtown Hollywood and the postmaster general of California presented me with the first sheet of Elvis, and I presented him with the first sheet of El Vez. They had these great big giant cakes with a peanut butter and banana center. One was an Elvis stamp, and the other the El Vez stamp. We sang the same songs. It was a fun day.

What happened to the German film you once described as a "Faust-Phantom of the Paradise-Chiapas Revolutionary Fantasy"?

It's one of those showbiz things where things come up [laughs]. I have been close to many great things. It was really nice because I had just finished the Zeros tour, and then they flew me to Vienna and put me up in this great, giant apartment and gave me a Mercedes to use while I was there. We'd go through these meetings and everything we talked about would be written down by these secretaries, so we'd have the notes. If we needed any books or references, someone was there, so I could say, "I need to look at *Rock 'n' Roll Swindle*," and they would go out and bring it to me that afternoon. Or I'd say, I need to see the Alan Freed book, and then they'd go out and get it. They put me up for a week, and I'd just take notes, ideas, and movies clips and say, "Let's make something like this," and we'd brainstorm these ideas for movies. We came up with three different scripts, and it was a nice thing. But that's showbiz, one of those things. I've had a lot of great chances. In my first year of doing El Vez, I was speaking with people at Disney and been under contract at Warner Bros. once with a guy who now manages Jennifer Lopez. He was working for me for a while, and we were working on a show for Warner Bros. I was under contract. They sent me to acting schools. It was a Patty Duke idea of me playing El Vez and Raul Raul, who is this Latino-Chicano angry young man, kind of a Chicano Kerouac beat kind of poet character that I had done before. I got all this money, pre-filming money, but it fell through. I did a thing with HBO last summer, and that was a nice thing. Things come and go. I always have a ton of stuff on my plate, so I don't mind when things fall through because that means I get some break time. Then I have the other band to work with, and so many El Vez projects to work on, so I don't worry too much. There's always something placed in front of me.

Is there a part of you who wishes to be back at a gallery, like in the 1980s?
Sometimes because when I see a real good artist, I say, if this was marketed in the right way, it could be very popular, or done better, this and that. I love art, whether it's visual, audio, or painting kind of stuff. It's always attracted me.

You were quoted as saying Morrissey was trying to steal your ideas.
[Laughs] No, he said that. The year before that we did a small tour with him in Vegas and California, and he wanted us to do the U.S. and England, but I got too busy with my own shows. In the press, he said he thought I was great and was trying to steal all my ideas. He just point blank said that, but I thought that was a nice compliment. Some people said they had seen his shows in Brazil and he was wearing copies of outfits I had.

If Elvis rolled out of the grave and showed up at your house, what would you say to him?
What was it like coming back from the dead? I don't have any questions about songs, or what he did. I'm happy with my Elvis lore and the ways things went, but I would like to know what it's like to come back from the dead.

Charlie Harper
(UK Subs)

In 1985, I flew into New York with my sister and watched the city unravel in the million-fold glitter of glaring windows wedged between the murky Meadowlands and the black hole of the Atlantic Ocean. We took a cab into Manhattan and stared in awe at the dirty corners and relentless inhuman blocks as the Jamaican cab driver blasted some heavy dub. My brother lived in a basement apartment in the Lower East Side, where the whole hall shared one bathroom and mice darted in and out of the foam mattress. I sat around and taped Government Issue and Joy Division records deep into the a.m., ate cheap Chinese food, drank orange juice as my sister smoked marijuana that was laced and made her sick, shied away from skinheads in Token Entry T-shirts loud-mouthing around a Tompkins Square pizzeria, and watched as a Puerto Rican skateboarder with LL Cool J songs webbed in his brain called the fire department on an art punk roof party. One afternoon I stopped by a tiny cramped record store staffed by a dude with wily dyed black hair and flipped through the bins, eager to spread my cash on the counter for the first Youth of Today LP, and Discharge and UK Subs "best of" compilations. As soon as I heard "Stranglehold," "Party in Paris," "Telephone Numbers," and other chunks of Charlie Harper's soul, I saw the street-minded second wave of Brit Punk open up and turn my world upside down.

Originally published in *Left of the Dial.*

The UK Subs just played Brazil. Was that the first time they played South America?

We actually played in Argentina twice. That was quite a trip. One time we were called there because the biggest Argentine punk rock band were breaking up, and they requested that the UK Subs come out there and party with them. It was great. The actual singer was Irish-Argentine. He didn't speak hardly any English, but he was a complete Irishman in the way that he drank. Most people kind of tolerated him. I thought he was brilliant because he was just this drunken mess, a bit like an Argentinean equivalent of the guy from the Pogues.

Shane MacGowan?
Yeah, exactly. Except this Argentinean is worse. We'd go to this place for dinner, and he'd fall asleep in his soup. His hair was caked in gunk. He was a legend out there. The strongest place in South America that he is most popular in, where he has sold the most records, is Bolivia, a country west of Argentina. So, he moved there because he's big in Bolivia. They're not just the biggest punk rock band in Bolivia, they're, like, the biggest band in Bolivia. And he has the most amazing Bolivian girlfriend.

You guys have always been trailblazers, like being the first punk band to play in Poland, behind the iron curtain. Was it an accident that you ended playing there in front of thousands of people?
Well, not really. Obviously it was done by a big agency in Poland. It was kind of a propaganda thing because Lech Walesa, the Solidarity leader who would later become president, was in jail at the time. They thought they'd get these concerts over, like Elton John went over first for the pop fans, then we did it for the underground. It was a heroin-for-the-people kind of thing, but the country was still quite divided. It was on the brink of civil war.

Did you see Soviet troops?
Not Soviet troops, but Polish troops were always at our concerts with machine guns. Instead of having bouncers, there were like thirty of forty troops there. The smallest concert we done was four thousand people, and the biggest were two shows of twelve thousand people. We played to twenty-five thousand people that night. They were these big shows in ice hockey arenas.

Do you feel that you connected with the kids?
Oh yeah, oh yeah. We'd speak to them before or after. It wasn't until after that, maybe five years later, that they'd tear you to pieces just trying to get a bit of clothing or hair or something. We've been out there a few times. It's still very divisive. It almost feels that the whole of Poland is just Nazis except for these kids. You'll see these Nazi skinheads, which we haven't seen much of lately, but it was very bad out there. It seems like the whole country is fascist except for the Poles who escaped over to England or America because you've got millions over here. It's like all the good ones escaped.

Was it your parents who fled the Spanish Civil War?
My grandparents.

Is that what influenced your politics, or did you learn politics on the street?
Not really, because my uncle grew up to be communist, and that was always
frowned upon back then.

A communist or Trotskyite?
A member of the Communist Party. He was a bit talked about and admired.
Family politics was straight-down-the-line Democrat, I suppose, but "Democratic"
means a different thing in America, it's kind of right-wing, but in England it just
means democracy, or left-wing socialism.

As a kid in the mod scene, you used to see Rod Stewart busking on the corner?
We were friends and buskers together.

How you get from there to punk rock?
[Laughs] We still do one of my favorite busking songs, which is an old American folk song called "Bottle of Wine," an old hobo song.

From the 1930s?
"Bottle of wine . . . When are you gonna let me get sober?" I think it goes back even further, because if it were from the '30s, then they would know who wrote it, so it probably goes back past even the turn of the century.

You can hear that influence on records like *Another Kind of Blues* with the harmonica and soulful singing.
It's not done purposely by any means because when Nicky came along he said, "You said you've got to drop all this rock'n'roll shit." But that's part of me, you know what I mean? I can't burn out of it. I tell you how it comes out because Nicky will come up with a hell of a lot of music for a song, then I'll say look, this bit is neat, you don't want to just pass it over. This bit could be the verse, or between the chorus. It needs to be played eight times over. That's my kind of blues, R&B upbringing. We do everything in eight bars, twelve bars, or four bars. We repeat, we don't just go across one bit of music. I just think that it's just too throwaway. I do come from the 1960s, twelve-bar thing, where you do something for twelve bars, or say you do a riff, then sing a line, and then play again. I repeat that in a few songs, not enough, but I like the way you do a little riff then sing a bit. For anybody who plays guitar out there, and you have to sing and play guitar, it's very easy, because I used to sing and play bass. You just sing on straight, then you do a kind of riff, then sing on the next bit.

Do you think bands like the 101ers and Eddie and the Hot Rods were the bridge between the R&B sounds of pub rock and punk rock?
When the Hot Rods came up, it was slightly different than pub rock. That was the South End. The South End of what? The South End of the county they were in. There was this great place by the sea, and all these great bands came out of there in the 1970s, like Eddie and the Hot Rods and Dr. Feelgood. Lovely great bands came from the South End. It's like they had that Manchester explosion with Oasis. Sometimes you get this nest of great bands. They went more towards punk than the pub rock thing did. The pub rock thing was almost country. You know the song "American Pie"? It's got piano and guitar in it; well, that's pure pub rock. Maybe that's why it was so big in England.

How would you define pub rock?
Out here in America it's called trucking music. It's kind of got the R&B and country sound. It's strong and powerful. It drives along, like for guys on the road for ten days.

On trucker speed.
[Laughs] Trucker music. That's what it was.

Why did you guys always get lumped in with bands like Angelic Upstarts and Cockney Rejects?
Well, they came out a bit later than us. Let's take it right back from Velvet Underground and Hollywood Brats and New York Dolls. When punk rock came out, we all got our inspiration from those bands, but we took it a bit harder, a little more bitchin' and spiteful, as it were. Then that launched the Sex Pistols, the Clash were very political, and Siouxsie made beautiful kind of music, the Jam went right back to the mod days and had the 1960s feel, the Damned more into the glam side, then our generation came along, like Sham 69 had a tougher line. Then the bands you just mentioned went a bit more strong, more punk, more virile, and then after that came Exploited, Discharge, and Crass. It got very hardcore.

Did it bother you to see hardcore take over?
It's great to see these changes in the music and wonder what is going to happen next. Now we've got old school, new school [laughs].

You've said that punk is just like blues and jazz: it will continually change.
Yeah, yeah. Like jazz will be, or blues will be. Some artist will come out, like some black artist came out and could actually write very good, and came out with a nice Fender guitar style, and took it right back there to Robert Johnson, but then everybody started copying this guy. Over here, Nirvana came out, and every band started sounding like Nirvana. So, it does have its kind of good side and downside. Instead of bands coming out with something different, they just jump on the bandwagon. "Nirvana just sold a million records, and we want to do this."

But is it surprising that songs like "Stranglehold" didn't sell a million copies, because it's basically a pop song, and not essentially any rougher or harder than a Green Day song?
Twenty years later. Our songs are written almost out of necessity, which is a shame, but you need some songs for a set, and we write these songs in like five minutes. They're not written with any thought, it's just sheer . . . Well, before

the UK Subs I was in a band called the Subs a year before the UK Subs in 1976, and we were still playing a lot of Chuck Berry songs. The Sex Pistols even played Chuck Berry songs. We were by the bar and people were leaving the pub afterwards and they'd be singing "Stranglehold," and I turned to my mate and said, "They're singing 'Stranglehold' not 'Johnny B. Goode' or 'Roll Over Beethoven.' They're singing our song." I still remember [laughs] the chill running down my back thinking, they're singing our songs, not these great standards. I thought, we're in with the chumps there. That's the way to go. Then I write "Party in Paris" and "Tomorrow's Girl." I do suspect there are some good pop songs. With "Party in Paris," for instance, I sometimes pick up the bass and play without thinking. Suddenly, I listen to what I'm playing and think, that's not too bad. And I'll go and make a riff out of it and surprise myself with it. When I wrote "Party in Paris," I said, I wrote this song, but it sounds very poppy, but the band didn't hear it that way.

When Nick put the guitar to it?
Well, I played it on guitar for them. But they didn't hear it as a kind of pop song. What I'm trying to say, when you write something down it surprises you when it becomes popular. I never think it will. We never go out of our way and say, let's write something that will be popular. It's more like, let's write a skate song like "Sk8 Tough" because half of us skate, so let's write a silly little skate song because it makes us happy. Even that song, even though it was never released as a single, became the most poppy song on that album. We did it live in France one time and then forgot about it, but the next time we went to France it was shown on TV. They had done a little video of it. But this studio was so poor, so they couldn't do it with four or five cameras. They'd do me with one camera, then the drummer with one camera, over and over again and so on, then do the whole band, then cut it. But they were used to doing this, so they were masters of cutting, and when they put it together again it was amazing. Every time we went to France after that and did it, everyone would go crazy. We had a hit out there without knowing it. Those things are kind of nice.

Is it interesting how different songs become big in different places?
Yeah, we had one in LA where this very highly regarded DJ, originally from New York, didn't sell out. He'd just play all underground music all the time. He got one of our singles, one of which I thought was a particularly good song, but no one else did [laughs]. The song was called "Another Typical City." I had gone to see Flipper or someone and the guy really flipped off the audience and said, "You're just another typical city involved in a typical daydream" while bitching at the audience for not jumping around. I thought, that's good. That's a line that should not be wasted. I wrote this song. It was what I call an almost

bastardized kind of thing, and it came out on a single with a few other songs. This DJ picked up on "Another Typical City" and played it all the time. So, when we came to LA, suddenly we were playing to six thousand people, and that was great because I always imagined something like that happening. Too bad we didn't get any financial gain out of it. For four or five years, we were playing big shows in Los Angeles.

In fact, you've said that touring America is basically a money-losing proposition?

But it is a lovely place to go. People do pay to come here, and we get paid to come here. We only just manage to bring our rent money back home. We don't come here for the money. It's just that we have a great time when we are here.

You don't do it for the glamour, or the bus over my shoulder [Government Mule was playing upstairs].

[Laughs] They can keep that bus. It doesn't hold any romance. I've done three U.S. tours in RVs, which is kind of okay. But now we just have this people carrier, this van. We've got room for the four of us and the T-shirt girl when she gets fed up with the other band. We just like to get there fast. We were late for a show down in Tampa, and we had to come from Baltimore. We had two days to do it, but we were going a hundred miles per hour. It can really cruise at that speed [laughs].

A few years ago you had a Strangler and a Vibrator living with you? What was that like?

Yeah. Well, the drummer is still actually my landlord, Eddie from the Vibrators. Knox is one of my best buddies as well, and he's from the Vibrators. We are very close. Actually, it's Eddie's wife that makes our T-shirts back in England. John Ellis [Vibrators] is not so much a friend, but he's just a really nice guy.

Would you have a band with all of you together?

No, Eddie plays in a lot of blues combos when he's not playing with the Vibrators. And John is just now getting a blues outfit together, and I said, "Can I play harmonica?" But he's got this German guy playing harmonica. Quite honestly, we don't get the time. Me and Knox got a band called the Urban Dogs together, but we struggle to find time to get things moving in that direction. We're always doing little bits of recording, but disregard nine-tenths of it.

Do you ever speak to the guys from Stiff Little Fingers or the Buzzcocks, who still tour just like the Subs?

I've got a lot of time for Pete Shelley and Steve Diggle. I don't know if you've checked it out, but Steve Diggle looks like the twin of Alvin Gibbs, the Subs bass player. Alvin used to really hate Steve Diggle because every time he went up to Steve Diggle to say hi, Steve Diggle knows who he is but just blanks him and turns his back. He says, "Why does he do that, Charlie?" I say, you would too if everyone comes up to you and goes, "Hey, Steve, c'mon I'll buy you a drink," and Alvin makes out that he's Steve Diggle and takes this guy's drink and at the end of the night says, "By the way, I'm Alvin from the UK Subs." Well, the Buzzcocks are on a rung a bit higher than us. When we play to three hundred, they'll play to three thousand. "It must be okay for you," I told Alvin, "but everyone must be patting Steve on the back and saying, you're Alvin Gibbs," and that must really bring him down! [laughs] But he didn't quite see it that way. Pete Shelley is a great mate and great person.

Do you receive checks from the cover by Guns N' Roses?

Not anymore, it was ten years ago. But we'd just like to thank the guys, and ask if you want any more songs! Actually, I've written a song for Axl Rose. Well, my last girlfriend, who was Italian, was crazy about Guns N' Roses. She kind of stalked me after seeing us in Italy. She was very young then, about seventeen. After talking to me, she decided she wanted to go to the University of London and study and track us down. And she did when she was nineteen. She's a great girl, Lulu, but she's crazy about Guns N' Roses, so that's the connection. I wrote this really great song. She's a little bit of a musician, she plays fiddle, and she'd like to play bass and guitar. She's got a bass, and I used to try and teach her, but she's a university student studying ancient Greek archeology. She's very busy and has a night job as a bouncer. She's a pretty little skinny girl with tattoos. I wrote this song for her. She always wanted a steel guitar, but they cost thousands of dollars, so I wrote, "One day girl you'll have your steel guitar." It's a kind of a folksy ballad, but it's brilliant, and maybe Axl Rose will get to hear this from your fanzine and turn this song into a hit song. It's almost written for him. It's about this girl wishing for this steel guitar, then one day getting it, like a quest.

Is there one thing you wished you would have done over the last twenty years that you haven't?
Not really. My big thing in life away from the band is fishing. One day I would love to have a fishing boat of my own, just a little fishing boat. There's great fishing along the English coast. You get all kinds, and if you want to go out there and get shark, you can. But my main target species is a beautiful fish called sea bass, a lovely white silver thing that gives a bit of a fight. I never normally kill them. I return them safe and sound without a mark, not even bleeding. Another thing is, I am very fish friendly, because I rarely catch anything. But I have got a Japanese girlfriend at the moment, and you know how the Japanese are with their sushi and fresh fish. If she gets a hold of anything, she's butchering it straight away. So, that's a thing I've got to look forward to. I really don't have any regrets because I although we've had a tough touring regime, and it's kind of split up a lot of relationships and things, it's always come first, and I've had a great life doing this.

And you are a grandfather?
I'm a grandfather. Like Nicky said, he's forty-five now, and he'd like to marry and settle down, but I've had that life. It's there in the back for me. I have three grandchildren now. I'm in these shops around the country, you know, the garage shops, picking up these three-for-ten-bucks T-shirts with sharks on them for my little granddaughter. Indoctrinating these kids with fishes on their shirts [laughs].

Do they know their grandfather has seventeen records behind him?
Not really. The oldest one is five. They know I kind of like fishing, but the first thing the oldest one wanted for Christmas was a microphone. The younger boy got a set of drums last Christmas. They both get on the drums, and they're both very serious with their tongues out, concentrating. The music thing didn't skip a generation because both my kids had a lot of talent. One of them ended up being a rave DJ, and he could have easily been a drummer or a singer for a band. They are kind of musical. But I think my ex-wife ran it into them, like, your dad will never get anywhere, so they've always been a bit afraid to go there. So, I

think the grandkids might have a bit more courage and talent. I wanted my kids to be soccer players. I wanted them to play for England. I taught them to play soccer before they could walk. By the time they were five they could kick a ball properly. They still play today but only as an amateur kind of thing.

Did you play?
Yeah, but only school, but they played on teams. They took it further and still play on teams, like company teams, or local area teams.

The new record is not on New Red Archives or Cleopatra, your last labels here in America.
[Laughs] These are the kinds of questions you should ask Nicky because I kind of don't know what label it's on and I kind of don't care. I think you're talking about the French thing, aren't you? I've known this guy for a long, long time. He had a fanzine like yourself, and then he started his own record label, and he said, Charlie, if you put the Subs on it, I could get a lot of distribution, even in America. So, it was just a little throwaway thing we gave him. First of all, it was an experiment between me and Alvin to see if we could still write songs together. It was almost like a failed experiment [laughs]. Then Nicky had this thing, "Something in the Air," which I really hate, but I really love the dub version that he spent all day mixing, and it's come out real great. But I do like the song I wrote that was the first song on it, "Reclaim the Streets." I like that, but everybody in the band hates it and won't play it. All my people I look up to, like Mark Brennan of Captain Oi! Records, a great record label in England, one of the biggest punk and Oi labels, loves it. So, I'm like, Mark Brennan loves it, and he used to be in the Business, and they used to write some great songs . . . That's good enough for me.

The Deaf Club
An Un-oral History

This piece was originally published by *Maximumrocknroll*, the long-running fanzine that understood the historical importance of the venue that hosted two years' worth of ribald punk music, art and performance, and underground films that have become an intrinsic portion of West Coast "year zero" lore. I am indebted to Kathy Peck of the Contractions, who was able to network me to old guard San Francisco punks. The piece is also dedicated to Olin Fortney, who was both deaf and punk—an actual Deaf Club member before the venue hosted shows. He befriended me in 2005 when we taught together in western Oregon and provided me with remarkable visual materials and anecdotes. He also embodied the spirit of the era so well. He died on my birthday in 2010, so I was unable to interview him for this oral history, which shames me to this day. I miss him profoundly.

Ethan Davidson (fan)

In 1978 or perhaps 1979, a lot of punks were getting fed up with Dirk Dirksen and the Mabuhay Gardens having a monopoly on punk shows. Some people didn't like him, some didn't agree that punk was a "theatre of the absurd." Some simply wanted the community itself to have more control. We sought out alternative venues and came up with one of the most interesting social experiments I've participated in—the Deaf Club.

Nobody was famous, the shows were really cheap, and as soon as a band stopped playing, they got off the stage and simply became part of the audience. This all makes it sound like we didn't take anything very seriously, which is partly true. I had missed the chance to be a hippie and had regretted it, and now I was excited to be able to participate in a movement of my very own. I had spent a year in Central America alone and free, and was having trouble adjusting to the restrictions of an American suburb. Punk gave me a way to be free again. Certainly I believed in the left-wing ideals, which I had always believed in, though I was acutely aware that the hippie movement had failed to achieve its basic goals. The nihilistic hedonism, which many punks advocated, didn't make sense to me. But besides all that, it was the funnest scene in town.

Lu Read (club promoter)

I remember the Deaf Club regulars signing and talking to each other, dancing and enjoying themselves. I remember going there one night to see a show, and when I arrived with my friends, there was a strange figure on the sidewalk out front. I assumed it was a mannequin or such, since many musicians also attended art school. As I approached, I realized it was a dead body, splayed in a very strange way, since the neck/spinal cord broke from the fall; the way the body lay on the sidewalk did not look human at first. Thick cerebral fluid surrounded the head. It was intense! I hurried upstairs, somewhat nauseated from the sight. I returned to the sidewalk to watch until the police and fire department pushed us all back. "I guess he didn't like the band that was playing," I said. It was a suicide leap from the roof, not a homicide or fall. Later in the evening a Latina woman poured buckets of hot water and bleach on the sidewalk to wash away the blood, though much of the chalk outline remained.

Fredrik Nilsen (BPeople)

We played the Western Front Festival, and we played there with Barbie and Ken (Boyd Rice and Laurie O'Connell) and Monitor. Somebody jumped out the window one of those nights. Michael Uhlenkott from Monitor probably remembers better. He is fluent in sign language, so he was talking to all the members present when it happened.

Ethan Davidson

One night I arrived to see a puddle of blood on the sidewalk in front of the club. Somebody had jumped from the hotel next door. Chalk outlined where the body had existed. "Don't go near that line," said a police officer. But some primitive impulse moved me to stick my finger in the blood and rub it on my face. The police officer said, "Don't be stupid."

Klaus Flouride (Dead Kennedys)

Somebody falling out of a window? I've never heard of that. I've never heard of a suicide there or people jumping out of windows, but that doesn't mean it didn't happen.

Esmeralda Kent (Noh Mercy)

Another night I was really stoned standing outside on the sidewalk smoking and talking when a dead body fell out the window from the whore hotel upstairs

and scared the fuck out of me! It was already dead when it fell, they reported. The police painted a line drawing around the body in red, and it made the Deaf Club even more notorious.

Lu Read

The neighborhood was no rougher than the Tenderloin, or the Lower East Side of New York City in the '70s. I actually don't think parts of the Mission have changed that much. I recall the Tenderloin being the rougher of the two neighborhoods, which is still true today.

Ethan Davidson

A number of the clubs were in slummy neighborhoods. The Geary Theater was in the Fillmore. The Sound of Music and the Hell Hole were in the Tenderloin. A lot of us lived in those kinds of places, too.

Ginger Coyote (Punk Globe)

The Native American Cultural Center, which was also open to having punk shows, was located near Fourteenth and Valencia, and the trek between there and the Deaf Club was very dangerous at the time. It was near the projects, so there were numerous Latin and Afro-American gangs and just mean nasty kids that loved attacking the punks. Lots of attacks with blades and on occasion the gangs would pound long heavy-duty nails into 2×4s of wood and would see punks walking on the street or waiting at bus stops and whack them in the

back and face. I know that happened to Johnny Genocide, the lead singer of No
Alternative and Fast Floyd. I remember a group of punk girls walking around
the bus stop and a huge guy cold cocked Mia from Frightwig smack in the face.
Girls were often raped and everyone was subject to being robbed. I remember
a young woman telling me that she was pulled into the projects and beaten
and raped.

Ethan Davidson

One Halloween night I was walking towards the Deaf Club when a group of guys
sped by and shouted "Hey faggot, what's it like to suck dick?" Used to being
verbally harassed in high school, I yelled, "Fuck you," and flipped them off. A
couple of blocks later, the car had stopped, and the passengers stood facing me.
I said, "Excuse me, do you know how to get to Sixteenth Street?" I don't remember being hit. I remember wandering confused until a Mexican American man
found me and took me to the emergency room, where they stitched the cut
over my eye. And then I took the bus back to Sausalito. The next day I inspected
the damage, and I looked like the character Two-Face from Batman comics. On
my left side, I was the same cute guy I had been before. On my right side, I had
a black eye, a fat lip, stitches above my eye, and scabs from my forehead to my
chin. Suddenly, my social stock escalated. I got respect from the kids in high
school, and from the people in the punk scene, too. This led to me moving into
the city and living the life full-time.

Klaus Flouride

It was the Mission. We lived in the Mission at the time. It was Latino and
Catholic, obviously, to a high percentage. There was some gang stuff. One of
our female roommates, who became a great journalist, figured out she could
pass for a Latina if she wanted, because she was Mediterranean, tall and attractive. If Amy went anyplace where guys would be schmucks and hit on girls and
stuff like that, she figured out if she wore a crucifix and a fake wedding ring,
they kept her safe in the Mission. It was just a matter of street smarts, literally.
But it was a funky area, which has all been gentrified now. You still don't want
to be there way too late, which would have to be 4:00 a.m. by yourself on a
Friday or Saturday. Back then, it wasn't gentrified much at all. It was basically
around Sixteenth and Mission, which now has all sorts of hipster clubs that
come and go.

Ethan Davidson

The Mission was a dangerous place in those days. BART was under construction,
and the noise and dust had closed many businesses down. Those who did live
there were mostly low-income Mexican immigrants and their children. It had a

serious gang problem. The so-called Cholos were running rampant. There were regular gay bashings. I don't know if the Cholos thought punks were gay (as I suspect), or that they were members of a rival gang, but they didn't like us, and communicated this physically on a regular basis.

Of course, they were not alone. To be punk in that era was to be harassed by people of all races, from the dimwitted suburbanites yelling "Devo" to the gangs that physically attacked us. Our budgets, as well as our temperaments, often took us into low-income neighborhoods where people tend to express their opinions physically.

People sometimes stumbled into the Deaf Club with bloody faces. But once they were inside, it was a safe haven. I enjoyed it so much that I commuted by bus all the way from Sausalito, regularly.

Ginger Coyote

The Deaf Club was one of my favorite venues in the early days. The deaf people could feel the vibrations from the floor and the music excited them a lot. They all seemed to enjoy the music and the people. Every once in a while, a problem would arise with either one of the deaf community or a drunk punk and a fight would break out. Robert Hanharan, who worked with the Offs, was doing the booking there. There were not many venues that catered to punk, so we tried our best to keep the Deaf Club open and available. I had a birthday party at the Deaf Club and all sorts of San Fran folks came out for it. My magazine *Punk Globe* covered a lot of the shows booked there.

Ginger Coyote

The deaf people also drank the beer being served and would get drunk. Depending on the show and what people brought into the club, fights would break out. The rational (sober) deaf people could see it was a matter of too much beer, and they would control the deaf patrons. But they also would cut off the punks. Sometimes that was the core of the fights that broke out. Basically we all got along. There would be people who paid at the door that would get freaked out and end up being in a gang in the area and punks would often have fights with each other. Booze being the reason behind most fights.

The punks really did not have gangs although there were cliques that people belonged with. The punks would often walk in groups with chains and bottles for protection.

Jello Biafra

For the most part, the people there were cool and weren't out to beat each other up.

— Can You Hear Me? Music from the Deaf Club liner notes.

Ethan Davidson

The most interesting thing about the Deaf Club was that it was a real Deaf Club. The members stood around with the rest of us drinking the powerful drinks. I don't sign, so I never "spoke" to any of them, but what I was told was that they enjoyed our music because they could feel the vibrations on the floor. I imagine that they also enjoyed the visual display, for we were the most visually interesting visual community at the time. People would dye their hair a different shade of blue, green, or purple every week. It can now be said that I never had trouble buying a Bloody Mary, even though I was sixteen.

Bonnie Hayes (The Punts)

The club was utterly uncontrolled, which was one of the best things about it. It was basically like a big, really messy party at someone's house. It seemed private, like an inside thing—you would meet everybody and be in the family. Everybody was drunk and a lot of people were using heroin. I remember a fair amount of throwing up. I was always drunk as hell myself, as I couldn't perform without getting wasted.

Esmeralda Kent

The Deaf Club was down the street from our "house" which was a ginormous storefront, 1920s dry goods store on Valencia Street that is now Artists Television Access (ATA Gallery) at 992 Valencia St., where me, Tony Hotel, and our manager (and Tuxedomoon's manager) Adrian Craig lived. We had a huge basement that had secret passages (connecting all the block) where we used to record and practice.

The Deaf Club was my favorite club because of how strange it was. One night after we played at the end of the night, I went backstage and changed and I thought everyone had left because it was so quiet I was sure I was alone. I went out and the room was full with over a hundred people all signing. I wondered if drunk deaf people slurred their sign language.

They *loved* the music because they could feel it. Deafness knows no specific demographic, so rich, poor, old, young, black, Asian, anyone could be and often was deaf and they were all there. Who knew? It was great to write a note of what you wanted to the bartender and see old ladies drinking with spiked mohawk punks.

Bonnie Hayes

I spent many happy hours at the Deaf Club listening to great music and soaking up the new freedom of the punk scene. I saw X, the Dils, the Contractions, Pink Section, and others. Maybe the Mutants? The Mommers and the Poppers, D. Iyall's band. T Moon played there a lot. I played there with my band the Punts many times. The music was amazing—whatever you wanted it to be. Experimental, messy, off-key and off-time but really original and alive-sounding, not all fixed up and careful. The deaf people sat on the edge of the stage or on the floor near the stage and placed their hands on the stage to feel the music.

Klaus Flouride

I don't remember people touching speakers, though I recall someone telling me that for most people, deafness is a percentage level. Profoundly deaf is where nothing works, apparently, due to nerve damage, etc. Things are totally gone. That was not the largest percentage of people that were there. This music they could really get a grip on and hear because it was loud, and that club, which generally had card and bingo games and stuff like that when there wasn't a show, was literally a club for deaf people, so not only did they have something they could hear, it was also punk rock theater. Back in the days when the Deaf Club was going on, there wasn't one hardcore band after the other like it is nowadays. Back then, there was a range between art bands, or the experimental Tuxedomoon-style bands, which fell between art and stuff. Bands like Pink Section. The record *Can You Hear Me? Music from the Deaf Club* also had KGB, which included Johnny Genocide, who is still out there playing.

F. Stop Fitzgerald (photographer)

I do remember some great nights at the club. It was very clear that what seemed a blue-collar neighborhood club for the hearing impaired had taken an interesting turn. It was at first unusual to see these folks—regular members, I would assume—at the bar, and dozens of strange-looking punks and punkettes all about. The contrast was wonderful. It was also obvious that the deaf patrons were enjoying the music—at the bar, in front of the stage, near the speakers, or backstage. They definitely seemed to dig it.

David Javelosa (Los Microwaves)

I remember playing as Los Microwaves at least two times. There really wasn't much of a stage except a low platform. I realized that I had to enunciate my drink orders to the bartender, because he was reading my lips for drinks! When we opened for Tuxedomoon, they surrounded the stage with plastic sheeting and started to spray-paint it from the inside. That drove us out of the dressing room and many from the club because of the fumes. Everyone wanted to play the club, until they actually did! It was in a bad neighborhood back in those days, but there were great tacos across the street. It didn't last for more than a year or two. The scene pretty much moved to Broadway where there were four or five clubs within a few blocks' radius. The high point of the club was the Western Front music festival that included everyone in town.

Deaf/Punk by Richard Gaikowski.
1979, 16 mm, b&w/so, 8 min.
Summary: "A dada-documentary of an unlikely liaison between punk rockers and the deaf who for a while shared the now legendary San Francisco Deaf Club. We see punk poseurs juxtaposed with the animated presence of deaf-mutes. Hands talk and wave around as we hear the dirty R&B of the Offs. The film works because of the concept of the environment." http://www.mail-archive.com/ambit@mediascot.org/msg00998.html.

Anonymous
I remember going with my older sister to see punk bands at the Deaf Club. The punk music, the club members with balloons to "feel" the sounds they cannot hear, the TVs to watch because they could read lips. The bar was a folding table and a refrigerator full of Budweiser. A perfect match of outsiders with absolutely no pretensions.

Klaus Flouride
I remember it being working-class, but I don't remember it being that dingy, but we played an awful lot of pretty dingy punk clubs. That didn't ever impress upon me that much. I think that "California Über Alles" might have come out by the time we played there, but I really don't think so, because we still had 6025 in the group. So, it was still before we had a single out. We were still early on in the thing. There was a folding table in the back. They sold cans of Budweiser. I think it was for like a buck apiece. Back then, you could get Buds for $2.50 or $3.00 a six-pack, or something like that, so they were doing okay. That was your bar. The thing that impressed me the most was that when we were watching the Germs I was right up front, and I was trying to talk to the person next to me. Everybody was grabbing somebody's ear and hollering to try and talk, whereas the deaf members, the people who were deaf and frequented the place on an everyday basis, would just lean forward towards the stage and sign each other— no problem with communication.

Bruce Conner (artist and filmmaker)

It was reassuring that, when the music got loud at one end of the room, you could crawl to the other end of the room and talk to the deaf people. They always had TV without sound.

—*Can You Hear Me? Music from the Deaf Club* liner notes.

Johnny Stingray (The Controllers)

I remember the Deaf Club well! We only played there once, but it was the best. The people *actually* were deaf, but loved punk because of the vibrations and the punk fashion. We were the headliners that night. It was our first headline gig in San Fran and the place was packed. Over capacity, in fact, and the fire marshal closed down the show. We never made it to the stage. The highlight was Darby Crash and Jello Biafra kicking in store windows after the canceled show. I believe Jello cut his Achilles tendon as a result. Fun times.

Klaus Flouride

When we played, it was weird. We weren't introduced by Johnny Walker, like it sounds on our *Live at the Deaf Club* album. He came up in the middle of the set and just grabbed the mic because he was Johnny Walker and who in the fuck were we? We were just this band out of San Francisco that was starting off. We had a fairly good following in San Francisco at that point. I can't recall if we opened for the Germs. It was one or the other. I think the Germs headlined. Walker just jumped up in the middle of the set and did his spiel about, "We're going to show them that San Francisco is the center of . . ." That sort of stuff. I don't recall the fire marshal closing down the show, and I may be wrong. I don't recall the Controllers being on the bill, but I may be wrong too. I know Biafra went out with some of the Germs and they indiscriminately kicked out windows. Biafra kicked out one, then realized that his fancy little pointed shoes weren't like the big old boots the Germs had on—big leather things past their ankles. So, Biafra's foot slid on the broken glass and he cut himself. He did a miserable injury to himself. Sliced a vein and a bunch of tendons. For four months after that we played shows with him in a wheelchair because he had to have his leg in a cast because everything had been operated on. It was a lesson for him: if you are going to kick in a window, make sure you have the proper footwear.

Kathy Peck (The Contractions)

The place was filthy. My boots would stick to the floor. The deaf people would dance to the vibration of the beat. Robert Hanrahan would do a radio show with Johnny Walker (BBC punk rock DJ) on the side of the stage, it seems. Robert Hanrahan, manager of the Offs discovered the San Francisco Club for the Deaf in 1978, and was able to rent it on a nightly basis.

It was great fun. The Deaf Club was more a like a neighborhood place, very underground, in the Mission District. People would give the deaf sign for a beer as the Offs, the Contractions, Middle Class, No Alternative, and the Dils played. People like Ginger Coyote (Punk Globe) would hang out, dance, and drink. The bathroom was full of graffiti. We'd load in, and the punk bands would always get in crazy fights, especially Brittley Black, drummer of Crime, who fell out of the upstairs window many a night.

The deaf people were receptive. They could "hear" through the wooden floor—a simple floor, made from planks or linoleum. It could catch the vibrations. Frank Moore from the Outrageous Beauty Pageant was there in his wheelchair that people dragged upstairs, since it was on the second floor. Dirk Dirksen (Mabuhay club promoter and San Francisco music icon) nurtured his career.

Klaus Flouride

I don't specifically remember Frank Moore being there, but he was at everything. It wouldn't stand out because he was at so many things. He was a really cool guy. He was really disabled. He had a Ouija board on the front of his wheelchair and a pointer on his hat so he could point out things he needed, because he couldn't talk. His hands were too uncontrollable to run the wheelchair himself, and he had a group of people that he lived with that almost worshipped him. They would get him to shows, and carry him up and down. They lived in Berkeley, and I think they still do. Everything is all tie-dye now, even the colors of the house and the car they drive around in.

Ethan Davidson

At the Mabuhay, I remember quadriplegic performance artist Frank Moore Performing with his Sexually Explicit players. In one memorable performance, Frank played a severely physically disabled man being tortured and given an enema by a nurse. It was extremely black comedy and would not have been socially acceptable even in the punk scene if Frank hadn't organized the whole show himself. As far as people of color, I don't remember them at the Deaf Club. At the Geary Theater, I hung out with Tony Zero, who was Mexican American. I remember a black Rastafarian working at GT. Some of us briefly got involved with Rock Against Racism, which was organized by a black woman. Later in the early '80s I remember hanging out with a couple of Asians. Oh, I met a Japanese woman at the Sound of Music and married her. We were together for about four years.

Kathy Peck

It was an era of disposable beer, disposable art—the Xerox art movement—as well as disposable bands. We played there with Wall of Voodoo, Zeros, Jennifer Blowdryer, and Johnny Genocide. I used Lysol spray to clean the stage at sound check. It was pretty dirty. People would party and get drunk and spill stuff. There was no real staff to take care of the place. The deaf people would do what they could to take care of it.

People were recording bands. V. Vale (*Search and Destroy*), Brad Lapin (*Damage* magazine), Lu Read, and Randy Seanor were there, along with bands, the Mutants, Crime, Dead Kennedys, Tuxedomoon, Noh Mercy, Pink Section, JJ180, Los Microwaves, Units, Punts, Jars. It was really mixed. It was more about the music rather than what somebody was or, "You Don't Know Who You Think I Am"—the whole identity thing. The deaf people would dance at sound check. Dirk cancelled one of our early performances at the Mabuhay, so we switched over and played our first show at the Deaf Club thanks to the Offs.

Ethan Davidson

Now, I have to admit that when it comes to the music, a lot of us weren't paying attention very closely. I remember Tuxedomoon coming on and I joined somebody in yelling, "Boring!" and "Art Frat!" Tuxedomoon is actually a good band. I just enjoyed yelling.

I remember Johnny Genocide of No Alternative singing, "Giddyup, little horsey, I just can't wait to fuck my horse again." This was his parody of a country song.

Klaus Flouride

Can You Hear Me? was all recorded by Jim Keylor, who recorded "California Über Alles." He recorded our first single. It was recorded on the same equipment as *Can You Hear Me?* He just set up at the side of the stage and winged it. It was for one solid week that he did that, basically. Well, I can't imagine him breaking down and setting the equipment back up again. So, I think it was a solid week of shows. Johnny Walker was there, who was one of the DJs at Radio Caroline, one of the first offshore pirate radio stations in the UK. I don't remember KUSF (University of San Francisco) or KALX (North Gate Radio), which would be two stations that would broadcast live. Both used to do remotes, but I don't remember them being there. I think Kathy might be remembering Jim Keylor on the side recording. He had his whole setup, like a splitter for all the mics.

The punk crowd was not all that diverse, even though the bands were more so. There was a Mission crowd, a North Beach crowd—but they'd all turn up at the Mabuhay, they'd turn up at Ben T. Rat Productions, which were Rat shows, and they'd rent different halls all the time. There was a guy named Montgomery—a black guy that did shows in Berkeley. The only really solid, all-the-time venue had been the Mabuhay.

The Deaf Club was one of the few places that had established itself as possibly a place that had more than two shows. Most of the time there were maybe one to two shows at the basement of a place. We played the Finnish Hall, all these places, like one time. I can see Dirk saying, "If you play that place, you'll never play the Mabuhay again," in some sort of bluff, but I don't think, or I don't remember there being anything along the levels of anybody threatening anybody other than when Bill Graham put on one show, or two shows.

At the show we played with the Clash, it was a big show, his goons got out of hand. He didn't like how stuff went, and he said, "I'm never going to put on another punk show." This is after he said, "I'm going to show punk rockers how it's done. I'm going to show these goddamn punk rockers how you put on a rock'n'roll show." Then by the end of it, he's like, "I'm never going to book one of these kinds of shows again." People were not behaving like he was used to, like just swaying to the music and going "ooh and ah." He went on radio once and was interviewed by Tim Yohannan and the people of *Maximumrocknroll*. They really confronted him. It wasn't like David Letterman and Donald Rumsfeld. They really did confront him about a goon throwing some kid without a proper stamp on his hand in front of a truck. But I never heard of any band being told by one club or the other, "If you play that club, you'll never play here again."

Ethan Davidson

Dirk Dirksen had a certain vision of punk as theatre. Other people saw it more as people as singing and talking about our real lives. The Mabuhay was focused around the personality of Dirk, no matter who else was playing. He deliberately drew the audience's anger towards himself, so his sneering voice was part of every show. North Beach, by this time, was not, mostly, an Italian or a beatnik neighborhood, but a center of sleazy, voyeuristic strip-club tourism. The aura of sleaze seemed to permeate everything. And not the seedy punk sleaze, but the manipulative, money-grubbing kind. The Mabuhay got the most press, and

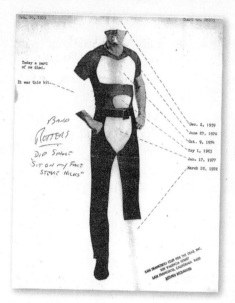

drew people who were brand new. The Deaf Club generally got folks who had been around at least a little while.

And then, the Deaf Club died quickly, while the Mabuhay died slowly and painfully. As the media took hold of punk and kids started flocking in from the suburbs in the early '80s, it became a tourist trap. The brick walls with spray-painted graffiti were covered with fake brick with fake spray-painted graffiti. I couldn't believe that it had so blatantly become an imitation of itself. The rules got stricter: no ins and outs. The bouncers got more uptight, and then sometimes actually violent. I saw somebody get thrown through a glass door. The police started hounding the sidewalk in front. It turned into a "no fun" zone. The Deaf Club never did. The Deaf Club did seem more DIY than the Mabuhay.

Craig Gray (Negative Trend)

What I remember about the Deaf Club is that there weren't many deaf people there, mainly the staff. I don't remember any deaf punks being there per se, but I didn't know everybody in the scene. I don't know if it's fair to say they were square and sidelined. Once in a while there would be some, who I assumed were the staff, standing up front with their hands on the PA. I don't think most of the people at those gigs were really aware of the deaf people and assumed whoever didn't look like a punk rock kid was one of the deaf. No one was consciously excluding anybody, more than anything it would have been a communication problem—not a lot of signing punk rock kids in 1978–79.

Klaus Flouride

You couldn't tell from the stage if the patrons were punk rock. When you were playing, you could see people signing, and that was about it. In terms of the punk rock stuff, as far as the fashion, if you want to call it that, the look and stuff, we thought, we are not going to wear spiky hair because we didn't want to take one uniform and replace it with another. So, there could have been people there totally into punk rock, as far as the visuals go, because they liked the theater of it, or whatever, but you couldn't really tell. Back then, the shows were so, well, look at old show photos of the Mabuhay in 1977 and '78, which you can find all over the Internet. You look at the styles. You see people right at the front of the stage at Mabuhay that look like it's 1975 still. That doesn't mean that they weren't into it or that their fashion didn't change later. They were right up front, dealing not with a pit, but a lot of action. I didn't notice one way or another whether the deaf people were punk. Well, I know there were a lot of people there for curiosity's sake because that was their Deaf Club, and deaf people would go there on Friday or Saturday night. Maybe they just sat at the back and watched, and thought, hmm, curious.

Ethan Davidson

I don't personally remember much in the way of interactions between the punks and the deaf patrons, except that they just stood around with the rest of them. I assume that the bartender was deaf, though he didn't seem to have any trouble with my drink order.

I remember that a number of people in the punk scene were gay or bi, which didn't mean that the rest of them were totally free of homophobia. But the general public tended to lump both groups together. This was, after all, the same time when the San Francisco gay scene was exploding.

Klaus Flouride

The whole thing lasted less than a year before they got complaints from the neighbors who were not deaf, basically.

Ethan Davidson

The neighbors had complained about the noise, so they had covered the walls with egg cartons, stapled on. But a member of the Mutants ripped them down during a show. For this, or perhaps some other reason, this unique social experiment was closed down, and we went back to hanging out at the Mabuhay Gardens and wherever else we could. Shortly after that, my scars and bruises attracted the attention of a young woman, who moved me into her one-bedroom apartment with four other punks and removed my stitches with a pair of scissors. And my life was permanently changed.

Kathy Peck

Ironically, for two decades, as cofounder and executive director of Hearing Education and Awareness for Rockers (http://hearnet.com), I have worked with musicians suffering from hearing damage, providing hearing services and education, and I started off playing at the Deaf Club, and suffered from intense hearing loss for ten years myself.

Once, the Mermen, White Trash Debutantes, Mo'Fessionals, Meri St. Mary and the Vktms played an event we called "Vibe-O-Thon" for a HEAR benefit (1996). I invited the deaf community and the punks to feel and hear the music through the vibration of the floor. In fact, everybody ended up lying on the floor like seals, a good vibration. Vibe-O-Thon was one of the first Media Cast Internet broadcasts. The Tactile Sound System (Clark Synthesis) allowed concert-goers to "feel and hear" the performances like never before at a volume that will not risk hearing damage to the audience "by vibrating the floor, and using the human body itself as a bone resonator, we were able to turn down the overall volume to help prevent hearing loss for those with hearing, while deaf and hard-hearing people were be able to 'hear' the concert via sound vibrations." It felt loud, but it wasn't as loud as it seemed.

Ginger Coyote

Now in 2011 the area has been gentrified and people are allowed to dress as they please. It is also a lot safer for people to walk in the area with ease. It seems the police patrol the area a lot more. There are patrol cars making the rounds at all times.

Esmeralda Kent

Valencia Street is now extremely chic. The rents are sky-high and it is filled with promenading twenty-somethings from India and the Midwest who work at Apple, Google, Yahoo, etc. with shitloads of discretionary income to spend in the trendy upscale restaurants and clothing boutiques. They call them "hipsters," but there is nothing "hip" about them. They are tech-addicted hardcore capitalists with huge 401(k)s. They remind me of straight people's parents in the '70s (and they like those straight '70s clothes!). They seem incapable of coming up with an original thought that does not include social networking or walking around bumping into things, looking at the device in the palm of their hand.

PART TWO

Hardcore Sound and Fury

Mike Palm
(Agent Orange)

Punk-as-pathology and dirty glamour may thrive as a cliché, but the ethos espoused by Agent Orange is not aural wallpaper for nihilism and senseless violence. Instead, they unmask false promises and reveal a struggle against stifling suburban wasteland, where mollification thrives and young kids cope with endless blandness, boredom, and consumption. Restless singer Mike Palm melds an endless affection for residual art rock like Krautrock and Roxy Music with fiery surf music. The early West Coast sound he gravitated towards was angry, smart, and female-led, like the Avengers, or local protohardcore contemporaries like Middle Class, who lived nearby in sleepy Fullerton, California. With a knack for melody and harmony, Agent Orange married punk's insistency with true tunefulness, an ability to graft hooks onto lyrical terrain about being "Too Young to Die." In turn, the songs evoked risky adrenaline rushes and vengeance as well, like "Bloodstains," which still causes audiences to catapult in frenzies. I interviewed Mike backstage at Rocbar in Houston, Texas, in 2010. *Houston Press* and *Artcore* originally printed versions of this conversation.

What brought about the affinity between surf and punk cultures?
I think you'd have to go all the way back to the 1960s. Actually, you could probably go even further back than that. Original surf culture guys were all about forging their own paths. They were kind of outcasts. People thought they were degenerate. In reality, they were some of the first people to embrace fitness, clean living, and actually living the life the way they wanted to, which is beneficial to your health in the long run. Mainstream society thought they were freaks. It's the same thing with punks too. People think, punk rock, what's it all about—spitting, fighting, bloody noses, and guys barfing on each other. Someone asked Joe Strummer (the Clash) what he thought the meaning of punk rock was, and he said, "an exemplary attitude towards your fellow man," or something like that. He was the kind of guy who, at four in the morning,

when everyone was drunk out of their minds, was the guy who made sure you had an ashtray if you needed it. People think that punk is just this nasty thing, but really, I think it was an intelligent movement that sort of paraded as idiocy, for the fun of it.

Did you feel like outsiders—melodic instead of raw?

Steve Soto (Adolescents) and I had a falling out, and that split the original lineup, and thank god that happened, honestly. The world got the Adolescents, DI, and everything else, the splinter-offs. Steve is a huge Paul McCartney fan. Actually, I love the Beatles too. More poppy and melodic music has always been something that appeals to me, and I right off the bat saw the potential of combining the furious energy of punk rock with something melodic and thoughtful, something more intelligent. It's just two schools of thought. You can either strip it down to something primal, strip it all the way down to the frame, basically that's what hardcore is, or you can take it in the other direction and go beyond that to do something more interesting. It's not like we were the only band doing it. Look at the Damned. They did all kinds of very adventurous things musically. Siouxsie and the Banshees right off the bat were expansive. In the pre-punk days, we were listening to a lot of German electronic music. Kraftwerk and Tangerine Dream are two of my favorites. That was very outside-the-box thinking for its time. We just happened to choose the melodic direction. The hardcore guys, of course, weren't into it, but chicks dig it.

You really liked Darby Crash's (singer of the Germs) voice and lyrics?

Sure. There are lots of people who have unique voices, and you go, "Wow, listen to that guy." Darby wasn't really copying anyone. No one did that before him. It's not that he had a great voice, it's that he had a great style of singing. Anybody could have done it, but he was the only guy who thought about doing it that way, for whatever reason. Lyrically, I think he was really brilliant. To this day, it blows my mind to read those lyrics.

Did studio engineers understand the band's style?

Those guys in the 1970s didn't have a clue. They didn't know what was going on. Tape your wallet to the snare drum . . .

Dampen it like Fleetwood Mac?

I was thinking of Steely Dan. It was really hard to try and talk these people into anything different. It's a real shame. Our first recordings were done on a three-track. The Beatles made great records on those machines. Here we were livid with this vintage old machine, but guess what. That thing had the potential to sound great. Unfortunately, someone taped a wallet to the snare and sucked

all the life out of it. That was the era. You live through that, and there's almost nothing you can do about it.

Did you feel connected to 1950s rock'n'roll?
Definitely. And there were guys that we knew . . . Right off the bat, one of the guys we latched onto was a friend of ours from Fullerton. He was in the original DI, playing guitar. He played bass for the Cramps for a little bit. That guy had a really broad knowledge of vintage recording equipment at the time: tube microphones, tube compression, old boards, and three-track machines. He knew what worked. When those machines were made, they were built in an era when quality counted and things were built to last. That's why those machines sound so incredible. There's no question about it.

Jack Grisham (TSOL) said the whole point was to be different than other bands, or risk even getting your ass kicked.
That's true. You'd get your ass kicked if you had a fake English accent. There was a whole list of things you could get your ass kicked for.

When did people start taking Agent Orange seriously?
About the time I wrote the song "Bored of You." I can't remember the rhyme right now, but something like, "I'm sick of the Rolling Stones and all the leather

jacket clones." I had this conversation. There were like twenty of us in this Volkswagen driving up to Los Angeles for a punk show, going to see the Damned or something. I got a couple of beers in me and started ranting, like "the scene is turning into a bunch of goons with matching leather jackets that all look like the Army in their uniforms." Dennis Danell (Social Distortion) was sitting in the back and I heard him go, "Ah, shut up." I looked over, and he was wearing jeans, a white T-shirt, and a black leather jacket. I said, "Everyone but you, Dennis" [laughs]. "You make it work, man" [laughs].

As a member of a bridge band that spanned both the first punk wave and emerging hardcore, how did you see the scene or genre change?
The hardcore era took over pretty quick, and once again I think it was mostly due to the press. You can trace this all the way back. Well, I don't know about New York, maybe they were a little bit ignored, but by the time the whole thing was picked up by the English press, God, everybody knows what they did with that. In the States, especially in LA, one of the big things right off the bat was, I don't know how people remember this, but there was an *LA Times* article where they coined the term "slamdance." In the same article, they said we were a band "banned forever," along with other bands as well. The article said all these bands had been blacklisted from all the clubs. I don't think a blacklist really existed until they printed that article. It was like, "It's well known that all these bands are banned." So, for me, I felt like, I don't care. If they don't want us, I don't want to go there anyhow. We'll find some place to play." I just had a "never give up" attitude, really, no matter what happened like that. I just figured that Agent Orange would find some way, somehow, to keep playing. I always looked long term at things. Yeah, maybe we're banned this month, but we'll just get out of LA. How about that? That's a novel concept [laughs].

Steve Soto stresses that media coverage ended up bringing in a thuggish mentality because the "violence" was highlighted by the press. All the people that were psychotic or had violent tendencies started showing up.
I think that was inevitable anyway. Yeah, advertise it as such, who's going to show up with a flowerpot on their head? They are going to show up with a leather jacket and a switchblade. That's what everybody thought it was. If you didn't know, you certainly weren't going to come unprepared. This whole false picture that the press painted, a lot of kids followed it. You still see it in out-of-the-way places. I hate to use any place as an example, especially now, because it took a lot of years, but basically everyone is pretty well clued in . . . There was a time when we would fly to . . . I am going to use Alaska as an example, even though it's not a great example. There's probably other places, out-of-the-way places, where you fly in and some kid would meet you at the airport with an

orange mohawk. He just cut it that morning because he made damn sure he was going to fit in, no matter what. Agent Orange is coming, and it's going to be punk as hell. Then they took one look at us, and they're like, "Oh, man. These guys look so tame" [laughs]. Cause it's not all visual. That's not what it is all about. Well, punk rock is a visual thing as well. It's just funny [laughs].

In early *Flipside*, you describe the rivalries between Huntington Beach and places like Riverside.

I had a girlfriend in Huntington Beach. I lived in Placentia, inland. It was all I could do to ditch school, get on the bus, ride for three hours, get to Huntington, spend the weekend there, barely make it back to Orange County for school on Monday morning, or whatever it was. There were scenes going on all over the place. Once again, it was one of those things where people had preconceived notions of what was going on, and the preconceived notions became . . . well, played out. Huntington is the only place where I would say it was really like people think it was. Maybe Hermosa Beach too, which was pretty violent. There were definitely factions that planted the seeds of hardcore and kept it simple.

When you look back at the media coverage of places like Cuckoo's Nest and Fleetwood . . .

The Cuckoo's Nest was notorious, but I tell you what. As far as what anyone thinks about the Cuckoo's Nest, it was amplified times ten at the Fleetwood. I saw so many things go down there. I don't know if people have any original footage of photos from that whole scene, but that was something incredibly unique, if you try to imagine the meanest, nastiest Southern California hardcore scene going on . . . I did avoid that place where they did all the Golden Voice shows—the Olympic. I avoided a lot of the Olympic shows, and I hear there was a lot of senseless violence. A friend of mine got beat up real bad and ended up in the emergency room. It turned his life around, changed everything.

Do you blame hardcore for pushing women out of the scene?

What girl wants to get in a pit with a bunch of guys that, you know, it's physically impossible? I wouldn't say it excluded them. The same way it didn't exclude the people who didn't have the guts to get their teeth knocked in . . . that's the thing that probably attracted the most attention. There was a lot of energy going on. But there were always a lot of women in punk rock, especially in the LA scene. One of the first bands I looked to, and I ended up kind of hanging out with them a bit, is the Avengers. It's the only band the Sex Pistols acknowledged in America. They're a great band. The list goes on and on. Don't even get me going because for me, personally, everybody has their own preferences. Personally, I mostly listen to female vocalists.

Really?

I don't know why. It appeals to me. I don't care if it is punk rock or jazz, bossa nova, whatever.

Do they capture something that male vocalists don't?

I think so. There's a certain quality to a female voice.

Were you at all aware of Darby Crash's ambiguous sexuality? People say it might have driven his misery.

I don't know if that is really the case. I don't think he was being tortured by anybody or anything. I think he had his demons. He had a little plan there too, you know, that maybe wasn't much based in reality. The suicide thing was probably a bad plan [laughs].

People say that as he became more aware of his own homosexuality . . . he was worried about how he might be treated.

I suppose that may be true. It never occurred to me. He always seemed so confident to me. It wasn't something I ever considered to be some sort of issue whatsoever. That's one of the things early in the scene There was a certain alliance, you know, with . . . I can't even explain it, to tell you the truth. Guys like that [Darby] got it, they got it. Much of it was based on pre-punk stuff. For me, it was like Ultravox, Roxy Music, and Brian Eno. I probably would never have known about any of those bands if I hadn't been running around with the guy that ran the AV department at my junior high. He was a really super cool guy. He was really knowledgeable about art and music and performance art, and he exposed us to so many really brilliant things, like the Los Angeles Free Music Society. If some old woman teacher ran the AV stuff, I wouldn't have learned a thing [laughs].

Didn't your older brother and cousin turn you on to surf?

My cousin was the bass player of a surf band, the original Surfaris, and my older brothers lived through that whole era. I guess those records were mostly passed down from my oldest brother. That's one of those things too. Back then, they just moved on to the next thing, whatever it was—the Grateful Dead, Rolling Stones, whatever it was. The old surf records just got passed on immediately. A big stack of 45 records.

Why did it speak to you so strongly whereas they moved on?

I don't know. It's weird. I almost feel like a natural archivist or something. I don't think that everybody has that in them. I find myself trying to save things that I think may be lost in the mists of time. If there is something that I think is important, I'll steal if I have to, to make sure that it doesn't disappear forever [laughs].

That's sounds like Greg Shaw of Bomp!.

I didn't go as crazy as someone like that. Back in the days, people would find records or books from the UK or different things that I assume no one could find, or I wouldn't see them anywhere, or never expect to find them again. I just knew those people were flaky and those things would be lost in a matter of days, so I'd trade them for a stack of *Flipsides* or something. Whatever it took to make sure that thing didn't get destroyed or lost. I sort of think of myself as an archivist and historian, I guess. I value musical history so much. That's the main thing. It's fascinating to see how things go from one thing to the next, how people are influenced.

Do you feel connected to the sound of 1950s rock'n'roll?

There's no denying that that old technology cannot be beat in terms of audio fidelity, which is another thing I have to say. It's kind of a shame. At the time, we all acted like we didn't care because it was the punk thing to do, but the punk rock era really produced a lot of substandard recordings. It's too bad that many more bands weren't recorded better. I was listening to the Screamers today, for instance. There's a band that was never recorded properly. I saw them live, and they were so incredible and different. No guitars: just keyboards and crazy treatments. It never came across recording-wise, and I know for whatever reason they chose not to record, but there's an example. A lot of bands chose to record and ended up with recordings that could have sounded so much better.

What do you think of the X records with their production?

They sound pretty good. They sound pretty close to what that band actually sounds like. I think they probably fought pretty hard to get that sound, just the way it was supposed to be, rather than overproduced, which is what everybody from our era battled constantly. That's what it was like back in the day. You had to fight with the engineers and try to get what you wanted. Half the time you didn't get it anyhow [laughs]. That's what's so great about now. We're in an exciting era. It's the first time since the 1960s when, well, even in the 1960s you couldn't even really record things at home. Now, you absolutely have the ability to record at home. No questions about it. It's cheap. With a little bit of invest-ment, with a little bit of thought, you can come up with perfectly acceptable recordings, especially for punk rock. Format-wise, you have your choice now. You can do downloads, CDs, vinyl, whatever you want.

Did you know the engineer Chaz Ramirez (Eddie and the Subtitles, Social Distortion records)?
I didn't. It's funny. There were guys in the Fullerton scene I never really kind of got close to. I think part of that was because I spent so much time in Huntington Beach. I was used to hanging out down there. A few years earlier my brother had a bike shop right next to the pier, so I spent a lot of time down by the beach. It made sense for me to hang out down there. I thought what was going on in Orange County was just going to get me into more trouble. I didn't need to be hanging around the Black Hole (the Mike Ness apartment). That's no place for me, anyhow! [laughs].

Punk always gets pigeonholed by academics as a white, male, middle-class phenomenon, but even tonight there were many women and Hispanics.
But that's over how long, you know?

But even back in the day . . .
There were black punk rockers. Of course, they were out there, and for the most part, they were accepted. That was the great thing about punk rock, up until that time. If you weren't one thing, or another, you had to be accepted by "those" people. Punk rock was the first unified group to not be a group of the very same people, and if anything, that was what created more frustration than anything. And all the things I complained about in those early interviews. The early days of the scene were just so vibrant. You just never knew what to expect. It was always something totally spontaneous. The more different, the better. The cooler you were if you just came up with something totally outrageous.

The Adolescents spoke about being locked out of the studio when tracks were being mixed.
That was common practice at the time. I think so. I poked my head in a couple of times to see what was going on. It was a fiasco. They were smart to keep us away. We would have beat the hell out of someone [laughs]. It's too bad we didn't have the control. That's the thing. We were young, we were naïve, we signed contracts we shouldn't have signed, we didn't have proper representation, and no one was looking out for us. To this day, I know I am getting the short end of the deal. It's all going to come down someday. Hopefully, it will go smooth like it should because things haven't been right for a long, long time. I think there

is a lot of guys who can say the same thing. It's too bad there wasn't someone there to look out for all these guys. Somebody in *Flipside* had an interview, and they talked about Robbie Fields was an idiot because all he had to do was keep everybody happy. He already had them under contract. He could have gotten multiple records out of each of those bands. Instead, he pissed everybody off and got one record out of each of them. That was it.

How did you not end up on Frontier?

That's a good question. My brother ended up working for Lisa Fancher for quite a while. I consider Lisa a good friend. She's still interested in working with us. At this point, I am not sure what any label could do. Now that everything is back in artists' hands, I think it's a good time for us to take advantage of that. Posh Boy came forward, and he seemed interested. We did the *Rodney on the ROQ* album. That was main thing. After that came out, he saw the potential, and stepped right in. I wasn't opposed to the situation.

The Angry Samoans mock Rodney, others praise him . . .

He's an easy guy to mock.

He's a straw dog, easy to knock down?

Especially if you're a punk. He's an easy target, a funny little guy.

How do you feel personally about him?

I think he's a great little guy. Everybody knows his history. He's the mayor of Sunset Strip. The whole thing with the LA scene. Being a DJ with KROQ, he definitely had some power there. His show was very influential. For me, I honestly sat there with a tape deck and taped his shows. I would start a song, and you never knew what he was going to play, and he was always playing something that was always so new. You didn't know what it was. You didn't know what you were going to get. It could be . . .

Like the John Peel of America?

I haven't really heard enough of John Peel to know what that means, I just know that if you're into punk rock and you're in Southern California, you would absolutely listen to Rodney's show on Sunday night. There's no question about that. In fact, when we started playing parties, playing more punk rock, we played a party in Huntington Beach. About halfway through the night, everybody was getting kind of lubed there, and we decided to pull out "You Drive Me Ape" by the Dickies. Well, the thing is, they hadn't released it yet. They had gone and played it on Rodney's show the weekend before, and here it was two days later, and we had already learned it, but we could play it twice as fast.

We pulled it out and played it, and guess what. There were only two guys who recognized it, and it was the guys from the Crowd! [laughs]. You know they were home listening two nights before! They heard it too. Everybody tuned it.

That show was an epicenter.

Really. He had certain connections. I think he was friend with the guy from Zed Records in Long Beach. I don't know what the situation was, but somehow, due to his day job, I think he had frequent trips to London where he was able to make personal buys and hand carry those records and put them in the racks of Zed Records. I think he was passing that stuff right on to Rodney, who got such advanced copies of that stuff. Hot off the pressing plant in London, right into Rodney's hand. It was great. What could be better? It was free too. Just tune in. The two things that were the biggest influence for us were Rodney Bingenheimer's radio show and the Capitol Records swap meet. I don't remember how often they did it, but it was an all-night event. I had to be like fourteen, fifteen years old then, and we'd stay out in Hollywood in the Capitol Records parking lot all night until the sun came up digging though records and magazines, eating this stuff up. Spending my entire inheritance [laughs] between the Capitol swap and Zed Records.

How involved were you with the visual representations of the band—flyers, record covers, graffiti, etc.?

That was one of the things that appealed to me from the beginning. I kind of always figured I would end up a graphic artist. That was sort of my aim, and then I got this impression that everybody in the world wanted to be a graphic artist, and that I was wasting my time, so I decided to be in a band instead. Funny how that worked out. Now everybody and their grandma's got a band [laughs]. But it gave me an outlet for my art too. I was able to design all the record covers, T-shirt designs, and the logo. In the early days, we were finishing it all up ourselves, turning it in as a finished product. I remember we turned in *This Is the Voice* and the record label could not believe it was so subdued. They were expecting something very punk, and we wanted to do something understated.

You ended up on the same side of history as Green Day and the . . .
Offspring. I'm a huge music fan. That's why I got into it in the first place. I wasn't
looking for the money potential or my goal wasn't to get chicks. My brother
worked at the Fender guitar plant in the 1960s. I grew up with the whole thing
of rock'n'roll as rebellion, doing something completely different, which is what
everyone is looking for, especially in rock'n'roll. So, it all fell in place.

What bands today speak to you now like bands did in 1978 or '79?
My brother is a guitar tech. He is getting ready to go out with Interpol. Listening
to them, there was something that struck a chord. I really like the two-guitar
interplay. I sorta like the monotone vocals, the drummer is really great, and
the bass player has a great tone. Every once in a while, I'll go back and listen to
something from back in the day, and Ultravox is one of the bands. In the last
couple weeks, I've gone back to listen to that stuff. No wonder I like Interpol
[laughs]. Once John Vox left the band, they shifted pretty drastically. But I really
started liking other things like Gary Numan in the early days. I've had multiple opportunities to see him play, actually bought my ticket, was absolutely
gung-ho, then I ended up with some crappy punk gig somewhere I had to do
an Agent Orange set [laughs]. I caught him one time. The other thing is all the
amazing opportunities I've had that I missed, like the times when he had the big
stage sets. It's one of those things I kind of miss now from rock'n'roll. A lot of
bands really did have great stage sets. I know, it seems like, what are we talking
about? Pink Floyd? You know who always had the greatest stage sets? Johnny
Rotten. No matter what band he was in, he always had something super cool.
Not necessarily expensive or over-the-top, sometimes something understated
and simple and cool.

Did you see that legendary PIL show at the Olympic?
I did. I was there. It was a great show. A very simple stage set-up that was very
effective. He had one of those fluorescent halos. He just held it over his head.
Simple. What do those cost? Three bucks? That is genius. Just something to
dress it up [laughs].

Gregg Turner
(Angry Samoans)

I met the venerable raconteur, rock critic, musician, and mathematics professor in Santa Fe, New Mexico, one time at a late-night bar hop for slugs of beer and small talk, but this interview, originally published in *Left of the Dial*, happened via e-mail. The man is garrulous, hyperintelligent, and driven by serious renegade wit. Although his more contemporary venture, the Blood Drained Cows, cruised far under the radar of the punk legions, the Angry Samoans remain everlasting ultimate specimens of the gunk punk, far before the term was coined. Ribald and resilient, the band kept punk linked to 1960s unkempt garage rock, yet they also tethered the form to stabbing satire that feels almost downright Swiftian too.

Is the drivel of "bad talent source . . . corporate McDonald's" FM radio today much removed from the drivel of 1978, even when warmed-over punk bands like Green Day get radio play, and Foo Fighters cover Angry Samoans songs?
The relativity theory of drivel maintains that new drivel inroads always seem more conspicuous as, um, drivel, whereas vintage drivel always seems better in comparison. E.g., Shannon's "Abergavenny" or even the Osmonds takes on

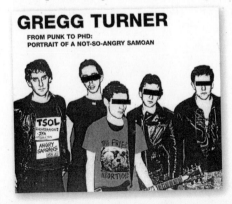

a more romantic sense, than, say, Eminem. On the other hand, *serious* (even vintage) drivel such as, say, Heart or Ted Nugent, will never be reconciled beyond a status of toilet film. In any case, I think it's fair to say that megacorporatization of music, like the co-opting of lit and film and so forth, strives to eliminate dangerous (to them) alternatives and mass dog foodization so that all ends of the aesthetic spectrum wind up in the center. Center is no good. It's where they make the money and we get no choices. Laissez-faire capitalism at its Orwellian best?

Where do you tend to locate the roots of punk, in something like the Ramones and Dictators comic NY rock, or way before, in the Stooges and 13th Floor Elevators, or even in the clang and clatter of jazz?
Punk's a loaded word. "Roots" confuses me even more. If p—k is a metaphor for the exit off-ramp in the road at each stage the road had been turned into a highway, then any of these could pass. The Dictators wiped the slate clean, when the slate was grimy with fatuous icons (the legacy of Yes and Joan Baez refused to go quietly). Calling Lou Reed a creep in 1976 was taking a chance! Then again, Gerry Roslie (Sonics ca. early '60s) as Frankenstein frat boy was twice a chance.

Although tagged as a 1980s hardcore punk band, at least in the beginning by people outside of LA, did you actually have more in common with the first wave of California punk, like the Dickies, Bags, and Weirdos? Why/why not?
We were really hatched out of the first wave. When Meltzer and I caught the Weirdos in 1976 singing, "I am mole, I dig your hole"—who could resist? Vom was the initiative, the Samoans followed in suit pretty naturally. And yeah, Alice Bag was a lot more alarming than anything Agnostic Front offered. The hardcore exercises in the 1980s were follow-throughs for us. That was the bathwater following the baby. I felt little in common or inspiration with most anything considered "hardcore" and would resist that depiction of what we did.

Do you still believe, like Joe Strummer, that punk was about cleaning house: no icons, no ruling class, no higher class . . . ? And do the heavily satirical lyrics of the Samoans embody this, or does it get covered up by the vitriol and outrageousness?
Well, the Strummer mantra you refer to was easily the credo (first wave) that we all adopted and pledged allegiance to. It was necessary to go this far to eradicate the cultural nonsense that had packed itself in up to this point. How our lyrics fit into this, I'm not sure. There was never any specific intent to espouse a view or adopt an attitude per se. I'm not sure we were consciously satirical even. More confused and misanthropic and too self-absorbed to care about making a point even. For example, "Lights Out" really was a plea for universal blindness. Some have likened the message to a parody of early-1980s nihilism etc. But we were encouraged by nihilism (as a bromide or alternative for others to explore, not us, of course)—if the next generation of wanna-be teenagers took it to heart, and so say 30 percent were walking the streets in the black (as it were)—what a way to herald in a new culture.

When the band was semiofficially banned from LA because of Rodney and began to play the beachcore and hardcore scenes of the California suburbs, did you feel the band was pushed into playing faster, louder, and cruder as hell simply to survive the boneheads and jocks, or would the band have moved in that direction anyway?

Saunders was the most aggressive voice to conform. He cared (despite the pose and claims otherwise) very much that he fit in. Ironic, since most of what he was about in almost any other respect was just the opposite. I was ambivalent at the time. Looking back, I think the first wave's audacity was a heck of a lot more in-your-face than hardcore's token anger and mohawks. True, there were shows we triple-timed tempos just because we didn't wanna risk the wrath of psycho twelve-year-olds (then, at age twenty-something were their de facto grandparents) and true again that fork in the road steered us onto a course hard to go back to where we started. *Back from Samoa*, if you consider that a "hardcore" record or not, was the one that caught the attention—but I think the first EP, *Inside My Brain* was infinitely more hostile and in-your-face, though sonically, that record alone would not have allowed us to play to Minor Threat fans.

As the band went back to its roots on albums like *Yesterday Started Today* and *STP Not LSD*, even though the band was going through some troubles, how refreshed did you feel to break out of the hardcore mold and play Jefferson Airplane covers in part for shock value, whereas in years before you played "They Saved Hitler's Cock" for the same kind of value?

Every novelty runs its course. The three or four years centering around the release of *Back from Samoa* became suffocating pretty quick. I mean, seeing two hundred kids erupt when we'd launch into "Lights Out" with white plastic forks making spastic eyeball impalement gestures for all eighty seconds as it played it out live was invigorating the first few times around (see above re: this)—then I felt like I was part of Sha Na Na (bad American doo-wop group from the 1970s–1980s) going through the motions of invective as a cartoon figure. It was all so expected and staged—there was nothing left to be appalled at. So, reworking the original 1960s proclivities (Mike and I were essentially connoisseurs of vile garage band workouts from the 1960s) seemed like the only alternative to invigorate. What came out in the form of *Yesterday* and *STP* were, maybe, hybrids of this and the 1980s trappings we'd been stuck with (at that point in time).

Do you regret never having toured Europe, where you had a substantial following?

We tried to do this a couple of times. It was difficult because we all had commitments beyond the band. Mike was an accountant and had but a finite number of days off each year, and I was going to grad school and so forth. Despite this,

we had (I recall) at least two opportunities to do a three- or four-week trip.
Each time Saunders torpedoed the
possibility. I was pretty sure he was
plane-phobic—when Bill (drummer
Vockeroth) almost annihilated his ass
for aborting an offer from a promoter
which would've involved a generous
amount of cash after all expenses
(this was in late '80s), Saunders broke
down and conceded he do it—but
only if he could "take the boat" (his
words—I use this liberally these days
for all sorts of contexts!). Figuring
it'd be say five weeks there and five
weeks back (i.e., on the boat) then

three or four weeks playing, then that would amount
to excusing himself from accounting duties for the whole summer. And so then
we should reimburse him for two months of work he wouldn't be paid for, etc.
Which is when Billy, I think, tried to impale him with a drumstick. It really is
unclear if it was this simple (boat over plane), but on the face of it, that's as close
as it got. The Samoans wanna-be Princess cruise across the Atlantic! Actually, less
depressing than this, there was the time the King of American Samoa wanted to
fly us over on his plane to play some special anniversary or commemoration of
Samoan-ness. One of the studio crew involved with *Back from Samoa* apparently
knew him and relayed our band name—and I guess on the basis of that, he
extended his royal invitation. This got almost serious, until he actually listened
to (i.e., got ahold of) the record! Then we were disinvited. Easy come, easy go.

**How does your writing—from your old *Creem* and *Rolling Stone* pieces to
your recent absurdist writing, "The Tapeworm Story"—link to your music?
Do they come from the same energies and focus, or from different ones?**
Gee, I've never really been conscious of any effective style or attitude in
print. To be honest, I just throw it up and see what sticks! Maybe too much
Richard Meltzer (rock critic/musician) has infiltrated (I wouldn't be the first to
succumb—and certainly wouldn't be embarrassed by an influence that influ-
ence-worthy)—but I just can't stand rock criticism as serious journalism. It's an
oxymoron, with way too many ox-morons loose at it. Maybe there was a two-
year window where communicating how you really felt about something vis-à-
vis rock'n'roll could matter or count. But elevating the analysis to egocentric-
ity, which filtered down and refused to go away became more than nauseating.

I always felt it was important to style your affectations, and the style should direct the rapport with the reader. Everything else was (weakly) secondary. "The Tapeworm Story" is just one of an anthology of short stories I might publish (if I can round up the time and money) to be called *The Tapeworm Story and Other Gastrointestinal Nightmares.* I've also scripted a play called "Necromaniacs from Hell" (originally titled "Hell's Whores")—sort of a hybrid of *Plan 9 from Outer Space* and *Hot Rods from Hell* (starring Dana Andrews, you ever catch this?). All my impetus to write, the source of the "energy" you refer to, my guess is that it must come from the first time I saw *The Four Skulls of Jonathan Drake* or *Invaders from Mars* on TV late at night as a kid. I measured the holes in the sand dunes (with a ruler over the TV set) that people fell into (then they had these metallic alien implants installed into their necks prior to turning into monosyllabic cretins). Then I extrapolated the scale, and figured that, *in reality*, the holes are like six feet wide. I was about eight years old at this point. So, I slept for the next year and a half with my arms clenching the sides of my bed, because I was sure that if a hole appeared in the floor of my bedroom, it wouldn't be maximally large enough to take the bed with it. After a year of this, my folks decided it was time to see a shrink. First of many shrink encounters, but easily the most trendsetting! The shrink said that my imagination was immature (in the clinical sense of how shrinks evaluate such things), but my creative synopsis in interpreting and magnifying things was . . . um . . . "advanced and threatening" (not sure if this was a compliment or ominous diagnosis).

Like Vic Bondi of Articles of Faith (high school teacher) and Milo from the Descendents (PhD), you have been through the academic trenches. Is it like the rock'n'roll trenches? And what makes teaching appealing?

I got hooked into math because all my professors were disaffected, highly eccentric cartoons. So, the entertainment value assumed center stage. Somehow in the process I got hooked on the substance they abused (abstract convolutions of thought with no redeeming social qualities) and after a certain point I was unable to turn back. Though finishing my PhD was hell on earth. I think I (barely) survived like two or three nervous breakdowns before the whole thing was over. In mathematics, the door prize for a doctorate is not a token of effort or reward for doing time. You need to create a problem that hasn't been addressed (and therefore not solved or proved)—then create the solution and (most important) the proof of the solution. But there are thousands and thousands of research level problems that have never been solved or proved. And if, by the luck of the draw, you take one of these (see, no one knows!) you're in for three or four years of unrewarded misery. So, it's like the worst form of delayed gratification in the world. Degrees in humanities and history are wussy PhDs. You go with a topic and do the time and wrap it up in presentable way—it's a foregone conclusion you'll finish at some point. I had dreams my equations were coming to life as little people—and (in the dreams—there were many versions of these) as I would approach they would scream at me—"FUCK YOU!! DON'T YOU TOUCH US!! GET THE FUCK AWAY—WE'LL NEVER LET YOU NEAR WHAT YOU NEED TO KNOW!" And so forth. I'd wake up in cold sweats. Being disowned by your own equations was humiliating and a step of shame I'd never considered owning.

Teaching's a different process. Unfortunately, when I finished my degree, the job market in four-year college teaching hit rock bottom. There were like three hundred applications per tenure track opening. I wound up here in Santa Fe, NM, after hiding out at UCLA with a post-doc, then taking the only tenure-track position offered at this shitty little art college with no math program to speak of. I stuck with that for five years before they informed me I wouldn't get tenure (they weren't tenuring non-arts faculty!), so I went to Worcester, MA, for a year (horrible, horrible place), and then scrambled back at this public four-year college in Las Vegas, NM. We currently have about eight math majors, and seven of them shouldn't have been encouraged past high school. It's truly frightening. So, I guess teaching college math is an okay gig if you were one of the lucky ones to be in the right place at the right time and be at a somewhat academically legit school. I'm burning out quick. Maybe "The Tapeworm Story" will sell (ha ha). But I do love Santa Fe and New Mexico. I collect petrified wood obsessively.

What makes your folk-rock with the Mistaken and your recent solo efforts different, other than in terms of style, from Metal Mike's post-Samoans music?

Well, from what I gather (what I've listened to), most of Saunders stuff post-Samoans refuses to budge from the Ramones/Kiss/etc. infantilism he's been not able to shed since the Samoans ended in 1991. The guy's actually an amazing improv of 1960s/1970s/1980s poses (but good ones)—seemingly he's unable to escape arrested development. I mean, he must be pushing fifty and goes around with Britney Spears T-shirts (for real). Age eighty never existed for Metal Mike—he atrophied at seventeen and a half. As for my crap, hard for me to assess its aesthetic virtues (if any). The Mistaken stuff evolved out of my years in Claremont, CA, playing on the side with these goofy people and being unduly influenced by Jonathan Richman. I think my latest CD as the Blood Drained Cows (more '60s Kinks/Shadows of Knight) is the best thing I've done—at least what I've been the most satisfied with. Whether this is not just as atrophied in a different time and place as the Metal Man is for you to decide. Most have likened it to a thread connected to STP, but that was anything but the intent. We're pretty good live, as a matter of fact. We don't blast your eardrums out (I just play through my Fender Princeton) and the stance is distanced and not assuming. Anyway, we do this once in a while. I'm too old to know better than to be determined about *any* rock'n'roll project circa the new millennium.

Is punk just another reeking nostalgia heap, or a different language within rock'n'roll that continues to be worked on?
I don't think there's even anything left of the heap. Rock'n'roll's a dinosaur—kids aren't buying it (literally and figuratively) and punk as a sub or alt genre, will be embodied on K-Tel compilations for a while. But aside from this, does anyone care?

Why, in the end, is Nico more interesting than Nirvana or Rage Against the Machine?
Here're some ideas about this: (1) Nico was run over by a truck, Cobain self-annihilated (five points for Nico). (2) Had Nico been *not* run over by a truck, she would have imploded (body mass can only expand so far before eagerly returning to equilibrium state). Cobain, had he botched the self-offing, would only have tried again, i.e., death metaphors are entirely from different contexts here—Nico cannot lose this. (3) *Marble Index*, *Desert Shore*, and *Chelsea Girl* were incredibly beautiful records. I never thought as much of *Nevermind* (though I did like "Teen Spirit") or *Bleach* etc. I think Nirvana were swallowed up whole by Geffen, so all you get to see or remember are the entrails of what was (what was?) there in the first place. As far as Rage/Machine goes, I'd vote for Throbbing Gristle. Nico vs. Throbbing Gristle? That'd take way, way more time to figure out!

Ian MacKaye
(Minor Threat, Fugazi)

While independent punk and alternative labels have flourished for the past two decades, Dischord Records, founded by Ian MacKaye and Jeff Nelson, is still indie music's most hallowed ground. For twenty years, the DC label, once a tiny operation that documented the music of a handful of friends, has grown to embody the principles of permanent rebellion, the seeds of which were sown during the stifling Reagan era. Throughout the 1980s, Dischord documented some of the most important bands in American punk: Faith (MacKaye's brother's band), which inspired both the Beastie Boys and Sonic Youth; Scream, a band that in one incarnation included Dave Grohl of Nirvana/Foo Fighters fame; Dag Nasty, whose guitarist Brian Baker is currently in Bad Religion; and Rites of Spring, whose core members—Guy Picciotto and Brendan Canty—became MacKaye's bandmates in Fugazi. Not only did the label provide a model, it pro-

vided a momentum, a burgeoning sense of possibility. Perhaps more importantly, MacKaye helped form Fugazi, punk's most beloved, respected, and tireless band. The band's frontman traded in the punk anger that he forged in the outfits Teen Idles and Minor Threat for an "introspective, almost poetic vision, using abstractions in strongly structured compositions," in the words of Trouser Press. For nearly fifteen years, the band toured every corner of the globe, insisting that every show they play have a five-dollar admission and be open to all ages. The band has also

sworn never to grant interviews to big corporate magazines, and they've turned down all the leviathans: *Spin*, *Details*, even *Rolling Stone*. In a bizarre turn of cultural events, *Instrument*, a video that documents a decade's worth of Fugazi concerts, practices, and portraits, was recently shown at the Museum of Modern Art in New York.

Originally published in *Thirsty Ear* in December 2000.

Is Dischord's twentieth anniversary just another moment in the label?

I'm not nostalgic for the glory years, but at the same time I do think there's something significant. I like the idea that the label has been around for twenty years, because there's a gravity to it that's undeniable. From the very beginning, people were telling us that we wouldn't be able to do the label, that we'd have to move to New York City. They told us we wouldn't be able to do business the way we do. We don't use contracts. We don't follow any of the protocol that most people do. We questioned things. As it went along, people said we should copyright all these songs, and we said, why? What's the point? And we just asked questions, and did what made sense to us. People told us that we wouldn't be able to continue, but after twenty years I feel like, Wow, I guess we did continue, huh? When we get the twentieth-anniversary release, I would like to draw a thread from the Teen Idles to whatever the latest band is. I would like to draw a thread because I see a connection between them all. I know why every band is on the label, and I know the people in the bands, and that's important.

Dischord tried to keep prices down by printing "Don't Pay More Than $5" on the back of the records. But many merchants covered that up with their own price tags.

It's impossible to stop the prices in the free market. The idea was to put the mail order price on the outside of the record to create an option. You could get it for five dollars postpaid from Dischord. Why pay more? Here's the address. Mail order it. All you can do is offer up an alternative, and I never minded if stores charged a little extra because if someone wants the convenience of going down to the corner and buying it for a buck more, who cares? Occasionally, it was really, really abused—people charging import prices because it said "Made in England" on the back or something. That happened. If somebody was really overcharging people, we would call them up and say they were out of line. You can't stop people; it's what the market will bear. It's a philosophy that I completely disagree with, but most of American business thrives on that.

You once said that you don't think anyone is going to change the world, but at least you want to live your life in the healthiest manner, with as much care, consideration, and love for people around you as possible.

Yeah, I still stand by that. There was a point when I felt that punk rock was all these people yelling about making life better, and part of what I thought making life better was about was being happy. I thought if you really wanted to reach that, then you should not just fight to be happy but actually start allowing yourself to be happy. This is not a trivial thing. I'm not talking about having fun. Fuck fun. I'm not interested in fun. I'm talking about when people are fighting for happiness, or fighting to be free. Then I think that their biggest fight is sometimes with themselves . . . Today I was talking with a guy who thought that the fierce individualism of the punk community is what got in the way of the movement, in the way of things actually being mobilized, because people were so fiercely independent. He really firmly believed in collectives and formal cooperatives, but I completely disagree with him. I feel exactly the opposite. To me, it's the rigid codification of the formal collectives, cooperatives, and other groupings that get in the way of progress, because they have these rules, and nobody can break cadence. They can't get out of that, whereas individualists can. I was interviewed by a sociologist guy in 1983 for a documentary they were doing on the DC punk scene. Unfortunately, that whole project went up in flames because those guys ended up in a bitter quarrel, and they split the tapes up, and I think one guy destroyed all the tapes. It was a disaster. They videotaped all these interviews with my mom and dad, and all these other people. It was a huge project. And actually, the Minor Threat [live] video is a remnant of that. They did an interview with this professor who was a sociologist, and he watched an interview they shot of me, and he analyzed me, and he said I was a tragic figure that was going to be so bitter by the time I was thirty.

Now you're thirty-eight and pretty happy.
I think he can go fuck himself.

You've always been an entrepreneur, whether it was a comic book shop, or a skateboard place with Henry Rollins.
I'm always for some kind of social activity. I've always been up for building forts or making bike shops. As kids, we were up for whatever. I think it started really early on, the idea of building or doing things. Having a club, having a gang, just doing something that involved a companionship. Keep in mind, none of these things I did made money. "Entrepreneurial" suggests that I was always trying to make money. Actually, what I was interested in was construction work. I was into the idea of creating things. When I was twelve or thirteen, a lot of my friends started getting into drugs, and I just didn't. A lot of the people early on just tried to spend most of their time getting high. For me, that was so boring, because I just wanted to go do something. We got a day, so let's do something with it. Maybe their detachment heightened my sense of involvement.

There's a photo of you in the early 1980s at Dischord House with a Hendrix record, and it caused me, as a punk, to have a gestalt shift. I no longer had to be embarrassed about liking people like Janis Joplin.
She was a total inspiration for me because she put it out there in a hardcore way. When I was around ten years old, I remember arguing with one of my older sisters about whether music could show somebody's emotions, and I was absolutely adamant that I could hear it in Hendrix. She was like, that's bullshit, but the idea that I could hear the emotion stuck with me for my whole life. To me, music has that. With Joplin, she was so powerful. I also feel [Ted] Nugent was naked in terms of his emotions. They weren't always pleasant, but he put them out there. Same thing with Joplin; she took a risk. It's not very often that people get to just go that hard. I'm thirty-eight and totally happy to get on stage and just completely melt down.

You're the only person I've seen who consistently sweats through their pants on stage.
For me, that's a great gift in my life. It's not something that everybody—not that they want to—will try. But it's worth it. When I was in high school, I was skating, and skating is in part about the redefinition of life. On a skateboard, when everyone else sees sidewalks, I see runways.

Everything is an opportunity?

In high school I couldn't see how people were going to redefine themselves in terms of life. I was sure that it would all come clear to me, that there would be this underground, subculture movement that I would be involved with that would challenge conventional society, because I was not interested in becoming part of it. There was no way I was going to go to college. At one point I thought I was going to be killed by a car, and if I died, I didn't want to have spent most of my cognitive hours sitting in school. Basically, when I was in high school, the only rebellion I was seeing kids do was getting high.

Which is really nonrebellion.

Or antirebellion. The political kids, the Yippie kids, were basically all stoners. Getting high was the one thing that anybody could do, but I didn't want to waste time. In the middle of all this, my friends started listening to punk rock, and I, at first, thought it was a dumb, junky thing. So we argued. And Nugent being the wild man that he was, and having seen his shows, which were so over the top, I couldn't believe that there was anything heavier. I remember getting in these polemic debates about Nuge versus the Ramones, really heavy arguments about what was what. In late 1978, I was given a stack of records . . .

The first Jam, the Clash.
All those records. I sat down and listened to them and became really intrigued, not necessarily liked them, but they scared me because it did not sound like rock'n'roll to me. They were challenging, like it was a whole new kind of music. The Ramones, at the beginning for me, sounded like a joke. Bubblegum.

You saw the Cramps early in their career, and it's a powerful memory.
It was something way deeper, and way darker. When I saw the Cramps in 1979, the room was packed with all different kinds of people, not just a room full of punk rockers, though there were punk rockers there of all shapes and sizes. The Bad Brains were there handing out flyers for their first show. There were junky-type people, a huge political contingent, and these crazy redneck hillbilly punker-type kids. It was the first time since the radical 1960s-type stuff that I had seen people like this. And I said, here it is. This is what I'm looking for. It was the people who were on the margins of society, and that's where I always felt I belonged. There were people challenging political conventions, musical conventions, artistic conventions, sexual conventions, and psychological conventions. People were testing every water there was to be had. It was all there, and the show was a cathartic experience.

After your first band, the Teen Idles, broke up, why did you decide to document the band post-facto and create Dischord?
At the time, there were no labels that were interested in us, that's for sure. We knew that if we wanted to document it, we'd have to do it ourselves. Jeff and I are crazy about documentation. At the end of the day, we had made this tape and had the money. We felt the music was important and wanted to have a record of it. We had been a part of something that was really important to us. We totally believed in what we were doing, the punk rock or underground. We were like: this is our family, and we need to make a yearbook of this shit. While I think some of the music is great, I'm not saying everyone should like it. I could give a fuck. I mean, I'm happy if they do, but if they don't, that's fine. I'm not saying these are the best bands in the world. I will say that for me, it's some of the most important music.

What was the challenge for the label in terms of getting the records distributed?
I don't think we ever really worried about that. We just made 'em and sold 'em. We never thought about it in terms of coverage. We just thought we'd make a thousand records and try to sell them. We approached it more like a craft or a hobby. We didn't think, we're going on tour, we need to get those records in the store. We just thought we'd better make some records so we can sell them on

the road. I don't think of records as promotional devices. At the time, if you got into punk rock, you quickly learned how to get the records. If you knew about punk rock and could buy a record, you could probably figure out how to get another one. That's also when mail order came into its own. Mail orders were so important for us, so strong at the beginning. We still have box after box of old mail orders. We didn't throw a lot of them away. So we still have mail orders from people who ended up being in bands later on. It's amazing.

What struck me back in the 1980s when I saw *Another State of Mind*, a film that features footage of Minor Threat, was the scene of you, energetic and polite, working at Häagen Dazs. Most people generally see punk rockers as shiftless, mindless, angst-ridden kids with pink mohawks begging for change.

I always thought that was the media's version of it. I was faced with the same dilemmas as everybody, and I was dealing with reality. I wasn't squatting. I was doing the same thing as everybody else, just navigating it differently. At the beginning, we were taking an extreme position and rebelling, but we weren't rebelling in the way that the media would like us to rebel, which would suggest that all teenagers were idiots who just wanted to steal stuff and get high. But we were actually doing stuff. I had to pay rent and buy food. I wasn't dependent on anybody. I had no money. That's what always drove me so crazy when people accused us of being spoiled, rich white kids. It was insane. I was working three jobs at that point. When the tape was shot, I was working at Häagen Dazs, a movie theater, and driving a newspaper truck at night. Plus running the label, plus I was in a band, plus I was putting on shows, plus I was writing for a fanzine. I was going around the clock, but I was up for it. People say to me, it must be nice now. You're just living off the music. That's bullshit. It's what keeps me alive, but it's not what I'm living off of. I work my ass off all the time. I run the label, I run the band, I drive the van. We work on our own studio stuff, we are the lawyers, we are the managers. So it's not that our art is our meal ticket. We've always tried not to become too dependent on that. Chuck Dukowski from Black Flag said that he'd rather work a day job for the rest of his life than be dependent on his music for his living. That was in a *Damaged* magazine article called "Apocalypse Now." That quote fucking blew me away. It hit me exactly where I lived.

Who were some of your punk role models?

DOA were in New York and wanted to play Washington. I told them the only thing going on was that we [Teen Idles] were playing this Valentine's dance at this high school. If you want to play, we'll put you on. And they came down and played this Valentine dance. We passed the hat, and they made, like, thirty bucks and stayed at my house. My mom made pancakes and stuff, and they were the greatest guys, and they were so psyched to play. To this day, I'm still an idealist because of that. To this day, I'm always up for a gig. I never blow off a gig. I can't believe when I hear about bands, particularly bands who align themselves with anything vaguely punk, that blow off a gig because they'd rather hang out in New York or something. Fuck that! If you commit to a gig, then you better do anything in your power to get there. That's just the way it is. We're so hardcore about that. Fugazi toured for ten years and cancelled only two or three shows ever, one because Guy was in the hospital and the other two because our van blew up. We physically couldn't make it to them. It wasn't until I was in the hospital in Australia in 1996 that we had to actually put down a string of dates.

But it wasn't necessarily about the shows or just about the bands. It was about the hang, about connecting with people.

To this day, I feel that way. The music is a thread or a currency. It's the center of attention, the point of gathering, maybe. My memories aren't really about standing there watching a band. It's always way more about sitting on a curb outside, or driving to the gig, or waiting in line. I have great memories of seeing the Ramones in 1979 in Virginia, a bit further out in the suburbs at a place run by the Marines. It had almost a Hawaiian theme, an old-school bar/lounge kind of place, with cocktail waitresses and stuff. There was a huge line of people waiting to get in the show, and there was a skirmish at the front of the line, and the word spread like wildfire and came down the line that there was a dress code, and you couldn't have torn jeans. But you were going to see the Ramones—everyone had torn jeans! It just rippled: dress code, they won't let you in with torn jeans. Suddenly—it was in a little shopping mall—people made a beeline for the pharmacy and started buying needles and thread. There was a whole fucking parking lot of people sewing their jeans up trying to get in this gig.

Fugazi tries to keep things interesting. We want to play the sock hops. One of the great aspects about booking your own band is the potential you might land in something weird. A person might call and say, do you want to play in an old circus tent? And most booking agents wouldn't necessarily feel that they could put a band in that kind of situation.

You have tried to play places that have a vaudeville feel to them, not the stereotypical big rock venues.

It's really one of the most frustrating aspects of music. It has become so difficult. You can't blame people for not wanting to rent their rooms to punk shows, because people have been so fucking disrespectful to property. Nothing used to make me more angry than people busting up bathrooms. I never understood that. I used to say on stage, "The toilet is our friend—it takes the shit away. So what the fuck is going on? Every show, you fucking idiots break the toilets. It doesn't make any sense." And in early DC punk, that was one of the strongest principles: Don't fuck up the room. And if there was ever an ass whuppin' to give, it was given to people who broke toilets and stuff. We'd just go after those people. It was not cool. We did not graffiti and we did not break windows. We were tough kids, and we'd definitely step up. There was definitely a lot of fighting going on. We understood that if we wanted the gigs to happen, we had to respect the venues—we couldn't fuck with them. Actually, I remember a turning point when people starting breaking things up, and it was really the end of the adventure of trying new places, because no one would ever give us a chance again.

In the '80s, the scene was very regionalized?
We were a DC label, and I saw things very regionally. That's what I thought was so cool about punk rock. I saw all these different towns had these scenes breaking out. They had their own bands, their own styles, their own way of dressing, even their own way of dancing. I could tell where someone was from by the way they danced. That was so cool, you know. The idea was, we've got DC covered, Alternative Tentacles had San Francisco, Touch and Go had the Midwest, SST was doing LA. It was like, everyone do your own labels, and then we'll be a network. I thought everyone was just going to document their own scene. I thought that was the idea. But actually it turns out we're the only ones who ended up doing it. We still only put out DC-area bands.

Shudder to Think and Jawbox left Dischord for major labels, but the parting was amicable?
The bands are first; I still stand by that. Even recently, the Make-Up just went to K Records, and that's their decision. They're dear friends of mine. Good luck, but they're not on Dischord anymore. That's cool; that's the way it goes.

Why haven't bands on Dischord, with the exception of the Make-Up, released live records?
For the most part, the idea that you can capture a punk show on a record is an illusion. There are not many great live punk records. Fugazi had a really

interesting conversation about live records because we tried to think of live records that are good that didn't have unreleased songs on them and weren't historical. In other words, Hendrix stuff is always historical, because he's obviously dead, so there's a historical notion to it . . . Well, we did live recordings, and they didn't sound any damn good. Bands were always out of tune, and the moment, what was going on in this room, couldn't be captured on a record.

So why pretend?
Right. The initial idea was to go into a studio and just record as live as possible. You have to understand, at least with Minor Threat's *Out of Step*, the vocals are live. Everything was done live. I recorded *Out of Step* standing in this little laundry room and just singing the lyrics next to a washing machine. It was one take. And I sang while they played. And if they fucked up, I just had to sing it again.

There's a lack of video footage as well.
I think we would have done video. It's just that nobody had the equipment. We couldn't afford it. Video cameras also seemed clunky at the time. Things are different, let me tell you. Now there's videotape everywhere of everything. But they haven't made the music good, I'll tell you that. Everyone is documenting every goddamn thing. The problem is now we have everything covered. Everyone knows how to do everything. They have distribution down, they got the labels down, they got the documentation down, and the only thing they've forgotten is that there's so few great songs. It's interesting because I've been asking a few people, who are the ones? In 1981, if you asked me, [Jello] Biafra, Dez Cadena, Joey Shithead, and, without a doubt, Jimmy Pursey . . . These guys were visionaries. People like Penelope, these people were the fucking visionaries. All these people were like gods. I've asked a couple fanzine people, who are the visionaries now, the people who you just can't miss a gig? It's real interesting because I'm not getting a lot of answers. Some people say, Fugazi, you guys are a good band, a good find. But I know there are other bands that are decent. Yet there are very few people who say, that person, I cannot miss him. I'm curious. I'm always asking. I want to know. I listen to so much music that it's crazy. Today, I actually had somebody over and we listened to all these different new things, but also a Beach Boys bootleg, the first Queen record, and this human beat box guy.

Your partner Jeff Nelson is a completist?
Jeff is not really into any of the punk rock stuff at all now. He listens to country music, like you. We had an interesting conversation about that today, actually. He just doesn't feel a lot of connection to the punk stuff. He likes the older stuff, but with the newer stuff, he doesn't know what to make of it. It's tough,

because I'm still very connected to a lot of bands, and would like to continue working on this stuff. It's an interesting time.

You've said that at some point the community you document will no longer exist; and in a certain sense, neither will the label.
I like the idea of an ending. But, I mean, I've certainly underestimated the community because I didn't realize that it was a constant, steady changing of the guard. That people would keep coming along that I felt so connected to that picked it up and kept rolling with it, although it's certainly shrunk down quite a bit . . . I don't want to suggest that Dischord is the only arbiter of what's important. It's not. We just documented what we thought was important. At some point, it just stands to reason that our taste, or our view, is just not going to be able to take in what's important. We want other people to document what's important to them too.

You've said in interviews that, for the most part, you don't have a problem with major labels. You've also said that you ultimately write songs because you want to say "fuck you" to the music industry.
I think you're confusing that a bit. In the beginning it was like, the rock'n'roll industry, we're anti-that. We're punks. We try to operate outside of that system. That's not the reason we write the songs. But it is a nice effect of that.

Do you have problems with major record labels?
They're the musical manifestations of the corporate culture that we exist in, so I have a problem with them on that level. I don't think of them in the same way as oil companies. I certainly prefer DGC and Interscope over Northrop or Remington Arms manufacturer. I have much bigger problems with those companies and the pharmaceutical companies, which I feel have gone totally insane over profit. They are unethical, because they are not thinking about what's best for people and for life because it gets in the way of profit. Major labels' bottom line will always be profit, which is distasteful, but I don't lose sleep over them. They do what they do, and some of them do a fairly good job. They can basically take something that is pretty tepid and get millions of people to buy it. That's kind of impressive. People say, Jesus, these records are great because they're selling so many copies. Now, I don't have any documentation for this, but I think that for every wholesome soy burger/sandwich, there's been five hundred Twinkies sold. People have said to me that Fugazi should have signed to a major label, because we would have reached so many more people, but I think that if we signed to a major label, we'd reach far fewer people because we would have broken up and not put out new records. With who we are, and the way we operate as people, I don't think we could have survived. It would have been

too horrible to have been at the beck and call of those people. To feel that we were a point of investment, which bands are, basically.

You've also defended the notion of preaching to the converted.

People have used this preaching to the converted thing for so long as a sort of argument, as a kind of negative thing. It's not preaching to the converted that's important, it's what the converted do. I have no problem with preaching to the converted, because then the converted can go out and kick some ass. People try to dismiss you by saying you're just playing to your fans. Well, of course, that's what happens, that's why people come out to see you play. What's interesting is when you can make a moment happen, when you can take advantage of the great potential of having a crowd and music . . .

You have taken it to places like Chile.

We played fucking city parks in Hong Kong in the middle of the afternoon. Those, I tell you, are not our converted flock. But by playing all these places, you just see yourselves better.

I remember you firing off a letter to *Flipside* when a girl took you to task on "Filler," a Minor Threat song. Do you take responsibility for things you have said?

To the degree that I can. I don't think I can ever reconcile or clear up the straight-edge stuff or the "Guilty of Being White" stuff. [Minor Threat inspired a subculture within punk known as straight-edge, which advocates abstain-

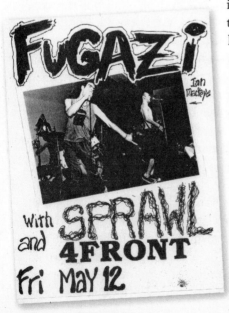

ing from drugs and alcohol. Kids loyal to the trend would draw Xs on both hands with a black marker as a kind of counter-symbol to the marks underage kids receive at clubs that sell alcohol.] A lot of those songs were written at a time when it never occurred to me that anybody outside my [circle of] forty people would ever even hear the songs. You have to understand the context. Anybody who didn't grow up in Washington, DC, might have a little bit of a hard time understanding what "Guilty of Being White" is all about. It's a little discouraging to be sort of her- alded by Nazi Polish skinheads because they think "Guilty of Being White" is such a great song, a great anthem for the white man. Knowing those lyrics are being posted on some Aryan Nation web site is discouraging, but life has that aspect to it. It's absurd. I never would have thought it. The same way, I think it's discouraging that there are kids cutting up other people for smoking cigarettes. That's totally ridiculous. If somebody is actually interested in my lyrics, I'm happy to explain what I intended. But I cannot control those lyrics. They're not mine. They're out there . . . That's the thing about sticking around—you continually have to answer for stuff. I recently got e-mailed from a kid maybe fifteen years old giving me shit about something. On the one hand, I'm like, fuck you. What the fuck do you know? On the other hand, I'm kind of psyched that I have people writing me saying: well, I understand that you guys are doing records through Caroline, they distribute records that are part of EMI . . . all kinds of shit. But the fact that I respond, I love it. I'm still answering the fucking mail to this day. It's amazing to me. That's the punk thing. All the other people, the bands, my earliest peers, I know where a lot of them are, but they're certainly not singing in bands. They don't have to answer questions anymore. I see people and I tell them I still answer the mail. They can't believe it. They never answered the mail!

Even if it's troubling, it reinforces the idea that you have lived your life a certain way?
When I was in high school, I was not a good student per se. I wasn't getting good grades, and I didn't like doing book reports and shit like that. I didn't read the books, and I didn't do the homework. I wasn't interested in that stuff at all. I had to get good grades to the degree that I had to graduate. I did not want to fail. I was assigned *One Flew Over the Cuckoo's Nest* for a book report, or I chose it, and I had never read the book. I was trying to come up with something, because I suddenly had two days to do the book report. I was trying to read the book and trying to get through it, but I ended up calling Ken Kesey.

How the hell did you get Ken Kesey's phone number?
I called 555-1212 and asked for Ken Kesey's number in Oregon. His wife answers the phone. He's out of town. But she talked to me for, like, forty-five minutes about the book and what his ideas were. Not only did I immediately write a report and get an A on it, but I fucking read the book because I couldn't believe she had been so kind to me. I'm doing book reports all the time now. Kids are always calling me about shit. I'm always happy to talk to them.

Jello Biafra
(Dead Kennedys)

Jello Biafra literally needs no introduction. His legend precedes him. Although the Dead Kennedys' internal squabbles have become almost as vitriolic and vehement as their music, their albums still continue to thrive in the imagination of every punk that hears their blitzkrieg beats, schizophrenic surf guitar, and shrieking sociopolitical tirades. Portions of this were originally published in *Thirsty Ear* and *Left of the Dial*.

How do you feel about the encroachment of NATO on Eastern Europe? Do you think there is a third way for these nations outside the influence of the United States and Russia?

Perhaps they could start by listening to their own people. The scary part is that now that capitalism has triumphed over communism, it's trying to destroy

democracy too, so there is an even bigger threat than NATO, and it's called the World Trade Organization, and the GATT treaty that created it, which signs into writing, if not blood, that corporations have the same rights of sovereign nations. Maybe nations aren't even sovereign anymore if the corporations can find a corrupt dictator somewhere to go to the WTO and say, this other country's antipollution laws are interfering with our trade, therefore that country's laws have got to go. America is really abusive within the WTO process too, getting all these sanctions against Europe

because Europe has banned Bovine Growth Hormone in cattle and wants labels on genetically modified, or should I say genetically mutilated, food. It's not capitalism anymore; it's feudalism. So, I'm really glad that people from America to Hungary to India to Africa are starting resist the WTO en masse. Corporate dictatorship is as bad as communist dictatorship, maybe even worse.

What were the major differences between running for mayor of San Francisco in 1979 and running as the Green Party ticket of New York's presidential candidate?
I wasn't even running this time really.

I mean, you were nominated.
They put me on the ballot in the hopes that it would attract people that were down with what I was into and what I was saying, who had never heard of Nader and the Greens—that it would attract people to the Green Party. To some degree, it worked. There's a huge constituency out there in America that wants to see things changed and not just be ripped off by rich people and corporations. Half of the eligible voters in America didn't vote at all in the last presidential election, which means that Gore and Bush were arguing over who won slightly more than 24 percent of the vote in Florida and the rest of the country. I mean, mayor is different because it's a local office. There was a lot more media attention. There were more equal time laws in place there, so if a candidate got in the paper, they had to give everybody a chance, or give every candidate a say. The same for television. But a lot of those laws have disappeared.

You caused a runoff between the top candidates?

I came in fourth, so me and the third place candidate forced a runoff between Diane Franken-fein-swine and another right-winger.

Did you ever feel at any point that you were challenging Nader?

It took me by surprise, and I wrestled with it. I decided to leave my name in there, not as competition to Nader but as hope that it would help the Nader candidacy and the Green Party reach out to youth. I voted for Nader in 1996, and I voted again for him this time, and did some of the super rallies with him, but I was not the best candidate for the Greens. It would have been vain of me to say otherwise.

Are the people you just described as the "huge constituency that wants to see things changed" the same people that were once called the "invisible majority" by the old Republican regime?

Some are, and some aren't. It's interesting to me what a groundswell of support there is for a candidate that runs against the grain, whether Jesse Jackson, Ross Perot, or Ralph Nader, or even George Wallace, because they all got some of the same people to vote for them. And it's a disaffected group who speaks for a lot of us because their main issue is a simple bread and butter one. It's not left versus right; it's the top versus the bottom, it's "Why can't I put food on the table?" And of course the corporations have people in place like Rush Limbaugh and King George II [George Bush] and all the Newtsies left over from Gingrich who

point fingers at welfare cheats and restrictive environmental laws and "feminazis" and other myths to use as a smokescreen to the disaffected. It's the idea that you are supposed to blame someone else rather than getting together and overthrowing the rich people who are stealing all the money in the first place and causing the problems.

If the media shuts out you, Nader, and the Green Party, how can Middle America be reached?
I think that's answered on my new album. Sometimes it takes word of mouth.

Does it surprise you that the students who helped oust Milosevic in Serbia were inspired by Rage Against the Machine?
No. One of the great buried stories of the twilight of the Reagan years was that it was not Reagan who brought down the Berlin Wall. It was a lot of different factors, but one of the main ones was rock'n'roll, especially in East Germany, Poland, and other places. It was of the main ways people vented their rage against the system, and it finally poured into the streets.

Like the Velvet Revolution?
That's what they called the one in what is now the Czech Republic.

What's more important, becoming the media, or being in a band?
If you're in a band, you have become the media. You can either use your voice with the music to sing stupid boring love songs or to say something interesting, inspiring, and provocative. The corny, dippy love songs are a media statement themselves that say, I buy into the commercial media myth of what music should be, therefore you should obey me, the great rock star, and shut up and shop.

What happens to the messages of a band like Chumbawamba when they end up sounding as mainstream as possible? Do they have more impact than the girl down the street who starts a garage band?
Far more people have heard Chumbawamba, so in their case they penetrated more. Their music was more melodic from the very beginning than most of their peers. Other people caught on to that and wanted to listen to them. It was sort of inevitable in a way. They had very catchy material.

Is the message compromised when it comes from a major label or from the mainstream radio?
Each artist has to make their own choice. I've chosen to avoid the mainstream entertainment industry like the plague.

Do you side with Chuck D from Public Enemy on file-sharing, who said that it forces record companies to reimagine artists' relationship to their fans?

I started out siding with Metallica, but the more I learned about Napster and its culture, I crossed over to the other side. Ideally, it's a good thing, at least so far because it gives people a chance to listen before they buy and completely disengage themselves from MTV and bad corporate radio to decide what they want to listen to. And a lot of Napster users tell me that they don't endlessly download songs and say, "I ripped off the artist and don't have to pay them." They do it to see if they like a song and might want to hear more and go buy the album. And the reason they do is because it takes so damn long to download a whole album off of Napster, then look how much space in your hard drive you have taken up. It's easier to go out and get the album. So, it can actu-

ally be used as a tool to promote an artist. An artist can even experiment by putting out several different versions of a song and seeing what one people like the most, if that's the way they want to go.

On the other hand, I do hope that people who file-share will remember that most artists don't make near the amount of money that Metallica does, if they make money at all. So, if people find something they really like by an independent artist, I hope they will go out and support that artist and buy the album. Say someone has been working a job they hate

for years to save up money to record and release their own CD of their music from their heart and soul, and they can only afford to make a thousand CDs. They'll be lucky if they can sell them all because so many other people are doing the same thing. But if they lose several hundred CD sales to free downloading, then they are never going to have enough money to make a follow-up CD. They'll probably just go back to their boring job. That's what I'd like to avoid. I mean, people downloading songs from major labels doesn't bother me a bit because major labels go way further out of their way to rip off bands, their own artists, than Napster ever did. Independent artists do deserve support and respect.

As you probably know, the former members of my own band have been suing the shit out of me because I wouldn't put "Holiday in Cambodia" in a

Levi's commercial. They refused to compromise or settle. They took it to a trial and marched up like little parents to the witness stand. Ray, Klaus, and D.H. all claimed they wrote all my songs, that I plotted to hide all this money from them, which I paid before they even sued. They even brought in an expert witness from Grateful Dead Records, who claimed I owed them a half a million bucks because they weren't, among other things, regularly on *Rolling Stone*, *Billboard*, and VH1. He also said that if x amount more money had been spent on advertising, then x amount of CDs would have automatically been sold. So, I got hit for all these debts, for $200,000 in damages as well, and now I'm trying to appeal. So what I'm getting at is, right now the other guys have run off with the Dead Kennedys catalog and are doing very sleazy things with it, including releasing a really poor quality live album behind my back that I don't recommend that anybody buy, and so while this is going, I think people would be better off going to someplace like Napster to get the Dead Kennedys rather than line the pockets of people who run around filing vicious lawsuits.

Did it surprise you when "Die for Oil, Sucker" was the best-selling single on Alternative Tentacles outside the Dead Kennedys? Is spoken word a force in the market as much as a band?

It doesn't necessarily need to be compared to bands. It was just that somebody needed to say something about the Gulf War. I had to get it done quickly, so I did it as a spoken word piece and had it out on the streets the day the bombing started, and people picked up on that because they were so angry. I think the fact that so many people poured into the streets to protest the Gulf War is what brought it to such an early end. As crazy as the Bush crowd is, they didn't want another Vietnam on their hands, and they knew that was what was going to happen right here at home if they didn't get out of there fast. That's why Schwarzkopf's plan to invade Baghdad and Dick Cheney's plan to nuke Baghdad were never implemented. The reaction at home was so swift that all the yellow ribbon bullshit and corporate media couldn't keep people from pouring into the streets.

You started taking film classes as far back as 1977 and have starred in a few films, including *Tapeheads* and *Terminal City Ricochet*. Are your film roles another version of Jello Biafra's media insurrection persona?

It can't be in movies because if I'm acting in a film I can't very well be Jello Biafra at the same time as I portray a character.

It doesn't carry over?

Well, that's for you to decide. I did manage to get an ad-lib into *Tapeheads* about my own obscenity trial that was going on simultaneously and they left it in the final cut of the film. The FBI agent I portrayed who was busting John Cusack and Tim Robbins for trafficking in pornography because they showed a video of a politician getting it on with a prostitute in a bedroom on TV, said, "You see what they did to Jello Biafra . . ." I don't remember the rest of it, but basically the movie ends with them in jail.

Is that the character, or is that Jello?
I think it was an injection of Jello into the character. I don't like to get that analytical about my own work. If I analyzed myself to death like that, I'd never get anything done.

What makes your work with Steel Pole Bathtub (Tumor Circus) and Dead Kennedys' *Frankenchrist* album some of your favorite work?
I like them. I don't want to do professorial analysis of my own work. That's for the listener to have fun with.

What did you see in the Avengers, Dils, and others in late-1970s California that you didn't see in Wire and the Saints when you visited England that made you want to be in a band?
That's another academic question where you assume something that wasn't true. All those bands made me want to be in a band. I mean Eric Burdon and the Animals, Paul Revere and the Raiders, and the Rolling Stones made me want to be in a band in 1965 when I was in second grade. That desire had always been there, I just assumed that was never going to happen to me because it only happened to pretty people who lived in New York and Los Angeles and could play as good as Jimi Hendrix. That was the mantra being preached by the major labels in 1970s when punk blew the lid off. So it was all of the above.

You've suggested that *Let Them Eat Jellybeans* spearheaded the hardcore breakout across the UK [this was a genuine mistake, I meant to say Europe].
I've never said that.

It must be a misquote.
The UK had a different thing going both with the commercial corporate bands like the Exploited and the anarchist underground bands of the Crass label, with Discharge falling somewhere in between and musically falling more into hardcore. But the more intense American hardcore broke out in Finland, of all places, where *Let Them Eat Jellybeans* was domestically released and apparently was a huge hit over there, then came out in Italy, then Sweden, and eventually Holland, of course, with BGK. It eventually spilled back into England. *Jellybeans* had a much bigger impact on the European continent than in the UK.

Do you ever think that the small punk cottage industry of labels like Touch and Go, Dischord, and Alternative Tentacles would morph into the big market players like Epitaph?

I always knew that was possible. The melodic side of punk rock, the people who do it well, make very catchy songs. It surprises me that it didn't happen sooner. The earlier side of that sound, like the Adolescents, DI, TSOL, and Agent Orange should have been all over the radio in 1982, but someday it had to break through.

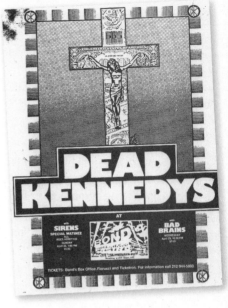

But Alternative Tentacles seems far more punk because the label puts out a variety of bands.

A lot of the bands that call themselves punk and cop a certain sound have no punk spirit in them whatsoever. Anything that sounds like the Eagles with loud guitars is thrown straight out of my stereo. And far as I'm concerned, if you want punk spirit, there's more of it in Wesley Willis than in Blink-182 [laughs]. As far as what other labels do, I figure live and let live. If I don't like what they are putting out, I don't have to listen to it. Life is too short to listen to boring music. It would be nice to open up the minds of more listeners to what we're doing than what we have been able to do in a place flooded with pop punk. I wish we could have done more justice to a band like Logical Nonsense, a band from Santa Fe, New Mexico. As more and more people start cool bands and there's more and more cool labels, the slices of the pie get smaller, smaller, and smaller, so to grab a bigger slice of the pie, you do what people in the commercial industry do, you go commercial within your own scene or within your own pie, thus so much cartoon retro formula pop punk, which Alternative Tentacles is proud to stay away from. We didn't put out any grunge bands when the Seattle craze hit either. We stick to our original vision of helping people out who want to work with us, and operate outside the mainstream entertainment industry, and if corporate punk labels are part of the mainstream entertainment industry, then we'll go outside of that as well.

The label seems caught in the middle, because your bands are too "different" for either the mainstream or *Maximumrocknroll*?

Well, I'd still rather put out music I like than put out something I don't like because I think it will sell. That's not what Alternative Tentacles is for. There's so many other labels now, if people want to go the mainstream route, the cartoon punk by numbers route, there's plenty of other labels at their beck and call. We just don't want to be one of them.

Does it become more difficult to find interesting things in such a deluge of mediocre music?

I've never had trouble, I just look harder. I stay curious. Even when I was in ninth grade, I turned off the radio and just started buying records whose covers looked interesting [laughs], and lo and behold within a year I stumbled upon the MC5, the Stooges, and Hawkwind, and many other wonderful things, and weaned myself from Jethro Tull in the process [laughs].

Do bands make a political impact, or do they, as critics charge, substitute politics with spectacle?

I'm all for spectacle as a way of penetrating people's brains and getting them to wake up and think. Marilyn Manson is brilliant at this, and yes, I think Marilyn Manson has had a political impact because he's let some other people who are disgusted with the way they're treated by their schools, parents, and churches know that they are not the only outcasts out there. You are not alone, and they have the right, or they should stand up for their right to be who they want to be. I think many people have had a political impact over the years. One of the first people executed in Chile when Pinochet got in was a folk singer named Victor Jara. They must have been afraid of his message and how people responded. Or everyone from Bob Dylan to John Lennon on up to Crass, the hardline anarchist punk band from England who basically persuaded a whole generation of punk fans to think twice about buying into the system or becoming mindless consumers, that maybe there's a better way to live your life. I think that people have carried that into adulthood, even middle age, if they got it at an earlier time. The rise of vegetarianism and the animal rights movement is directly related to punk rock.

Gary Floyd
(Dicks, Sister Double Happiness)

Gary Floyd is an underground music legend, almost bar none. For years in the late 1980s, I listened to *These People* by the Dicks, which Floyd fronted, as if it were a punk Bible, and he was a preacher entangled in fiery blues, queer outrage, punk vendettas, and barbed-wire politics. Yet, when I moved to Texas, in the heart of ozone city Houston, people made sure to remind me that the Lone Star version of the Dicks, which produced dizzying mayhem like *Kill From the Heart*, were the authentic originators of the bombastic form. That audience divide might not ever mend. Floyd evolved into a kind of mysterious and mystic figure who studied Eastern religion and explored roots music in fine bands like Sister Double Happiness and the Gary Floyd Band before returning to raw rock'n'roll territory with Black Kali Ma. This interview is culled from that louder-than-a-bomb Kali era printed in *Left of the Dial*, biographical material I gathered from Floyd in the late-2000s, and a recent 2012 phone conversation.

As lead singer for the Dicks, you came on stage with the hammer and sickle symbols, or chocolate panties and condoms filled with mayonnaise and water. Did that constitute youthful shock value, an art statement, or subversion of traditional rock stars?
I always felt that if it made anybody feel more deviant, then my work had been done. I did think of myself as very political back then, and I did consider myself a communist back in those days, but I also never aligned myself with any kind of political party like the Revolutionary

Communist Party or any of that shit. I have always been very happy about that. Politics, to me, is like an inward thing, and if you happen to find people that you can communicate with, then that's all the better. To just join things has always irritated me. As far as the other thing, I liked to shock people, and it seemed to work at the time. When I moved to San Francisco I stopped doing it.

It was redundant?

Yeah, plus I wanted the music to be what carried the Dicks, not the antics. Antics are fun, but I didn't want them to be the main thing.

    The Dicks was way back in 1979. I had been back in Austin a very short time when my friend Lynn introduced me to a new guy in town. His name was Dan, and he worked at a high-end beauty salon. He had worked at Sassoon's in San Francisco and had only lived in Austin a few months. He was the most smart-mouthed and incisively intelligent person I had ever met. He loved to bleach my hair, then put Crazy Color on it. Okay, this was 1979 . . . Austin, Texas. State government yahoos and frat boys in Camaros and Woodstock wanna-be's and leftover cosmic cowboys and me walking around with super-red, sorta dayglow-looking hair jumping off my head. People would almost have wrecks looking at me from their cars. I loved it and was the first person I knew who had this kind of electric hair thirty years ago, when boys aimed for Aerosmith aesthetics. I didn't have a car, so I got around on the university shuttle bus or the terrible Austin city buses that cut the city in half. Lots of contact with the "normals." People would say really stupid shit, like, "Is that your real hair color?" I would

usually look real serious and say, "Yes," to which I would always hear the thick Texas fighting voice drawl, "It is not!" come from their mouths. Mad . . . they were mad at me. The red hair, my lack of caring about their ways of living and dying brought out some emotion—searing hate—in them. Again, I loved it, the trigger effect.

Randy "Biscuit" Turner of the Big Boys and I would try to outdo each other, and that certainly gave the people their money's worth. Biscuit was more creative than me. He would spend hours, or days, literally, putting a whacky, carefully arranged outfit together. Me? I would throw on some torn-up dress, some nasty panties, a wig, and I was ready. But it worked, in a demented way, like an old John Waters film, live and loud. Biscuit and I loved each other. We both remembered the boring pre-punk time, before we had our own bands and were taking full advantage of the edgy new era. We remembered the perfectly faded denim and tousled long horse-haired boys and masturbating guitar solos. The bit of creative competition between he and I was always a fun thing, never catty, scowling, or done to be prickly and mean. Our friendship was deep. Like survivors. Being lead singers, who just happened to be gay, in popular punk bands and big showoffs, too, kept us close-knit.

How did you begin to meld the blues into punk, and why did that seem like such a natural thing? Is punk, like the blues, a form of great American music?

The last part of your question I tend to shy away from because I'm not some big scholar on that, and I actually think that nobody is. I think punk rock is music and people got into doing it in England, Belgium, and they did it in America, so it's an international expression of music. It happens to be a common thing among some people. I always liked the blues. It's always been one of my favorite kinds of music. With the Gary Floyd Band, I actually did hard blues albums, and with the early Dicks my voice just seemed to project that, especially on songs like "Shit on Me" and "Shithole," which had a little bit of a bluesy feel. When people expressed that (my bluesy quality) after the fact, I was shocked.

People say a sense of "soul" made the Dicks more unique and different than the Dead Kennedys.

You know what? The more comfortable I got with singing and with my voice that I thought was mine, the more people would say that and identify the voice as an instrument in the band. When I first started singing, if you tried singing any way other than like raw punk rock, then you were sort of a poseur or something. After a while I thought, me being a poseur would mean I was doing someone other than I wanted to do. I've always been a guy who pretty much did what I wanted to do and said "fuck you" to people who didn't like it, like when I tried to move out of the punk thing. Even when the Dicks were playing, people would be yelling, "Faster, play faster." You know what? "Fuck you, fuck you." To express myself through music is the most important thing to me, whether or not it lives up to some person's ideology of what I should be doing.

"No Fucking War" is not a fast song by any means, and that's fairly early on. Or "George Jackson." Some songs off *These People* are rock'n'roll songs. If I wanted to be restricted, I'd work in a gas station or a factory. With music, if I feel restricted, then I feel like I'm not doing music. I'm doing somebody else's thought of what I should be doing, which I can't do.

What was the Rock Against Reagan tour like?
RAR was a traveling caravan from hell. MDC had their own van, fixed up for touring with a loft and all the comforts of a road ready punk rock touring band. We had a van, but it was not all fixed up. It was bare bones. I'm not sure if DRI had a van or not. Some of the travelers had beat-up cars, and the Crucifucks were stuck on the big banana-yellow school bus, which had the cooking things used by the "staff" of RAR. Some guy—a tall, skinny, longhaired hippie dude driver—had his baby on the tour. I mean a little kid, maybe three, always in a filthy diapers scurrying round the bus. Ratty dogs, overflowing bags of weed, and lots of different types of misfits and outsiders were in there. The big guy with huge hair that I had seen on stage doing a sound check when I walked into the well-worn club the first night was a poet, of sorts, doing spoken word while playing a little plastic Casio keyboard thing. He wore a clothes hanger tangled in his hair, and his very skinny wife waited on him hand and foot. What a couple! His revolution didn't include his wife telling him to fuck off.

When we played Kent, Ohio, we played the Neil Young song "Ohio." We loved doing that song and put it into our set list most of the rest of the tour. One of the biggest shows was in vast green Central Park in New York City. Thousands of people milled around. It was wonderful. The Dicks were about ready to leave the tour, so it was almost a goodbye show for us. The cops were getting ready to close down the show due to noise permits not being right or something. Really, they were just afraid it was all about to get out-of-hand. MDC had stirred up the crowd to a near frenzy, then us Texans came on. The crowd was slamming and sweating like animals devouring each other, like a midday insurgency amid chic uptown. The police had gotten sick of it all, and they were bracing, ready to pound some pasty punks. I yelled into the mic, "We dedicate the next song to your friends and ours, from New York to Texas to California. It's called 'Dicks Hate the Police!'" Well, everyone went nuts. About halfway through the first verse, the cops pulled the plug! They scowled and stared at me from the dead generator, just daring me to say or do something

to incite the crowd. I just raised my fist and yelled, "Thank you, New York City," and left the stage.

You pruned trees and worked as a janitor at a mental asylum when you were young. How much of that has carried into your music?
I'm not very nostalgic or attached to the past, but everything does bleed over into what the music is. I've done things with a bit of discomfort up until a certain point in my life, and then when you become comfortable with it, you use the past to serve you rather than depress you. As far as being nostalgic and saying, "Oh, I should write a song about those janitorial days," or about people I've known . . . No. I'm not a very attached guy. I have a few good friends, who I cling to and love, but as far as being attached to some kind of memories, like playing at Raul's in Austin in the early 1980s, I don't have any attachment to that. It happened, and I'm glad for that, but I'm also happy that today happened. So, tomorrow I'm going to be a little less attached to today.

Does it embarrass you that people say you have the best voice since Tom Jones?
That's a compliment [laughs]. I'm not embarrassed either, but I'm happy to hear that.

How did you get turned on to Kitty Wells, Janis Joplin, and Muddy Waters?
I let a lot of guards drop that had been held up in front of me for different reasons. My parents are music fans to the point that they listen to a lot of music. On Saturday evenings, there would be this long horror story for me of different country people like Porter Wagoner, Buck Owens, and others. So, it was something I was listening to, also the Grand Ole Opry and Panther Hall, which had Willie Nelson. It was my young hippie days, and I hated it. But you know what, it was there, and I was listening to it. My mother used to listen to some bluesy things too. As music started progressing, there were people like Canned Heat doing the blues. They did an album with John Lee Hooker, which opened a lot of people up to what John Lee Hooker was doing.

What about John Mayall and the Bluesbreakers?
Never too much into them. I did love . . .

Johnny Winter?
I love Johnny Winter. That led me into a lot of the blues stuff.

Your dad was a complicated man. He was a World War II veteran who wrote you a letter to the draft board explaining your sincerity as a conscientious objector, yet you've called him a redneck.
I'm a little bit of a redneck myself.

Are you as complicated as your father?

You know, the apple doesn't fall far from the ass [laughs]. You know that story, don't ya? My father was very complicated, but isn't everybody complicated? Even the most simple people have their weirdness, but my father was all those things. He did write the letter, because he believed I was telling the truth, and he told me this guy named Anthony Foster, a black kid who played drums in a band I was in during high school, was always welcome at my house.

Yet he was a redneck?

He was a redneck in the way that his politics were conservative, and he didn't mind telling people what he was thinking, you know, and I'm proud of him for that. He supported me, and I support him on that. Once again, I'll say I have a few redneck tendencies myself.

Which include?

Ask the wrong question, find out.

Why did you turn to Hinduism?

Why shit and not vomit?

But why not something like Catholicism?

Because I had already been a Catholic.

There's nothing redeeming in that?

Yes, it led to where I am now. The bottom rung of the ladder is as important as the top one, if you want to get over the ladder. I had been sorta spiritual as a kid, but then through politics and the Vietnam War and all that, I adopted a much more leftist ideology that sorta negated spirituality, and I fed into that. I was very happy. After a long time of looking within myself for something that was very natural, it became like an irritation. I'm not a Christian. I think Jesus is fine, but most Christians are pretty fucked because they became so political, so I went after my own ideology. I studied Buddhism a bit, then I found some offshoots of Hinduism that I found very attractive—the mother worship of Kali and Vedanta philosophy, which I found very interesting. Once again, this was something I wanted to do, but to do it to the maximum I had to quit Sister Double Happiness, who weren't very happy about that because we just had an album on SST. I always had a feeling within me that a bigger "thing" was some-where out there but also within each of us—the same God-stuff, both in and out. Our ability to tap into that "thing" is a two-way street. It's always ready to take us to its center and be our guide, but only if we take a step or two to realize its helping nature. So, I studied for a year, was very close to a monastery, and found it very wonderful. But after about a year, I knew I wasn't going to be a monk in this life, and if I wasn't going to be a monk, then I should go back to music immediately. That's when Sister Double Happiness got back together, and within a year we were signed to Warner Bros.

A *Rolling Stone* writer said that Black Kali Ma both embodies and demystifies masculinity.
Well, I'm a pretty masculine queer, and people are often fascinated by that because they are very influenced by stereotypes.

In rock'n'roll, which is supposedly all about freedom, why is queer sexuality so covered up or dismissed?
Because it's not free, it's extremely homophobic. That's why. It's not free at all.

What shapes that lack of freedom?
Society in general. There are several things. First of all, I do not like to criticize the gay community for their lack of support of rock'n'roll music. There are a few, and they work really hard to make rock'n'roll to be part of an accepted thing.

Didn't Sister Double Happiness have a core of gay followers?
I have plenty of gay people who come see our shows. But generally there's not that many gay people who love rock'n'roll. There's a lot, but if you're talking overall, there's not. But part of that is that oppressed minority kind of shit will come up, like people are telling people to listen to this type of music, and they do it. But you always have a few rebels, a few rock'n'roll queers. The smartest people in rock'n'roll are queer. I always remember that . . .

After you have a bit of success, and people start buying your records, and you get used to having some money, and you're finally able to be successful at what you want to do, if you come out and you're really queer, people will stop doing that [support]— you get pegged as a queer. Fat-ass Elton John is able to do it because who gives a shit. That's why Michael Stipe never did it . . . because general people might stop buying their records because they don't want to buy records by queers. Believe me, that is true.

So many people, believe it or not, don't know I'm gay, and if it happens to come out, they act all weird. They don't want to feel emotional about music that a queer is singing, because being queer has such a weird connotation in this society. My thing is that I'm not a real advocate of going out and screaming in my songs about, "I love him," and so on, so I keep my work gender-neutral, because I want everybody to be able to relate to my music. And I get a lot of shit from queers about that, and once again, I don't give a shit. I do what I want to do for music, and I am pretty open about being gay. I always have been, in a kinda redneck way.

Did Europeans treat you differently?

I would never get asked about being gay much in Europe. I remember once in Zurich, when we got there, they ran an interview that they had done with me during an earlier trip. The title was something like "Big Gay Buddha Comes to Town," and I was like, "Oh my god." They didn't say anything about me being queer in the article, but I thought, everybody's going to come and give me a lot of shit. But there wasn't anything to worry about. Nobody seemed to care. Of course, there is a homophobic element in Europe, as is everywhere, but personally, I never got any grief there. Everybody seemed very tolerant and never made a big deal about it. We played in front of some rough crowds there, like those big festivals in Holland, a couple of really big concerts in Germany, so people could have given me grief, I'm sure, if they wanted to. I've never gotten that much grief here too, from the audience. Somebody at Warner Bros., though, did say once, "We don't know what to do with you," in terms of marketing. So, I do think Europe, in general, is more tolerant. But they have a lot of fucked-up shit going on there too.

You took a break again a few years ago. While working one night, you heard one of your songs on college radio, and thought, "This is not who I am. I should be playing music." So, who had you become?

I felt I was a musician, and felt pretty good about it. But I had a very bad tour of Europe. Sister Double Happiness wasn't together anymore. I released five albums with the Gary Floyd Band in Germany, but I came from that tour and decided not to play music anymore. I was a musician, but didn't want to act like one for a while. I was cleaning houses for money, and I was cleaning a garbage can, and then the radio played "Sweet Talker," and I looked up and said, "I do that better than I do this." It was catalyst of sorts. There's a certain thing in Hinduism and Buddhism called dharma—you do what you do. I realized I wasn't doing what I should be doing in life. As weird as my career has been in music, this is what I do. That woke me up a bit.

I called a guy I knew from the San Francisco scene when Sister was doing really good, Matt Margolin, from the Smokin' Rhythm Prawns. He said, "I'd really like to play with you, but you probably don't know this, but I live in Minneapolis now." I was like, "I thought you were in San Francisco." He was excited by the idea of playing music with us so much that he moved back to the Bay Area. It was unbelievable. He was always like, it's such a stupid thing for me to say, but he was always such a great gentlemen. He was always polite. He was never a big sloppy drunk. He was a great, talented guitar player, and he just died in his sleep one night, such an ugly thing to happen.

The first person I wanted to call about drumming was one of the best drummers I had ever seen, drummer Bruce Ducheneaux from the Gary Floyd Band, who said he wanted to play harder music too. We had the revolving door bass players thing though—about fourteen people it seems. Ed Ivey played most of the bass on the album, though he was never actually really part of the band. I really loved making that record, but once again, it became a big drag. We went on tour, and every city seemed a thousand miles apart, everybody got sick. We headed to Austin for SXSW, which everybody thinks is the shit. We got back, our personal lives became too much to be in the band, and the next thing I know, Black Kali Ma is gone. We weren't together anymore. I really, really loved that band and album.

Now in your late fifties, do you have a slightly different perspective?
Usually, getting older means you get some kind of knowledge. Good or bad, you're still picking up things. Just life knowledge brings comfort to yourself, so I feel very comfortable with what I'm doing. A lot of times what makes people progress is not being comfortable. That's what's happened to me a lot. That's made me move forward. Do I feel like I'm smarter than other people? Of course [laughs]. Because I'm me. And that's why they're smarter than me. That's not really true, I'm joking a bit. You know, I really don't feel like I'm a punk.

I use the term loosely.
I'm a musician whose made punk rock music that I think is really good, but I've also made blues and folk music. It's like when gay journalists ask, "Are you a gay musician, or a musician who's gay?" It's like, you know, I'm a musician who's gay. And I really believe that, and they get all uptight about it.

There was a time, when I was in the Dicks, when I would go on tour, and I didn't know where I was going to live when I would return. I would sleep on the promoter's floor next to the dog shitting. I didn't care, though I do now. I'm too fucking old. I don't want to sleep on the floor, or next to the dog. I cannot tour like that anymore. You get older and you have health issues. I want a little better. I don't think it's too much, or it's selling out, to say, I want to sleep on a bed and have a bathroom that doesn't have a lot of foreign hairs all over it. I don't dig that. I've done it, so I don't need to keep on doing it.

I offer no paths for to you follow or anything for you to do. Being happy and feeling whole within yourself is the goal. If you are, stay there. I moved only when I felt the need. I never asked if it was right. It was right—for me—and I live it now.

Mike Watt
(Minutemen, fIREHOSE)

"Just me and Mike Watt playing guitar," murmured D. Boon on the tail end of the Minutemen album *Double Nickels on the Dime*, which was lined with drawings by Raymond Pettibon, close-ups of all three San Pedro working-class heroes in their used cars, and photos of them playing cramped clubs and outdoor parks. D. Boon half-sang the lyric, as if he were talking to a beer glass or an empty telephone booth. He loved Richard Meltzer, John Doe, E. Bloom, Joe Strummer, Richard Hell, and Mike Watt . . .

When I brought my copy of the *Tour-Spiel* seven-inch to the Appletree Records counter, where I later worked and guys would cut out and paste pictures of dorks with goatees and insert the caption "Hymie" in permanent marker, the guy with the unruly, oily Beatles haircut said, "I just heard that D. Boon died yesterday." I bought the record and I went home with hunkered down shoulders and the feeling of Styrofoam in my legs. The show *Cutting Edge*, hosted on MTV by deadpan and quirky Peter Zaremba of the Fleshtones, dedicated their next show to him. They had aired the "Ack Ack Ack" video earlier that year, about the same time MTV used to run a clip of the "This Ain't No Picnic" video. They also ran footage of a UCLA show interspersed with interviews that took place on some skinny steps outdoors surrounded by trees. D. Boon said, "There should be a band on every block" and scratched his thick beard. I had a Ludwig jazz kit at the time that I bought from a guy who lived on a dairy farm in Wisconsin. With gusto and floppy wrists, I barely mastered the heavy metronome chops of "1969" by the Stooges and the single version of "In-A-Gadda-Da-Vida" by Iron Butterfly, but hearing those words cemented the whole idea that I was a band guy. I gave up on second guessing the whole thing, and have been in bands right up to now. D. Boon was an archangel of sorts. Mike Watt is his bass player, even now, even after fIREHOSE and two decades as solo artist.

Originally published in *Left of the Dial*.

You just stayed at Ian MacKaye's house?

Yeah, he's a nice guy. A no-bullshit guy. If he says something, he does it. There's no career hustle, and I like people like that. Other than the bands like the Clash or something. They've sold hundreds of thousands of records out of his house, and never had any major label hustle. I'm very inspired by that. I try to run things down to earth too.

But what it is like to be hanging with him twenty years later?

Well, bro, he's come to all my shows. I was just at his house. I hadn't been there for about two years. But he comes to all my DC shows, like Henry, or a lot of those guys.

Let's talk about D. Boon. His daddy was a big Buck Owens fan?

That was all his daddy would listen to. D. Boon knew nothing of Cream, the Who, and others. Creedence Clearwater was the only band he heard that was kind of rock'n'roll. So we learned all those songs, and that's why I wear plaid. We were only thirteen. Our first gig we went to was T. Rex, when we were fourteen, when they came through. His dad was cool, that was just where they were from in terms of music, but it wasn't like he was closed-minded, it was just that he wasn't exposed. It wasn't like his Dad was a big T. Rex fan, but he wasn't afraid to take his kid to see them. He loved country, and that was what he came from. I remember when we took some of his dad's records and put firecrackers in the holes and threw them all over the place. The John Fogerty influence is very heavy. The other guy who influenced him on guitar was Donald Roeser, who played lead guitar for Blue Öyster Cult.

Was the first song you taught him "Red and Black"?

You got to remember he was the guitarist. He played much better than I did. His mother encouraged us to be in a band because they lived in the projects and it was a way for us to stay in the house so she could keep an eye on us. It was a kind of childcare, you know. She had a big influence on us. She died when we graduated from high school. It was a very traumatic experience for us. First time we had to deal with death. That's why I wrote "The Engine Room." I lost D. Boon when I was twenty-seven, and I lost my father when I was thirty-five.

You almost lost yourself recently.

That was very hard. That's what the next record is about.

You spent five months in bed.

The surgery kept me in the hospital for a week and a half. You know where the perineum is? It's between your legs.

They thought it was a fungus, but it was really an abscess?

They didn't know what the fuck it was. They were just keeping me on antibiotics. I think they thought it was a VD because of the antibiotics they gave me. The test came out negative, but they had the idea fixed in their mind. The shit they gave actually helped spread it around my colon, and it got so big it exploded. I had thirty-eight days of straight fever. I was dying. I can't tell you what thirty-eight days of fever is like. But they were young doctors, young men out of medical school, LA County Hospital, of course, full of poor people and the indigent. The next record is about my sickness. It's my version of Dante's *Divine Comedy* where hell's the sickness, and purgatory is the healing where I play my bass and ride my bicycle.

How many circles does your hell have? Dante's had nine.

Well, I tell you, the fever was like the bottom one. It's very strange, the body and mind. Your body is burning up, and every three hours you go into the shakes like a junky. It was insane. I never got any sleep longer than a minute or two for months. It's an incredible experience to go through. I hurt so bad for so long. And then I had nightmares. Of course, I'm on morphine for the first couple of days of surgery when they cut me open. That's when I went through intense trauma. Then it healed slowly. I was much better after that because I had hope. I didn't have hope before they cut me. Before it exploded, they gave me some prescription stuff, but that didn't heal it. The only thing that helped was hot baths.

You ended up with three holes after surgery?

Well, it blew a hole in me, and I went to the emergency room, and the doctors were shocked. They cut two more holes in me so they could clean all that out. One of them was like a cunt. Another was like my ball sac, but bigger. My balls were swollen up like grapefruit. You can't imagine what that's like. After all that stuff happens, you don't know what's happening. You're putting your trust in these guys, and they're acting like nothing is wrong. I'm not telling you to hate doctors or anything because obviously it's the doctors that saved my life. They're not gods. It's a new science. It's only been around for a little over a hundred years. If you've ever seen a Civil War doctor's kit, it's a chisel and a saw. But anyway, I lived, and I'm very grateful. It was traumatic, the sickness and the healing . . . my sister packing and unpacking me, like starting a lawn mower, packing me up, loading me up twice a day. I had tubes in me, so I could not play bass. They took the tubes, and I was pissing out bits of the lining of my bladder because I had a bladder infection. That shit was like pissing fishhooks. It's insane. You raise your arms and get up on your tiptoes all the way stretched out screaming your brains out because the acid is really high in your bladder.

So, I went back and tried to play bass. I had not stopped playing bass since I was teenager. I started doing Stooges songs.

Because they're fairly easy?
Not a lot of chord changes.

At that time, did you know anything about the Fog project with J Mascis and Ron Asheton from the Stooges?
He had come to some of my gigs before of mine and I did a song with Ron for *Velvet Goldmine*.

   With him coming on board with J, I kind of asked him. We did nine shows. He's very sweet. Up to the time, I grew up with the Stooges, so it was like playing with Marc Bolan or John Fogerty. I'm not really a musician, you know. I got into it because of D. Boon. I graduated high school in 1976, and that's when punk came. It was a lot of circumstance, and a lot of luck, the right place at the right time. And sure, because the opportunity was there, we went for it. It's not something I took for granted. I have to say, it would be hard to top the time of 1976. There was a lot of chance and luck. There were some very inspiring bands. You could not be scared to be on stage. These guys were really incredible. It's like you're never out of school. You got to get in front of class. You hope everybody likes you, and you think one day you'll grow out of that shit, but you don't. It's what you have to deal with every fucking night. But I don't want to say that things are too tough. What about working in a coal mine with five starving kids? This rock'n'roll stuff is for sissies. They think they are so precious. You should just be grateful for the opportunity, but you just hear them pissing and moaning. But I also have to qualify it by saying that I think I am a born entertainer. Right now, with the Jom and Terry Show [Jerry Trebotic and Tom Watson], I'm still curious all these years later, twenty-eight records later. I have it set up so we're all facing each other like at practice. It's the drummer's first tour. He just had a baby. It's quite something to sacrifice that to go out and tour.

You didn't play with that same stage set-up with the Minutemen or fIREHOSE?
No. You're right. Ed was very charismatic, very confident, but at first he didn't like looking at me. I asked him about it one time, and he said, what, I have to hold your hand? And you know, that was almost the thing that made me say, maybe I'm done with this. Ever since then, I have put the guys around me. I think bands are kind of a young man's thing in a way. They are like a little state. You come together and make decisions. Do things together as a team. You try and focus through the music, but it's like getting gray hair, things change. I use a littler bass now because my hands got sore. I can't make the same moves anymore.

You've been using picks again?

That was with J. But I do it on a few songs. If you don't use it, you lose it. It started with *Double Nickels on the Dime*. You see, with punk rock I couldn't use my fingers. It was too fast. I picked until I got better and could use my fingers. Again, if you don't use it, you lose it. That's why I say I'm not natural at it because I'm always working on this shit. I'm practicing all the time in order to do gigs. You got to just keep doing it. I now ride a bicycle. I got a car when I was sixteen and stopped riding a bike. But this guy sold me a ten-speed for five dollars, and I began to ride again. I live in the harbor. It's different than LA. It's forty-five minutes away. I wrote the whole opera on that bike. But anyway, I don't want to lose learning how to play the bass.

Was the tour with Perry Farrell such an impetus for the opera?

You got to understand, Perry doesn't play. It's the first time I've ever played with a guy who doesn't work like a machine. When he teaches you a song, he doesn't show you the chords, the notes, or the riffs, he tells you a story. It's all very interesting, and I thought, I should tell my own story. I was on tour with him, but we didn't play that much, three times a week or so, so I had a lot of time on my hands. I went to a used bookstore. D. Boon's favorite movie as a kid was Steve McQueen's *The Sand Pebbles*, which came out in 1966, and turned out it was a book written by a sailor named Richard McKenna, who was a chief engineer down below, just like my father. So, I get this book, and I read it, and it really inspires me. Then there's this other book that was a favorite of mine from the 1920s that I enjoyed called *Ulysses*. It takes places during the span of a day. I thought, I'm going to put the life of my father and the life of my band in one day. Let it be an opera, but with these kinds of songs. I had not written for D. Boon for fourteen or fifteen years, or my father, so I wanted it to have the right kind of sound. You know, I loved them, and I wanted to put it down. I've always written songs for people. Always. So, it shouldn't be that hard. They were gone, and I had to deal with that. What's weird about that movie, we loved that movie, but we couldn't tell what it was about. We were just kids, and it was complicated. It took place in 1928, in times of the Chinese Civil War, as such: military fears, psychological things. In the book, Jake Holman [played by McQueen] wants to belong to something, but he can't put up

with the bullshit. The hypocrisy. This takes place on the Yellow [Yangtze] River, on an old Spanish riverboat that we've [United States] got now because we won that earlier war. The crew don't do anything. They got coolies doing it all, like cutting their hair. The only thing they're not allowed to do is use their dishes. The captain's got two sets of books. There's corruption. They got the coolies basically keeping the ship running. Like when the Chinese built the railroad through the Sierras. Incredible job they did. The Chinese, the Irish, and the Germans. Those Chinese came over to build it, then they were kept out the country.

There's a museum of Chinese American culture in the West.
Yeah, in Sacramento. They came over and sweated building the railroad but couldn't even live here because of the Yellow Laws.

The Oriental Exclusions Act.
They couldn't even have children here. It was all just a bunch of shit. So, this guy is just a simple man working. He wipes his hand of the whole mess. He doesn't like the way these guys are doing their jobs. He gets one of the Chinese guys, Po-han [Mako], and teaches him. What the others do is called "Monkey See, Monkey Do," where they just copy because the white guys don't want them to really know knowledge. He teaches him by using metaphors to talk about things like how steam is used and stuff. A working man wrote it. It's his own book. He wanted to be a writer, so he went and read Hemingway. He retired from the Navy in Chapel Hill, while my dad lived in Fresno, which is nowhere near the ocean, which tells you about the Navy. But the book's all about the military fear, and how it runs. When they lose it, it all falls apart. I recommend it to anybody. It's not complicated. In a way, it talks about getting cured. Of course, in the movie, they simplified it. It was a war movie, but the book is more than that. So there were all these things coming together. Now, I've written things down and call it *The Secondman's Middle Stand* because I'm definitely not at the beginning, but I hope I am not at the end. Did you think about being in your forties as a kid? But this is where I am, and time is a train.

Are you the same age as your dad was when you started putting out records?
Hmm, I was twenty-two. So, was my dad in his forties? Yeah, he was. He died when he was fifty-two. He never understood my vision of the band. Thought it was a just a limited thing. As it got towards the end, I was sending him postcards from all the towns, which is also in the opera *Contemplating the Engine Room*. I think a part of being a piece of the consciousness in the world is the ability to learn. In one way, you could say being humble, remaining engaged and not a shill or a pawn. One guy did this interview with John Coltrane and said, John Coltrane, what are you trying to do here? What are you trying to do with this music?

What period of Coltrane was this?

When he was going on and on, and people couldn't handle it.

Like *Om* or *Interstellar Space*?

No, more like *A Love Supreme*. But to get back to the statement, he said, What are you trying to do? Coltrane said, I am trying to uplift people. Well, he says, Sun Ra says you're ripping him off. John Coltrane says, you know, there might be something to that. I listen to a lot of John Gilmore. He says, I think music is a big reservoir.

He's probably the biggest inspiration in my life right now. You know, I didn't grow up with jazz, didn't know anything about it. When I first heard it, it was groups like Albert Ayler, John Coltrane, and it sounded like punk to me, just from a different time. It was insane. And I couldn't systematize it like all the other music I heard into verse chorus, verse chorus. It sounded free and reached me in different ways than other music. I was ecstatic. Kind of like the state I like to get in when I play because you're so scared I try to whip myself into a kind of frenzy, a Dervish kind of thing in a way. I don't let the fear win on me or make me insecure or not let me engage. That's why I think songs are a dialogue, a conversation, between instruments. It's not just everybody, like the piano, playing their little part. It's actually them engaging each other in conversation. That's a lot of my style, lexicon, or whatever, on my bass: humility. When people ask me, what kind of bass player are you, I say I am D. Boon's bass player. He made me feel important, so I could grow. He was very generous, very giving. So, it helped. I didn't even know what bass was. When we played, gigs were so far away that on stage I couldn't tell the strings from my fingers. I played it like a guitar with four strings. I didn't know anything. You can't believe how music was in the 1970s. You could buy guitars at record stores. We didn't even know that your A note had to be the other guy's A note. We just knew that the notes had to do with tightening the strings. Some guys liked them loose, but I liked my strings tight. When we played "Down on the Corner," and it sounded right, you were in tune. We didn't know that your "Down on the Corner" had to sound like the other guy's "Down on the Corner." We were twelve, and if punk wouldn't have come, we were ready for it anyway.

In one interview, did you say that you didn't even know that you could play your own songs?
Maybe, maybe you're right. We didn't, we didn't because there was no culture. The 1970s was about copying records. There was no clubs. It was arena rock. Nobody wrote their own songs until punk rock happened down in Hollywood.

So you began seeing the Dils . . .
The Dils, the Germs, X, and the Screamers. They were the first big band, and they didn't even have a guitar. You have to understand, 1970s punk was much different. I don't dis the 1980s hardcore kids because they were very important, but because they were at such a young age, and not much musical, everyone was playing the same fucking song. It was different too because of the parents and the suburbia. In Hollywood, there was a lot of glitter and glam. The only kids you saw were like runaways. But a lot of them were artists, so there was a lot of experimentation, like Black Randy, Nervous Gender . . .

Which Phranc was in.
There was a nine-year-old boy in there, too. But we lived down in Pedro, along the harbor. I had never seen any of this stuff before. The distance between the people on stage and the audience was very small. I got to talk to Darby, to Pat. It was just a different way of doing music. It changed my life forever. It blew my mind. Like *The Rocky Horror Picture Show*, we'd all run up there. They all knew the music. They'd throw toast. They took over the movie.

You were at places like the Masque.
Yeah. It was kind of inbred. Bands from outside of it couldn't play. That's why we became friends with Black Flag. Did our own thing. It finally got big. The Orange County kids came and took it over, and we played those gigs with Black Flag. We played very fast. I'm not ashamed of anything. I don't think it was

lame or anything, I think it was what it was. It did get a little more narrow. A
lot of these cats played that way just because they were young kids, and as they
learned more, they started to grow out of punk. You have to understand, for us
it was much different because we had already learned how to play. That's why
we had a different sound and punk meant so much to us because we thought
we were tainted, polluted. We didn't want people to think we were rock'n'roll.
We hated it, thought it was fascist, and kept things far away. Our parents were
working people, so we didn't have swimming pools to take a shit in. We weren't
oriented that way towards society or oppressive suburbia. We were more interested in working conditions and who people were voting for, not like rock'n'roll
oppression, and people not letting us play clubs. Things in our life were a bit
different than in their life, but that didn't mean we were too good to play for
them. Now, I don't know what they thought of us because by that time the
scene was full of good-looking young men, like TSOL, at punk shows. And you
know, old punk was not full of good-looking people. Whatever, I'm not trying
to make judgments or anything, but it had changed.

But those guys were all surfers . . .
Exactly. Jack Grisham and the guys are still playing, but you could tell that he
might not have been the biggest bozo in high school, like me and D. Boon. So,
I can imagine what they thought seeing us up on stage. But we did it our way,
and met other bands, like the Meat Puppets, Hüsker Dü, and Saccharine Trust.
But we all had our different styles. We thought the thing to do was not copy
each other. That was the thing about punk: it was important that you had to
somehow come up with your own thing. You had to get your own thumbprint,
not rubberstamping a sound or being a cookie cutter.

Jack from TSOL said they hated bands that jumped on other people's sounds.
They went through a lot of hell when they changed because people didn't want
it. But I can't blame these kids because for a lot of them it was the first time they
had ever gone to gigs. It wasn't like us to appeal to those kids. It doesn't mean
we were better, just different. It's not like today, where for ten-year-olds it's a
regular part of growing up. In those days, if you were an Orange County punk,
you took a lot of shit. They had mug shots of kids. It was ridiculous. Because of
their haircuts, like what the fuck? So, I always had a place in my heart for those
guys. They did get together as mobs sometimes and acted like idiots, but by
themselves these guys were getting the shit kicked out of them.

Are you speaking of the Starwood?
Well, not that much, but they would beat up people for having long hair. I'm
not talking about that so much as one-on-one. To be different, those kids had

to go through hell, so my heart always went out to them. I never thought I was better. Even though I came from a different place, but Joey Ramone was like this, hey you're a little weird, c'mon in. You know a lot of that old punk rock attitude like Johnny Rotten was . . .

But hold on, Joe Strummer did name the Minutemen as his second favorite punk band of all time in _Spin_.

But I'm talking about the whole attitude of being angry at people, especially Johnny Rotten, who I met a few times. I don't know what his favorite bands are, but there's always been an aggressive attitude. I don't know what happened. Maybe he was forced into it by his role. I don't know if he's naturally that way. But Joey was definitely a guy that thought punk was big enough for everybody. It just seems like some of those English punk guys, well, it got big there really early, so you can't blame them personally. They were all on major labels. They were rock stars, popular musicians. So, maybe there was a competitive edge there, but if we tore down other bands, it would have been counterproductive. If you tried to keep together and be original, and not be a rip off, it was a good thing. Over there, there were managers, a whole different thing. More like an actual scene, the Jam, Clash, big bands. Somebody told me that Joe Strummer said that, but it's strange because I don't know how he knows about us. You've got to understand, we didn't even know that people in Denver knew about us. That's why fanzines were so important because people just told you about different scenes. You didn't know, and when you toured, you stayed at their houses. It was very much a network, kind of what the Internet is today. Fanzines were a big part of punk culture. Wire and Pop Group had a huge influence on us. In Hollywood, some of them got very successful, and went on to hard rock. It was like, you graduate from punk, now we're in rock'n'roll, the real stuff. I mean, it happened with Brian Baker . . .

From Minor Threat.

Who was in Junkyard. I mean, it happened to Bad Religion, too. That second record sounds like REO Speedwagon to me. But music is for guys to try out things. There are no rules that say you have to go by certain things. They just came from different places. We were at war with rock'n'roll, and we were different than them. Not better, we just reached different conclusions. Like Coltrane said, music is a big reservoir. But I don't want people to say we lost the war and that's why music sucks today. What the fuck's that? Like we're better than Matchbox 20 or something? That's why I try to be conscious of what I am saying. What I try to do is get people inside my mind, and I still call myself punk rock, so I have to deal with this all the time. Back in those days, if you considered yourself punk, you didn't say, "I'm punk." Now, people say, how are you punk rock? You look like my dad. I just try and talk about those days and why I still feel a part of the punk movement. That was an important part of my life. That scene was fertile enough to get me and George out there.

What was it like to see the reformed Wire?
Um, well what's it going to be? Nostalgia, sentimentalism? They moved on too. They used to not play the old songs until a few years ago. It's like John Fogerty said, "blah blah, my back yard." Or like my daddy used to say, those were not happy days. He hated the 1950s. It's always better looking back. I just talk about it because sometimes it sounds like I am being hard on people, but Wire were a big influence. A lot of people think they were one of the better punk bands. I side with Richard Hell, who I talked to once about punk rock.

Who was walking around in New York with a ripped shirt even before Johnny Rotten was singing Alice Cooper songs on the jukebox at Malcolm's shop, SEX.
But I think Rotten's singing is the one thing that makes the Pistols different, because he doesn't act like all the English singers before him and try to hide his accent. Like in New York City, when everyone saw the Dolls, they thought this was new music because there was new clothes and a new look on this Jewish guy from Lexington, Kentucky. One of them was kicked out of reform school in Delaware. He ran off to New York in 1970 and didn't really fit in. He told me he really liked the poets.

What about your book?
It's a book, but not really something I wrote. It's a collection of my lyrics I wrote in the Minutemen—tour diaries from the Black Flag and some words from Richard Meltzer and Thurston Moore. I probably got sixty lyrics from the Minutemen. In fact, it will be in French and English, which is a trip. I have been asked many times to write a book, but I don't think I'm at that point in my life yet. I'm still in the living the life part. I'm passionate about my diaries. I put them up on my website, which is kind of part of the fanzine tradition. The web has no gatekeeper; it's anything you want.

You've mentioned that rock writers in the future might only write webpages instead of print articles.
Every writer should have his own page.

D. Boon once said that every block should have a rock band?
Yeah, you could do it. A band. I told you we had a thing against rock. We loved Little Richard and Jerry Lee Lewis, but by the time it got to the 1970s bands,

it stopped working. They got all the people lumped together, got them all to sound like the same thing, and all have the same goals in life.

But even Ian MacKaye said he loved to see Ted Nugent because of the naked, magnetic animalism.

They mean different things to different people. I don't think there should be a line you walk. I'm just saying one of the reasons why I'm at war with that is my own fucking deal, my own business. I see very dangerous things about it. Those people get away with everything. It creates a whole upper class. To me, rock'n'roll is some dishwasher from Georgia who wants to put on a dress and yell "Tutti Frutti." It's not about being popular, or making someone big and they get whatever they want. If you talk to kids about what they think about music, it's all this bizarre stuff. It's not about proving you're alive, it's all about, I wish I were him. It's all like hollow men who know they can't live up to that. I'm not into Pink Floyd, but I'm into Syd Barrett, but I think that Hitler was one of the first rock stars. I'm not afraid to admit that. It dangerous, like all swastikas, and every unit had a drummer boy.

During the Gulf War, the soldiers were playing "Rock the Casbah" before the bombing campaign.

Well, I heard the pilots got "We Will Rock You" while the soldiers got "Mandatory Suicide" by Slayer. And when you hear it, you do get those kinds of feelings. You gotta watch out though, you can get a little swayed, like Edgar Allan Poe said, your mind will explore thoughts just because they are there, even if they are bad ones. There's some fascist shit about this stuff. A kind of herding mentality that goes on, which is scary, because you would think it's an empowering individual thing. I would like to play up that tendency, not the fucking herd tendency. We have enough of that, mainly through consumer culture. I feel that rock'n'roll panders to consumer culture. I don't know if that is what it was about in the first place, and it was never about that for me, so am I supposed to make a career move and just don that church of rock'n'roll robe? That's why that shit

bothers me. It's power and control. With me, I am trying to show the experience I first had when I started going to punk shows. I'm trying to do that for the kids in a weird way. I'm not trying to live up to that shit, I'm trying to live up to the personal utopia I felt in my life where I could play anything I want and D. Boon could help me. We don't have to live up to anything. We are too weird-looking, we are too lower-class, hell, we could do anything we want. Hell, we could blow minds one day like ours were blown. And in turn, improve these kids, or whoever, people our age or older, and show them that they can take chances and not cater to the flavor of the week.

Do you think the lasting legacy of the Minutemen may not be the music but the philosophy?

I hope so, but I am proud that the Minutemen have their own sound. It's weird, because we got to the point where we could play slow, fast, whatever, and you could still tell it was the Minutemen. I don't know how we did it because we were so drenched in Creedence. But those English guys helped us. They were inspiring and gave us ideas, like "fuck format, get rid of solos." Then Pop Group and Beefheart showed us how to take it farther. I know it sounds naïve, but in those days it was like, why not? The Minutemen is a combination of a lot of accidents, so we'll be known for all those accidents. And, of course, there was philosophy because it was the first time we fucking thought about things. I didn't even know what the fuck lyrics were for. I thought they were like lead guitar. You talked about women and bongwater. My favorite song was "It's Alright, Ma," and I thought he was trying to talk about some kind of sensibility where you just had to fucking think about things and not get caught up in images. I really didn't think there were instructions or it was meant to be connected to events and stuff. Some people tried to figure out what the words were, but I didn't. Lyrics had a whole other meaning to me after punk. Blue Öyster Cult? I didn't know what the fuck they were saying. I didn't even know the fucking "Proud Mary" was a boat. After I got older, I realized the big wheels were the paddle wheels, and thought, this guy's working on the fucking boat. I just didn't think about music that way.

I'm trying to get better. I'm trying to be a sponge. I'm trying not to get stuck in one perspective. You have to be open to new sensations. Sometimes you don't choose it, it just happens. I was married for six years, and that was very hard when it ended. But to get perspective, you can't take things for granted. When you are a young man, you think you are indestructible, and those lessons are hard to come by, but it takes a life to live because it all comes from different angles and shows you different things. That's why I have a lot of respect for teachers because it's a lot easier to tell people what to do than inspire people to do things. When you're in the military and have a gun at your back, you have to listen. When you are in a band, you can't just tell them, you have to inspire them. I'm still learning how to pull the best out of them like D. Boon did. That's why I need people like J or Perry sometimes.

Shawn Stern
(Youth Brigade)

The Stern brothers (Shawn, Mark, and Adam) are the positive punk stalwarts of hardcore California. Their label Better Youth Organization not only provided a plethora of legendary releases but also forged gigs and a sense of international brotherhood that still resonates. The label also witnessed the punk morph from gritty anthemic tuneage to pop-flavored indie rock leanings to retro swing music and back again to lean mean barrages. Still touring and feisty, Youth Brigade is a bridge that connects the past and present, and Shawn is the convincing, coherent captain, articulate as always.

Originally published in *Left of the Dial.*

You once said, "To organize punk music, we didn't want to get exploited by people who didn't give a shit about the music, which is ridiculous because no one is ever going to make money off punk rock." At what point did you realize that it was possible to make money off punk rock?
If you are talking serious money, in the 1990s, when we got back together. I kind of look at Nirvana, even though they went to a major label before they got really successful, that sort of broke open a lot of doors. Obviously, in 1994, when the Offspring and Green Day started selling millions of records, then it was apparent that hey, ten years later, bands can sell millions of records and make a real a living off this. I wouldn't say the reason we got back together was because we thought we could make money. We got back together just because hey, people were asking us to do it, and it seemed like it would be fun.

If I am correct, your band That's It, and your brother's band, were touring Europe at that time?
Well, no. Actually, what happened was, we were both in Hamburg, Germany, on the same night. They were playing at this jazz club across town, and I played at this squat, so this guy Yaz, who was in this band called the Smarties, whose

record we put out in the States back in 1986, was traveling with my brothers in Royal Crown Revue because he lives in Hanover and there's a big jazz club there and he hooked them up with that and traveled with them. I guess he was playing an acoustic guitar with them a lot, playing a lot of old Youth Brigade songs because he's a big Youth Brigade fan, and everybody was drunk, and they called me up and said, hey we're at this bar, come meet us. We all went down and met up with them, drank, and that's when they said, hey, we went to a disco with Yaz and they were playing Youth Brigade and people were dancing, and he's been playing the songs

and hey, what do you think about doing it? I said, yeah, if you want to get back together and write some new songs and see how it sounds, sure.

Were you reluctant?

I was only reluctant in the sense that I wasn't interested in doing a reunion thing where we would just get back together and try and make some money and cash in, and even at that point that was a ridiculous assumption anyway because it was 1992, and punk rock was not that huge. I mean obviously Fugazi and Bad Religion, from that period of about 1987–88, had really started building things up again, but yeah, I didn't think we were going to get back together and make a bunch of money or anything like that. I just didn't want to do a reunion thing because I knew that would be tired and pointless.

But how did you feel about taking a break from That's It?

I put that to the side more because we had started up the label again than I did because of Youth Brigade. When we started up again, Youth Brigade was really a part-time thing because my brothers were in Royal Crown Revue, which was pretty serious for them. The problem with That's It is that people I was working with left the band. The main guy Tom Withers, Tommy Stupid, which is an appropriate name because he's quite an asshole, bailed out right in the middle of the U.S. tour . . . He met some drunk girl at this show we did in LA like a week before the tour and started professing his undying love for her every single day on the road, like making calls from people's houses, all kinds of fucked-up, stupid shit and basically said he would finish the tour up to New York, and he was going to meet up with her in Baltimore. Then he wanted us to give him a ride to Baltimore, even though we had no desire to do him any favors. We just left him on the street in New York with his drums.

He deserved it?
Oh yeah, he did. He deserved a lot worse, believe me.

Between 1987–92, BYO wasn't really active, but it hadn't disappeared either because the titles had been taken up by Southern, like 7 Seconds.
Well, the label never stopped. The deal was that neither Mark or I actively wanted to run the label anymore at the end of 1987 because we were burned out. Southern had been doing licensing with us for years, so we just said, you just manufacture and license the active stuff in the catalog, the stuff that is moving, for the whole world. John Loder at the time was a really nice guy, and he said, sure, fine, no problem. What happened was that he decided he was going to start doing CDs, and we had a really simple deal with him, a simple deal that we do with our bands, which is 50/50 profit share. Well actually, with him it was 70/30: we took 70 percent, he took a 30 percent distribution fee, and somehow he got it into his mind that it was okay to charge us a bunch of different expenses without telling us, so I started calling him on it. I decided to put out a That's It record and a Royal Crown record and become an active label again, and we went to him and said, okay, we need some records for the bands. He was sending them to us and saying, well, I'll just charge you the wholesale price, and wholesale price was really high. I said, we're not getting accounted at this price, and I got a lot of weird different excuses, and I said, you know what, I don't want to work with you no more, so we just took back all of our stuff. We always owned it and controlled it, and it was always our label. He was just basically doing a licensing deal.

You had always done your own distribution?
Everybody went through a lot of the same distributors. Dischord early on made a deal with Loder. Loder has never been through a major, but he manufactures and distributes Dischord's stuff and has been for years and years and years. Yeah, Epitaph never went through a major. They've always done it themselves, though Brent stopped for a number of years running the label like we did, but he's always done it on his own, basically through the twenty or thirty different independent distributors around the world. Alternative Tentacles, as far as I know, always did, but I am not positive. Yeah, SST tried something with Unicorn for a while, but that was huge disaster for them and yeah, Frontier, she might have made exclusive deals here and there, I'm not really sure. And Fat Wreck Chords—well, they weren't around in those days. There are a handful

of independent labels that are still going. Most of us, even though some might have strayed to try and make it easier for them, still go through a handful of independent distributors.

When people look back on Youth Brigade history, it all seems to begin with the Extremes, 1977, when you played with the Controllers, Screamers, and others, but I just recently discovered that it began even a bit earlier with the Mess, a three-piece Hendrix cover band.

That was more like a high school band, the whole reason Mark and I started playing music. We grew up playing music, but it was like my mom made us take piano lessons when we were kids in Canada, then we moved to California and I played sax in the junior high school band for a few years, and Mark played violin for a little while, but then my grandfather was in town visiting from Canada one time. I was sixteen, and Mark was fifteen. We were bored, and there was no surf, and we were sick of skateboarding, so he suggested to us that we should pick up instruments and start playing, so that's what we did. When we first started playing, we were playing Hendrix and Led Zeppelin and stuff like that because that was the music we listened to. That summer of 1977, I heard "My Aim Is True" on the radio, and I read an article by the big music critic here, Robert Hilburn, about the Sex Pistols when they were coming on tour in the fall of 1978. That's when I said, Wow, I am going to write my own music, screw this. We started writing our own music, and I have some tapes of it, and it's pretty funny. It's total English accents, and it's really hysterical.

Your high school class on existentialism left a big impression. There was a guy from the Screamers in the class?

Yeah, he went on to play keyboards with the Screamers, Jeff. He wasn't like one of the original guys, but there was me and Jeff and this guy Russell who played with the Extremes for a while, and he also ran a club in LA and called it the Anti-Club, which was kind of a famous artsy fartsy place.

I remember seeing a 100 Flowers video shot there.

At first, they moved it to a different venue all the time, then they settled on this place where there's a girl who goes by the name E.G. Daily, she was in *Valley Girl*, she's the girl in the bathroom that rips her bra off and her falsies fall out, and she's also had a singing career for many years. She went to school with us, and her real name is Liz. Her brother was friends with Russell, and that's how Russell hooked up with this space for the Anti-Club on Melrose because her mom owned it and she was pretty crazy, but E.G. Daily does voices on one of those kids' cartoons, *Rugrats*. So, yeah, there were a bunch of different people in that one existential class that went on to be in punk bands for a while.

You gigged alongside the Bags, the Zeros, and the Go-Go's?
Oh yeah, we played with all those bands. I know all those people, so we definitely did.

Was the band so obscure that people don't associate you with that era?
I think it's more a combination of things. My brother and I were a couple of people among a handful of people in that scene who were teenagers. Most of the people in that scene were in their mid to late twenties, some of them much older, so people in the bands that went on to become much more famous they didn't pay much attention. There's plenty of bands that people mention now from the early 1980s that were hanging around then that I would know that most people wouldn't, like the Screws or Social Task. There's a bunch of different little bands, Symbol Six, little bands around here that would open up. It's like, big deal, they never went anywhere. So, people don't remember them. So, I guess it's a combination of both of those things.

Do you think you would have ever started BYO if it weren't for things like the Elks Lodge riot?
It was sort of the straw that broke the camel's back, but I probably would have started something just because that's what people did in those days. They sort of banded together . . . You know, everybody was coming from different areas, like "Who are you guys?" So, they would make some name up of who they were, that's how all those sort of cliques of what would later become "gangs" happened and I just sort of thought, look, getting together and putting forth a positive idea about what we're doing instead of letting the media go around and sensationalize what we do and making us out to be a bunch of idiots that go around beating the shit out of each other just made sense.

But there's a leap from hanging out at Skinhead Manor and drinking beers to putting on shows with three thousand people and starting a label.
Well, my brother and I have been entrepreneurs since we were pretty young, from what most kids do by selling lemonade on the corner or raking leaves and shoveling snow. We were little kids in Canada, then moved to California, where they bussed us to school because we lived out in the country for the first few years, and there were no markets or stores around the school. They had a store selling really crappy candy for really expensive prices, so we started bringing in our own candy and totally undercutting the school and making lots of money for little kids who were ten or eleven years old. The principal called us in and told us we had to stop because we were taking away business from the school. In high school, we were putting on parties, and we'd get kegs and bands and then we'd charge at the door, and we were also drug dealers, so it was something

that we have just done forever, organizing stuff and doing business, whatever it was we were involved in. The whole reason we did most of that was because why spend money to have fun when we could make money and have fun. We've always been lucky enough to figure ways out how to do that.

Including shows at Godzillas?
Yeah, these things sort of just happened to us. It's not like we sit and say, let's figure out a way to make money. It's kind of like, hey, we're making music; okay, let's play a show; okay, let's put it on ourselves. We never thought, let's find someone to do it. That's the way we've always done things. We always just do it ourselves. We're very hands-on people. We've learned to delegate, but it's taken a long time.

There's a downside to it too, because although you had these great shows at places like the Hollywood Palladium, you had lawsuits such as the one from the Minor Threat show where the kid was stabbed or the girl who jumped off the balcony at one of the shows.
She was making out with a guy up there, they fell down together, and he landed on top of her. She got in on our guest list. We knew her. She's Ken Berry's daughter, the guy from the *F Troop* TV show. She was just stupid for suing us because she never got anything out of it. I mean, what are you going to do? Those things happen regardless. They happen today, whether we run the organization or

someone else does. There's really nothing you can do about stuff like that. It happens.

What happened that soured you guys so much to the point that in the late 1980s you only did things like warehouse parties?

There's a whole bunch of things you are talking about. First of all, we stopped promoting shows mainly because of Goldenvoice. Gary Tovar was running Goldenvoice, and we started doing shows together. It was never like we wanted to run shows. We just did because we were in a band. What we really wanted to do was play music. He came down and got a handle on it . . . We liked the guy and worked together with him, and he had the same philosophy as us. It was really just about putting on the music and being fair and paying the bands fairly and keeping the door priced low and putting on a good show and trying to make it so there wasn't fights and the cops weren't going to bust it and destroy the place and that sort of stuff. He was doing a fine job of it and really didn't need us anymore, so it was kind of like, cool. That was one less thing we had to do. You know, my brother ended up doing some promotion a few years later, but the thing is, the scene was dying. The heyday was 1983–1985. Goldenvoice was doing shows at the Olympic Auditorium every five or six eight weeks, and the shows were between three to five thousand kids on a pretty regular basis, but some of those kids got out of the scene, some of them moved away, and it did get more and more violent to a certain degree. It started dying down. I don't remember if the Olympic stopped doing shows, wouldn't let us do shows, or what the deal was, but it ended up moving over to Fender's down in Long Beach, which was substantially smaller. I think it held somewhere between 1,500 and 2,000, and then actually my brother started doing some shows with a friend of his. They were promoting, well, they had this little promotion company called Babylon, and he was doing some shows here, punk rock bands, but he did some other things. He did some rap chick. He did a few weird different things. The friend of his that he was working with ended up going to work for a big promoter in LA that ran the Pantages Theater up in Hollywood and some other stuff.

Our motivating factor in this was that we were musicians, and we wanted to play music and doing shows and things like that were out of necessity. Eventually, the same thing happened with the label. We were putting out bands that weren't doing anything, the scene was dying, and we weren't making any money, we were losing money. So, yeah, a combination of factors soured us on it. We burned out and needed to do something else and didn't want to play music with each other anymore. Our younger brother Adam had gone back to art school in 1985–86. We tried it and changed the name to the Brigade, which in hindsight was probably not the smartest idea. We should have just changed it outright. It was funny because right as we were quitting was when Ian was getting Fugazi together and Greg and Brett and Jay were getting Bad Religion back together, and that's when things started taking off again, slowly but surely.

But do you think that your post–*Dividing Line* music period would have even fit into the reemerging punk scene?

No, probably not. But that's okay. I used that as one of the reasons we said, okay, we're not going anywhere.

When you look back at the Brigade EP and album after that, how do you feel?

I have no problem with those records. The only thing I had a problem with is trying to be a different band . . . We should have just made a clean break and started something new because we weren't Youth Brigade anymore, so why try and play those songs or keep that name?

You said in old interviews that *Dividing Line* was a reflection of your observation of Europe and living in a Western society: the dualistic nature, like right/left, good/evil, and black/white. Did it mark a change in you philosophically or even spiritually, because later on in the same article you talk about the millennium, spiritual things like prophecy, and Nostradamus, even Edgar Cayce?

Yeah, when I came back from Europe in 1984, the scene was getting kind of crazy, but a bunch of my old friends from the early days, like Jane Wiedlin from the Go-Go's and Craig Lee from the Bags, and this guy Michael who had been in the Extremes with me, people like that had started getting into spiritual stuff and meditating and doing these weekly meditation meetings and some of the people were channeling, or supposedly channeling, other spirits. Some of it was pretty amazing, some of it was a lot of bullshit. It was kind of interesting, and that definitely influenced what I was doing at the time . . . A lot soured for me when I worked on a magazine called *Whole Life,* and they started doing these expos downtown, and I worked at them for a couple of years sort of helping out, taking money, like for guests. They would have speakers, and just oh my god, the amount of bullshit that was going on . . . I mean, first of all, the majority of these people were just about making money. Most of them had really bad attitudes. What I was doing was that they'd have guests come, like you would be a speaker, and you would get x amount of guests, and you would pay money to have a booth there, selling whatever you sold, whatever BS product, or being a masseuse or whatever the hell you were doing, and for your money you would get a couple of passes, and if you wanted to get other people in, you could get them in at a discount, so they would come to me and pay me for the discounted tickets. People would bitch, "I already paid," and I would be like, "Look, you only get two tickets, and you already got them," so yeah, that soured me on the whole thing. Then I ended up working on political stuff, which was kind of cool but was also frustrating just because people get so bogged down into their own little scene and they couldn't see the whole picture.

That was out in Venice, canvassing neighborhoods during the election?
Yeah, I stated working with some people called Venice Renters Canvass, and we would go door to door . . . LA has rent stabilization, which means you can raise your rent only a few percent each year, so that way if someone moves out, the landlords can't just go by the market and try to price gouge and jam the rent prices up to whatever they want. Santa Monica is the city next to Venice, which is its own city, but Venice is part of LA. Santa Monica, at the time, was very liberal and had really strict rent control, like people were renting units there, like New York in the 1970s, paying $400 for a one-bedroom. You were pretty much paying that in the late 1980s and the early 1990s too. So, we were trying to do stuff like that, and I ended up getting involved in Get Out the Vote in 1988 and 1990, these coalitions, and during the Gulf War I organized this big antiwar rally downtown: Red Hot Chili Peppers, L7, and That's It played there, and there were like ten thousand kids. It was a really fun experience, and I learned a lot, but it was also very frustrating because a lot of these people were old hippies or elitists who can't see the big picture. If their interest is saving the whales, that's all they care about. They couldn't see building coalitions and the big picture.

It was quite singular for them?
Completely singular, to the point where I just said, "Screw you people, you are wasting time." You know, there's a lot of ego involved, and people try to take credit for doing stuff. I thought the whole purpose of it was to see change and be effective, to try and educate people, but for a lot of people it was really about furthering their own ego and their careers, or what they perceived as their careers. I don't know what kind of career you have at being an activist for social change.

But you kind of held out for a long time that music and idealism were a good mix and could be effective. You enjoyed bands like the Alarm.
I still believe that. I am just older and I guess more cynical. But I still believe that people can change things, and I have to believe because if we can't, who the hell will? We're it. If we don't try, we're going to get what we get, like George Bush, which is a really frustrating thing because these people are getting into power because people are so apathetic, which I understand, and I can't even vote because I am not a citizen. I am a Canadian, but I still walked door-to-door trying to get people to vote.

You've never tried to be a citizen, or you are not allowed to be a citizen?
No, I could be if I tried.

Why do you choose not to?
Well, I got the form and it had stuff in it like, are you now or have you ever been a member of the Communist Party, and it asked me to denounce my country, and it's just so archaic and absurd, and I thought basically this is going to give me the right to vote, and that's about it. And I thought, I like traveling with my Canadian passport, and I'm proud to be Canadian, and as much as I love about this country and there are a lot of great things about it, there's a lot of fucked-up things about it and traveling on an American passport is not something that I would look forward to doing right now, and since I have a choice . . .

In an old *Suburban Voice* article you also targeted religion: "As we know civilization has been ruled by religion at the center from the beginning of time until this century." Do you think there's still a connection in this country between ignorance, religion, and war?
Hell yeah. I mean, ignorance is what is fuelling this whole ridiculous push to bomb Iraq. We played a show last year about a week after 9/11 happened with the Circle Jerks, and my brothers were saying to me, I know you want to get up there and say stuff, but just tone it down because people are really freaked out right now. I had a hard time holding my tongue, but I did. I mean, I understand. What happened was unimaginable. Who could even conceive of something like that? I guess someone did because it was in a movie before it happened, who knows if that did or didn't give them the idea in the first place, but then Keith from the Circle Jerks got up there and went off. He said, I think what happened in New York is terrible, but I tell you what, I am surprised it didn't happen sooner, and this was up in Ventura. It's not a redneck town, but it's conservative, and people were throwing shit at him and telling him to fuck off, but he held his own. I thought it was pretty commendable. The fact to me is that what he said is true. When the greatest export of this country is culture in the form of, hey America is home of the free, home of the brave, land of democracy, anyone can become anything as long as you work hard, you can be rich, you can be famous, you can be a celebrity, you can own a house, which is not the reality for the majority of the people in this country, but definitely not for the majority of the people in the rest of the world. This country is handing out images of MTV and Coca-Cola and Levi's to the rest of the world and eventually some guy who is worried about whether or not he is going to have food to eat the next day, a place to sleep, and clothes on his back is easy prey for religious fundamentalists and fanatics who say, fuck these people who come into your country and they take everything and leave you poor, and people in power treat you like shit

because the people in the West are working with them and screwing everybody here, which is true. Eventually, they are going to find enough people pissed enough obviously to go around and kill themselves in the name of whatever fanatical cause they want to do. That's what's going on.

One kid declared himself a vegan to you, and you asked him, "What do you think about abortion?" and he said abortion is murder. So, punk rock, which is supposed to be a haven from the right wing, actually embodies it?
I guess when something is around long enough, people get drawn to it for various reasons. I mean, there are bands that send us tapes that call themselves Christian punk rock. That's an oxymoron. There's no such thing. It's ridiculous. How can you believe in Jesus Christ or God or whatever, which is all about faith and following, and say you are into punk rock? Punk rock, for me, is thinking for yourself. That's completely the antithesis of religion. You want to be spiritual, that's fine. You're a religious person, I have no problem with it, but don't tell me you're punk rock and then sing about Jesus Christ and listening and following him to a greater life in the afterlife or whatever the hell they are singing about. I had a band send me a tape that said, we do originals, but we can also get up and lead the people in traditional songs and can even get up and do some preaching. I was like, are you serious, what in the fuck is this? It blew me away. But yeah, it's frustrating, but when it comes to kids, they're really easily influenced and unfortunately what passes for punk rock these days in some circles to me is a joke. I don't have anything against love songs, but if that's all you sing about, what does that have to do with punk rock? They are on major labels, they sing love songs, their audience is twelve-year-old girls, and they don't have anything that great to say. The only redeeming quality that they have is that hopefully that some of the kids will want to explore where punk rock comes from.

Hopefully it will spur them on to go look at a BYO catalog and buy a SNFU record from 1985, but I don't think it's true.
I think it happens very rarely. Okay, if we are talking about Blink-182 and the Newfound Dork Fest and Sum 41 and all these crappy bands, probably not. I mean the guy from Good Charlotte is all into the Unseen and Pistol Grip and he's wearing their shirts, so maybe hey, a kid sees that, maybe he goes out and checks out the band . . . Okay, it's a stretch because you figure the kid has to be intelligent enough to be able to go and do that and then listen to the lyrics and give a shit enough about it to go and do that, but if he's listening to these bands in the first place, then chances are he is not, but he's twelve or thirteen years old. I don't know if you remember being that age, but your tastes change very quickly and your interests change. Little things can spur your interest to making life changes. It's kind of amazing. The things that I was reading back

in high school, well, one book could change my whole direction of what I was interested in.

Of all those books, did the existential ones stay with you the most?
Yeah, but I think the things that you read that really connect with you are things that you already feel and that's why those things connect with you because they make you go hey, this is really something that I have thought for a long time and this puts it down into words that I can really relate to, and that's what to me good music does. You hear the music, you read the words, and you can really identify with it, and it stays with you for your whole life. It does for me, and luckily for us, a lot of people have related to our music and the things we've talked about. Yeah, reading *The Stranger* by Camus and those books in my senior year in school definitely had a huge influence on my life and what I write about, and I hope that kids are still doing that.

Would you say that your father sitting down and playing records with folk songs from the 1960s influenced you?
I think that it subconsciously influenced me to be interested in music and the things that he was listening to when we moved to California, for his record collection had everything from the Beatles to Bill Withers to Jim Croce and Janis Joplin and all that sort of stuff. I mean, when I was listening to the radio when I was a little kid in the 1960s, AM radio was full of Motown, Jackson 5, and stuff like that. So yeah, all that's an influence on me, sure, definitely.

Kids have a greater number of choices than they ever had before. Everything is so convenient, everything is a fingertip away. In the past, say when I was a kid in the early 1980s, you had to dig dig dig to find a Ramones record or a 999 record. Do think the convenience robs the music of some of its initial meaning?
Well, they are coming from a whole different perspective. They never knew having to look for the stuff. Yeah, it's easier, but the one thing that I think is bad is: the digital revolution has enabled, well, it's so much easier for anybody to make a record. Okay, on the one hand, it's great. It used to be that you're in a band, you learned how to play guitar, you bang some stuff out in the garage with your buddies, your friends come see you play at some parties, and if you were really good, cause mostly you start off by playing covers of whatever is popular at the time or whatever you are into, you emulate that, but if you were good you started to write your own stuff, and if you were really good, you survived. In the past, to survive meant you had to figure out a way to make a record, which was not an easy thing to do because you couldn't do it on your own. Now, anybody can make a record. It's so easy and cheap, and that's a great

thing because people who might have been obscure and left in the garage and never went anywhere, cause that's what happened if you weren't all that good, you ended up just being a high school or college frat band or whatever it was back then, then you went on and got a job and remembered fondly how you used to be in a band back in high school or college. Now, anybody can do it and people do, and I get tons of tapes, and unfortunately mediocrity rules the day because I think the struggle and the work you had to put in back in those days to actually survive and be a viable band sorta weeded out a lot of crap.

A filter?

Yeah, it was a filter, and now I am happy because at the same time there were guys I guess who could write great songs but just didn't live near a big town, didn't have the wherewithal, didn't have the finances, didn't have whatever it was, the stamina, to keep trying and banging away because having a day job and being in LA playing your original music can be frustrating after a while. Now, there are just so many bands. Bands make a career out of just being a local band that plays the little circuit of three hundred square miles and every little town and every little bar, or whatever it is. Bands like 311 and other bad Chili Pepper rip-offs. I get all these tapes of these bands that want to be Rancid, and I mean I'd rather hear that than a wanna-be Chili Peppers, but still. There's nothing unique to them. They just sort of mimic what they've heard. For a while, for a few years there, we would get tapes that we called "Epifat." It would just be this Epitaph, Fat Wreck Chords pop punk sound, really nondescript. There are so many more bands out there these days. It just kind of waters it all down. At least back in the 1980s, there were a lot of really good bands, but there weren't a lot of bands. Maybe it's just that I was really involved in it during those days. I guess it's a combination of things.

How do you think *Sound & Fury*, with its doo-wop, rap, and its Faulkner and Shakespeare allusions, would be received in today's climate if you released for the first time in 2003?

Well, *The Sound and the Fury* is a Faulkner book. I never even liked Faulkner. I did take a quote from . . .

But the title comes from Shakespeare, "sound and fury, signifying nothing."
I don't know. I haven't really thought about it, but you know I just kind of figure
that kids are still in school reading these classics. They can relate to it in some
way or another, but then again, they are reading less and less of this sort of stuff,
and people are dismissing how important it is for kids to learn this literature,
which is kind of a sad thing, because they're just sort of dumbing down kids.

But would the attempts at different styles also confuse the kids?
Yeah, that would be a sad thing . . . My brother and I talk about this often. Some
of the bands on BYO came up in the mid-to-late 1990s, most of them are fifteen,
twenty years younger than us, so they are like your age, a little bit younger,
and they come up and maybe they saw us play in the day or maybe their older
brothers turned them on to the music and stuff, but they are actually a little
too young to be there and didn't come around until 1985–87, and really they
went to high school listening to stuff we hated the most, which was the hair
bands that took over the Sunset Strip, which was the stake through the heart
of what was left of punk rock in those days. They'll always talk to us when we
are hanging out at punk shows and they'll throw in this metal stuff, like, "Dude,
don't you remember listening to Mötley Crüe or Poison?" and we're like, "No."
They come on like it's this little secret, like, "It's cool, dude, y'know everybody
listened to it," and we're like, "No, we never listened to it. We hated them. We
always hated it, and we always will."

It wasn't even a kitsch factor for you?
Right, there was nothing good about it. It was horrible. It was everything that
we got into punk rock to destroy coming back in the worst possible manner
because it wasn't even that good. At least the originals like Black Sabbath and
Led Zeppelin, those are classic bands that are still good, but the crap that came
after it like Iron Maiden . . . For us, the really bad stuff was the studio bands,
like Toto, Kansas, and Boston.

Asia, the first super group of the 1980s!
Yeah, all that crap. That whole second generation of Mötley Crüe, Poison, and
Dokken and all those bands, we couldn't stand them, and it always cracks me up
when these bands go, "Hey, c'mon . . ." But what really blows me away is the kids
that grew up with that then also grew up listening to hardcore and punk rock
from their brothers and sisters and then in the 1990s they put it all together, and
for me, I'm sorry, that just doesn't work. It's cool that people want to try that
out, but System of a Down, I don't get it. It's just not for me. Personally, I never
got the whole speed metal thing. It's just not for me. I want to hear melody
when someone sings, I want to be able to understand what they are singing

because it's important to me, and when the guy is just going ROAR, I just don't get it. Then they try and mix it up with punk rock and hardcore and metal.

But they might say, "Dude, DRI and Corrosion of Conformity did it." Then again, the Descendents had songs like "Hurtin' Crew" that totally mocked the idea.

That was the thing. We never understood DRI and COC because they came out, and they were okay punk rock bands, then it wasn't going anywhere, so they just reverted to what they really were, which was just metal kids. It's like, okay, these guys were never really punk rockers, so they just went back to what they knew, which was metal. I mean, they made a career of it. But see, metal, to me, is what punk rock was trying to get away from because it is just mindless, I mean those people, they're sheep. I guess there probably is Christian metal. That doesn't seem like an oxymoron to me at all, except that you are singing about God in a music that sings about 666 and the Devil, which I just think is really funny.

But there again, those are just Western dualities, good and evil.

Christian people don't like to think about it that way.

You have said that bands like "Black Flag, Fear, and the Mentors are really negative bands that have nothing positive to say, though some people call it sarcasm, but sarcasm is a hard thing to do, and sometimes I doubt it." Would the Circle Jerks fall into that category?

Well, it's a personal thing with me, but first of all, I would never put the Circle Jerks in that category. I think that they were a great band, and I think that Keith is a very intelligent person and very political, and they've always been a political band. Yeah, they are funny, but I think comedy and politics is always a good thing. You never want to take yourself so seriously that you can't laugh at yourself.

A Lenny Bruce thing?

The thing I don't like about Fear is they didn't come from the punk rock scene. We played a show with them, it was probably their first show, with the Extremes, and there was no place to play. There was this guy in the band, Michael, a little short gay guy. He somehow got into touch with this place in the Valley called the Rock Corporation, some biker bar, and somehow the only way we could do it was if this new band called Fear could play, and they sent us their single. It was "I Love Living in the City" and we were like, this is kind of crappy, which actually, I think, is a pretty good song now. There's a couple songs of theirs that I thought were pretty good, but we show up at the show. It was going to be the

Bags, us, and Fear, and Lee Ving goes up to Michael, who is about five foot two, and gets in his face and says, "Look, you little fucking freak, there ain't no way we're fucking opening for you. You're going on first, there's nothing else to it." I'll kick your ass kind of thing. I don't remember the exact words, but that was the basic gist of it. We're like, "Who the fuck is this guy?" but all right, fine. There were probably 150 people that came down with us and the Bags from the Canterbury because Michael lived at the Canterbury, and most of the people from the Bags lived at the Canterbury. That summer of 1978, saying one hundred punks is true because there weren't much more.

So, we played, and everybody was in there, and I think it was our first show actually, and then Fear came on and everybody walked out into the parking lot, sat out there, and drank and smoked cigarettes and talked and did whatever while Fear did their entire set in front of this fat girl that was with them. Then the Bags came on and everybody came back in and danced and had a good time, and then we left, so that was my first experience with Fear. We had another run-in with them at Godzilla's with their security when they were starting to get an attitude after *Decline...* They drew a lot of knuckleheads, and it was a funny kind of show for the first couple of times, but after a while it was like, what do these guys have to do with punk rock, really? They didn't really hang out. They were all about getting signed to a major and becoming rock stars, and to me, it wasn't like they were coming to shows and hanging out and trying to be a part of the scene. They were just outsider guys who just came in and tried to be a part of it. It always struck me that they got a part in that movie when they didn't have anything to do with what was going on at the time other than they were a band that was playing. And Black Flag, but you know, Black Flag, they trailblazed, I give them all respect for that. They were one of the first bands. I like the stuff with Keith, Ron, and Dez. I am not a big fan of the Henry Rollins–era stuff. That's when I think they started taking themselves way too seriously. Greg Ginn is a strange guy. Chuck I always liked. He's a nice guy.

But Tony Kinman told me that Black Flag really marked a shift in LA music from the early punk rock art weirdness bands and the hardcore machine bands—the muscular macho bands.

I would agree with that. Black Flag was in its own little thing. They never really were a part of the scene. I mean, they were, but they weren't. They had "The Church," they had their own little thing in the South Bay . . . I'm a surfer, and what marked it for me, who was coming from both scenes, was the early scene. You would walk down the street and people would yell shit at you, like "faggot," "weirdo," "freak," and throw shit at you, and longhaired people would come after you. I had long hair. I was a longhaired surfer guy walking around Hollywood with my hair shaved or colored or whatever, like spiky hair. I was getting a lot of shit, and the people around the scene, they weren't fighters, so it wasn't like you stood up to these people and fought. You pretty much had to run, because there's me, I'm sixteen or seventeen, with my little brother, who's a year younger than me, and what are we going to do? So, when the surfers got into it, it was like, wow, this is what we have been waiting for, like now this scene can fight back.

For us, the turning point was going to the Public Image show at the Olympic Auditorium in 1980, and I went with two of my brothers, and we're walking around with our arms around each other walking through the crowd, and not that I am saying that it was a good thing or the right thing, but if you had long hair at that show, you got beat up, just because it was like all this frustration for all these years of going around and getting pushed around by people in long hair, and now here was all these punk rockers here for this huge show. There were probably three to four thousand people there. It was crazy. There was this little kid from Huntington Beach who got up on stage and was singing with Johnny Lydon. He was probably like ten years old, this kid. We met a lot of people there that night, and that sort of was a big turning point, that and the Hong Kong Café downtown doing shows on a regular basis. And Starwood's Tuesday shows were a place where a lot of people started to meet, and then Okie Dogs, meeting there after shows . . .

Early Black Flag I liked. There were a lot of good things about what they were doing, and yeah, when Henry got in the band it definitely changed their outlook and stuff, but what really bothered me was that they really insulated themselves from the scene at a certain point when they started getting really popular. And they would go out on these tours. They trailblazed. They were one of the first bands out there, and they worked their asses off, and they helped create the whole touring scene around the United States and going to Europe. They were one of the first bands. But what they did was from a business sense. They started touring only with their own bands, bands on their label, and I always looked at it like it was shitty because what they were doing was taking their roadies out who had bands, like Nig-Heist and things like that.

Or Tom Troccoli's Dog.
Yeah, it was several things. Number one, it was a business thing, so it would help sell the records on their label, which is understandable. Everybody does that. That makes sense. But it got to the point where, from what I could see, they wouldn't let local bands open up for them because I think they were setting it up so they wouldn't get blown off the stage, which is something I saw the English bands do all the time. We thought it was pretty shitty because, for us, when the Angelic Upstarts came out the first time we were huge fans of theirs. They stayed at our house, and they started acting like rock stars and didn't want to stay at the house and made us get them a hotel for the next night, and we opened up for them at the Whisky, and they wouldn't let us use the drum riser, and our attitude was like, look man, this is punk rock, there's no rock star shit here. You get up on stage and you kick ass, and if the opening band blows you off stage, well then tough shit. You know you got to get up there and play and do what you do. Everybody should get the same use of equipment, because we had seen English bands do that before where they wouldn't let you use the whole PA, and they'd set up the mics and wouldn't let you use them. They'd be like, "Oh well, our stuff is set up, you can just use whatever's left on the board."

But you guys were big fans of English music.
We were big fans of the Upstarts. They were still a great band and put on a great show. We understood they were coming from England. At the time, there were three weekly papers that would build new bands up, but as soon as they built them up, they would just tear them down. So, it was just the system there. When you were coming up, you were treated like shit, and when you were the top dog, you treated everybody else like shit. That's just what you did. The bands would start coming over here, and we would say, "We don't do that here. I don't care what you do in England, because we don't do that here." The older bands were like, "Fuck you, we're going to do it," and what could you do? But the younger bands, like Chron Gen and Anti-Pasti and bands like that, they were totally cool. As soon as we showed them, look, we don't do that here, they were like, "That's cool, we don't need to do that either." They were nice guys, and we hung out. Actually, when the Upstarts came through just this last year, we saw

Mensi, he was huge, but he put on an amazing show, and he was great and a lot cooler this time. Still very political, still put on a great show. It was amazing. We played Holidays in the Sun the last two years in the States and with a lot of those bands the attitude is gone. Of course, things have changed, and they are not big rock stars anymore.

Why did you change the cover art for the 7 Seconds reissue of *New Wind*?
The band hated the cover. Those guys are such a pain. They came down here and they had no ideas for the cover and they're like, "Steve just had a baby, so let's use a picture of the baby," so they gave Mark a picture, and he's like, "What in the fuck am I supposed to do with this?" So, he put something together, and he sent it up there and he was like, "What do you think?" And they were like, "Great, we love it," so we used it. Then all we kept hearing was, they hate the cover, they hate the cover. It's like, why didn't they tell us? I don't know. So, it ended up getting changed.

There's been a lot of revisionism concerning the LA punk past, especially Darby Crash. How do you remember him?
The Germs could be an amazing band if you were fucked up, and if Darby was fucked up enough live. They did some groundbreaking stuff, and I always like everybody in the band. Darby could be okay, but sometimes he was a bit of a schmuck. I mean, memories of him besides the early days of seeing them at the Masque and stuff, which was a kind of cool, was that they were an okay band. Their records are interesting and different, I guess groundbreaking in some ways, but it's not my thing. I like some of it, and I saw them play live a bunch of times. Most of the times, they sucked because he sucked. The band was pretty good, but he wasn't that great. But if he was fucked up, he could put on a pretty crazy performance, but I just remember him coming back from England and coming to Skinhead Manor. He didn't live there, but he came and hung out. He came back from England and had been hanging out with Adam Ant and came back with this big mohawk and was all into Ant Music, and we all thought it was pretty funny. He started doing the Darby Crash Band, and they were rehearsing at our house for a while, and he was getting high, and then he died. I think sometimes people remember people, well, you remember the good things and not the bad. Do I think his life warrants a movie? No, not really.

Do you think that reformed bands like the Controllers, Kaos, and the Skulls merit a second look or are they better left in the past?
I don't know. I think that if a band gets back together, and they're making new music and it's good, and people are coming out to see them and support them, that merits it, regardless of what they did in the past. It's pretty much, what are

you doing now? Like, if you're getting back together and you are just going to play your old stuff from twenty years ago, I don't know, who cares? . . . I've gone to see Stiff Little Fingers, and I have to tell you, when I saw them two or three years ago, they came and they started playing all this new stuff. First of all, if you're an old band and you've got new stuff, that's great, but don't open up with the new stuff because kids aren't there to see that. I just went to see Channel 3's record release show, and their new record is just okay. I was a little bit disappointed, and it amazes me too when these bands get back together. It's like, listen to the old stuff and remember what it was that made those songs great and why people like you. Find that again, instead of revisiting *Airborne*, which was just not very good. I mean, I certainly, when we got back together, did not pull out the Brigade records. I listened to *Sound & Fury*, and I was like, let's make music like . . .

But your 1992 record was not like *Sound & Fury*. It was far less varied and did not take nearly as many chances.
No, none at all.

So, people might say that you are playing it safe for the new punk kids.
Yeah, it wasn't like we went in and said, "Let's be Youth Brigade of 1982 in 1992." It was like, we are not going to go in and make a record like the Brigade. That's not us. We are going to make a record of Youth Brigade, and we're Youth Brigade. We did different things. I think the stuff we did on the split with the Swingin' Utters is some of the best stuff we've done since *Sound & Fury*, and that stuff we wrote in a week and went in and banged it out. It's not like you make a conscious decision, okay, like I am going to listen to the old stuff and really try to emulate it, but you want to play punk rock. You want to play what you play. You don't want to start being something that you are not because the kids won't be into it. The kids have been listening to your old shit. That's why they are going to come and see you, so you better be able to hold up your end of the bargain. Your new stuff better be able to hold up to the old stuff. I am not saying it should be exactly the same, but it better be along the same level of good music.

When you decided to put the first version of *Sound & Fury* on CD, you realized the recording was good, but that the mix was poor?
No, it was the mastering.

Why did you just release those thousand copies and not work on the mastering?
Well, at the time, we had no idea it was the mastering. We thought it was the shitty Mystic Studios that we recorded at, and we just figured, fuck it. And we had come back from tour with a whole bunch of new songs that we loved, and

we went in the studios. I am super proud of that record, and I would have never thought, "Shit, it's the mastering. This record's not so bad. Well, fuck it, let's not go back in and make a new record." It would have been nice not to have waited fifteen or seventeen years or whatever it was. That would have been better. But I am glad it is finally out. I think the songs are really good, but I don't think it's as good as a record as the one that we ended up releasing as the *Sound and the Fury*. Like you said, it's not as varied, it's not as fun, it doesn't have all that stuff. The record really comes from us being on the road going through all the *Another State of Mind* tour and everything we had gone through during about a year's period since we went and recorded the first version.

Punk rock has become family values, due to things like your Punk Rock Bowling and Music Festival.
It's kind of cool that you can pass that on. There's nothing better than being able to pass on, in my view, something that is cool as punk rock. Becca, who works here, has a twelve-year-old, and she's kind of not into the music. My niece is three and has been to the Warped Tour and she came to see us play with the Swingin' Utters when she was barely one. She was crawling around all over the floor upstairs at the Troubador backstage. She was black from the dirt and my brother was telling the guy who runs the Troubadour, "That's thirty years of rock'n'roll on her right now." So, these kids are getting to see stuff from the time they are babies that some of the kids out in the audience would kill for.

Kira Roessler
(Black Flag, Dos)

Kira Roessler is likely one of the most overlooked talents of the American hardcore scene. Although she has been a presence since the late 1970s and continues to work in earnest as half of Dos (with former husband Mike Watt), most fans simply know her as the solid bass player for mid-period Black Flag, when she was the ductile anchor that held down the pummeling as Greg Ginn shrieked into noise-*cum*-metal bliss-outs. In part, along with women playing in bands like the Dicks, Sado-Nation, Sin 34, and Capital Punishment, she proved that hardcore was not merely a testosterone-charged boys' club but a potential level playing field for women with guts, determination, and savvy doses of intelligence. Her current work as a sound editor proves her craft is still alive and well. This e-mail exchange surfaced on the *Left of the Dial* blog.

At Black Flag practices, you once said in an interview, Greg Ginn could go for ten hours while the rest of you would drop out one by one.
Well, bass and drums are more physical than guitar, if you ask me. And sometimes I think that it is the one area where being female may be a factor. The muscle structure in my hand can only be built up so far. The concept of having someone's large hands attached to my arms was a fantasy during Black Flag. I have to practice, I have to warm up before gigs, I have to make the parts become somewhat automatic to my hands, or I will suck. There are those who may not need that much work. I am not one of them. Maybe that is true for all instruments. My hand will seize and not move the way I tell it to if I don't warm up before a gig.

Do you feel it was important to Black Flag that people saw you as a "journeyman" of sorts?
Girls grow up as tomboys all the time and always have, and they would naturally always participate in music and sports in garages and playgrounds . . .

Moe Tucker is a good example, and there are many we haven't heard from. There is no obstacle in the playing, in the interest, the capacity, and the role, sex symbol or otherwise.

The difficulties, from my perspective, come with some personality stuff between men and women, the physical challenges of some instruments, and of touring in general. Guys probably didn't want a girl with them on the road in the van, whether they were dating a member of the band or playing. Any signs of physical weakness or lack of technical prowess, like not understanding signal flow, would be accepted between guys, but not by a guy for a girl. And there is this underlying assumption that sex is somehow always at play. If I am in the van talking to someone for a while alone, sex must have occurred. Girlfriends of band members also don't appreciate the girl player who goes on the road with their sweetie while they stay home.

It is the political problems in any band that create the issues, and so many guys just avoid some of those by not having women in the band. I didn't particularly enjoy having an all-girl band either. I felt some of the same feelings about the other women I played with that guys must feel. Mostly, they are unfair assumptions or judgments we place on each other.

You experienced the Avengers and the Germs. Was hardcore more macho and sexist than punk rock?

In the examples you gave, the premise of the band included women, but in Black Flag it did not. It was already established as a hard-driving boy band: videos existed with Henry as a skinhead, songs had content which some might say degraded women. Don't get me wrong: it is the audience who may have assumed that changing the bass player to a girl might soften the result. I don't believe that they thought it would at all, but that they thought others might. Greg was all about the "process of weeding out," in my interpretation, removing "fans" that were only fans if Black Flag conformed to certain rules, like short, fast songs, short hair, or whatever. I was just another way to break the rules for some people. When we went to Europe, I had the shortest hair in the band, and there were lots who were pissed off about Henry's long hair and me being a girl. It didn't conform.

I don't think the genre matters. Punk rock was less alpha-male for sure. Look at your examples and many more, but the stereotypes were still there, and some women even fostered that. The Go-Go's come to mind. What did they do for women in punk rock?

How did you approach playing with Bill Stevenson? Did Twisted Roots or Nicky Beat prepare you?
Well, I certainly needed all the preparation that came before Black Flag. But I was nowhere near physically prepared. Playing with Bill and Greg was mostly about practicing a lot of hours, going over and over the same material, often at a slowed-down pace, in order to create the feel that Greg wanted. Nicky and I worked really hard with him writing drum parts that reacted to my every note, and that was probably good preparation. Listening back to Twisted Roots, I was doing some pretty heavy stuff then, but never felt good about it for some reason, and again, the physical demands only occurred with joining Black Flag.

Just so I'm clear on that point, the first week I joined Black Flag I did something to my right hand playing one note on a song called "Nothing Left Inside." I went to the hospital, and they said not to play for six weeks. I did not heed that warning because I am female and felt that was weak, and my hand has never really been the same. Maybe if that hadn't happened, I wouldn't feel that Black Flag was such a physical challenge, but I always look at it a little like college ballplayers who go into the NBA and blow out a knee in their rookie year. They pick it up a notch too quickly, and their bodies can't handle it. Some recover and some don't. Dos is easier on my hand because it has no drums. When I do rock stuff, which I do on occasion, I still have problems.

How do you feel about bands that delete the bass player and go with two guitars? Or use drum machines?
There is a big difference, to me, between omitting a player and making the parts work without it, and having prerecorded or preprogrammed material that you play along to on stage. The latter has always bothered me too, and seems to bother audiences. I am not sure why, the spontaneity that they believed was there? The "stiffness"? Mike always says that playing to a click track would make us play stiffly, so isn't that what a drum machine might do, at least in his mind? On the Europe tour with Black Flag, I was playing behind the amp for Nig-Heist, our opening band, and people were very pissed off, even dropping cans of beer on my head. Maybe they felt "duped," as you said. I know for me, as an audience member, it is somewhat nebulous why I don't like it, but I never have.

What do you see in Dos that reminds you of punk rock?
It is not like anything else, that is what punk is about: nonconformity, creating something new, without any rules. Let's face it, when punk started . . . the music then was so nonconformist. Many of the bands were just rock bands, but they looked completely different. They bucked society's norms in style and attitude. In lyrics, too. The Minutemen made short songs with no guitar solos because they were trying to buck the rock style. Mike and I wanted a band, so we just decided bass was enough. The first record had only one singing song. That was an afterthought.

TSOL told me that punk rock was everything from Joe Jackson onward, yet their fans might now disagree.
Yes, I do think that "punk rock," like so many labels, is misunderstood, misdefined, etc. It was time-specific, audience-specific, and less type-of-music specific. And yet, there were bands at the time that were not appreciated by punk rock audiences because they didn't conform to preconceptions. Twisted Roots was problematic for those audiences. So were Meat Puppets, Saccharine Trust, and

many others. Somehow, the Screamers were okay. It wasn't the instrumenta-
tion, though. It was somewhat the style of music. Twisted Roots was trying to
be a bit more pop, and the audience felt that. How does a new band develop its
audience? At first, you might play for the wrong audience and only a handful of
people liked the show. Eventually, people kind of know that the band is more
that style, so people who like that style go see them. Minutemen opened for
REM on a tour, but the audience may not have appreciated them. Meat Puppets
opened on a Black Flag tour, and people didn't always like them. Labels have
always sucked, and good bands have always been hard to label.

Dos has covered Billie Holiday . . .
My gut feel about Billie is that it has to do with the emotions she expressed,
and we who listen identify deeply with those feelings. Unrequited love is such
a base emotion. With other artists, it seems to have to do with breaking out of
old molds, like Elvis and the Beatles, and being remembered and appreciated
for that. They give young people an alternative, in their day, and then influence
scores of artists who come after.

Do you enjoy when politics becomes immersed in music?
Personally, it is in the emotion expressed that I find greatness. It is her emotion
about that incident, or D. Boon's strong feelings about politics that make
them good. Content does not matter, to me, unless I actually feel an emotion
expressed.

**Does an audience's nostalgia for rock'n'roll make it more difficult for people
like you to forge ahead and keep presenting new ideas?**
No, what they do does not affect me and what I do. I have no issue with them
doing that. I just am not dying to see it either. I will keep doing new stuff, so
will many others, and that will be what I go see, if I go see anything. It may,
however, be mostly to do with the same thing we discussed earlier. Greg [from
Black Flag] was willing to lose audience and try new things. Audiences may just
want to hear the old songs played the same way, and it is they, then, that are
having a stagnating effect. The bands have a choice to conform to what the audience wants or to practice artistic license, and there are plenty in both camps.

Jack Grisham
(TSOL)

Jack Grisham, singer of beach boys gone berserk TSOL, is a tour de force of American punk history still operating in full-bore style. His memoir, *An American Demon*, which surveys his cataclysmic youth and early career, is not for the timid and meek. Like a meld of Oscar Wilde's *The Picture of Dorian Gray* with *Fight Club* and *A Clockwork Orange*, he offers a savage poetry with an undertow of wit. In his lens, not-so-quiet Los Angeles suburbs become awash with dysfunction, revolt, and violence. Yet, in the end he offers a sense of recovery as well, a way to transcend personal chaos and find solace in the lurking memories. In the dramatic, razor-sharpened lens of TSOL songs, suburbia is far from a sleepy wonderland bedecked with slick malls and coiffured lawns. Those tracts of same-samey homes are chock-full of demons, such as singer Grisham himself, who wandered the bland wasteland of the American dream in the early 1980s like a priest of peril to the lost boys, misfits, and rebels.

Originally published in *Left of the Dial*.

How is touring different in 2001 compared to 1982?
Jack: I don't want to jinx it [laughs]. It was a little more out there then. They weren't that hip to the way you looked, you know what I mean? It was a definite freak show, not even necessarily being punk, if you got out of your vehicle with a dress on people were bummed. Now you walk into truck stops and you don't have to fight someone.

Do you prefer a show when you stop into town by yourself, or the package tours like Social Chaos and Warped?
Jack: Sometimes it's fun to go with your friends. You have more people to fuck around with. We all hang out. Sometimes in those groups with a bunch of bands you're friends with everyone, and you fuck around all day, like you switch cars and ride with another group of guys or whatever. It makes it kinda fun.

Supposedly on the Warped Tour, you guys were the oldest, but the most obnoxious?

Jack: We were threatened with getting kicked off the tour. It was stupid because it wasn't even a big deal. We were getting caught for chewing gum and lying, you know? It wasn't like we were doing anything fucked, but I was kinda bummed. We were kidnapping kids—that was our deal. We were kidnapping kids, and then we'd keep them with us for three or four days, right? And now I hear that Pennywise is doing that, it's like *Survivor* with Pennywise, and now everyone is going to be saying, "Man, Pennywise is kidnapping kids."

You've said that punk has been turned into a Sprite commercial, but what could have been done to prevent that?

People not selling shit out.

Meaning?

People not wanting to make money off the stuff. I don't blame them. There were always guys who were just punks, and guys who were trying to make money off of them. Like I remember guys going, "Hey, man, I'm making splatter shirts." Remember splatter shirts, Ron? [Ron Emory was present at the interview.] What was that guy's name? Somebody would come up with a scam, like hey we're making splatter shirts, and it was kinda a cool thing, so people started cashing in on it. But there were people who were doing things and not cashing in on it.

You've compared yourselves to the old blues musicians who got ripped off by the white 1950s rock'n'rollers.

Jack: Still do. Yeah, because we were stupid and didn't care. To us, it wasn't a business. We weren't making shrewd business decisions, we were like, "Give us a couple six packs of beer and a pen and we'll sign."

Ron: With our first record it was like, "Record contract? Okay, whatever."

Jack: If you look back at our early contracts, they're signed in blood. It was like, hey, watch this. We'd throw contracts down the toilet and say we didn't care. We didn't understand anything about the business, we never had a lawyer, we didn't ask about publishing, we had nothing, and they took everything.

Do you think a lot of bands, especially over the last ten years, use the tag "punk" to legitimize music that is basically really mediocre and faceless?

Jack: Yeah, because a lot of it is not what you would call punk rock. When we started out, Elvis Costello was punk. I mean the Go-Go's were punk. There was a lot of stuff like that, which was considered punk rock. It was different because back then it was in the attitude, instead of the music. I mean the music

was cutting-edge or whatever, more experimental, but it was mainly the attitude. Now, there's the music and the look, but there's no attitude to it. There's
nothing that truly makes it punk rock.

**What happened in the evolution of punk and hardcore that made it eventu-
ally become so rigid in terms of the look, sound, and feel?**
Jack: It started getting bigger.

**But at the same time, TSOL expanded its song structures and started using
keyboards.**
Jack: A lot of it was people who thought they knew what it was, you know what
I'm saying? They thought they knew what it was, so they started copying these

people. When we first started, you could be influenced, even rip people off, but if you copied a band's sound, you were immediately fucking burned. More and more, as people started getting into it, you had the Black Flag clone bands, the Bad Religion clone bands. It got to the point where it all conformed, to this is the way it is, this is the way you should sound . . .

No deviating?
Jack: Yeah. No deviating. And those were the people that didn't know what was going on anyway. It was a joke.

Why was anger and violence such an inherent part of punk?
Jack: A lot of people were pissed off—pissed off with no outlet. I know for us, a lot of us, a lot of people hit us up for being jocks or whatever. We were like sportsmen, we're all big guys.

All over six feet tall.
Jack: Yeah, we used to joke that we were the biggest band in the United States because everybody in the band averaged like six foot something.

But you also painted your face white and did unjock things?
Jack: We all came from broken families and dealings with the police and school, and then you start looking different, so everywhere you go you're getting shit, and we were big enough to say, "Fuck you. You're not going to yell at me for having pink hair, or you'll get a crowbar across the face." That's how a lot of that went.

Critics say the first wave of LA punks like the Avengers, Dils, and Zeros used violence as a metaphor, whereas as the beachcore and hardcore scene developed, the violence was tangible and physical.
Jack: I'll second it, 'cause none of those guys were going to use real violence. With a lot of the early arty bands, they were arty guys . . .

But when you reformed to play the Santa Monica gallery show, you teamed up with the arty bands, like the Bags, Urinals, and Zeros.
Jack: We loved them, but those weren't the kind of guys who were going to get in a Sunday football game with their friends. When it trickled out to the beach stuff, that's what it was. A bunch of athletes . . .

And rednecks?
Jack: No. A lot of the surfers were punk kids.
Ron: Surfers, skaters.

Jack: They were guys in shape. If you look at the early surf history of the 1950s and '60s, they were punks before there was punk, driving around with swastikas on their woodies, being fucked, you know. So, when it got down to us . . .

Huntington Beach, right?
Jack: And Long Beach, Venice, Hermosa, I mean these were the guys who were out in the sun all day, in good shape . . . These were people who were getting into drunken fights anyway. We were hippies and liked to get into drunken fights. It was just one of things.

You were the first West Coast phenomenon and could play shows up to three thousand people at the Olympic, but has that all been eclipsed by bands like Green Day? Will it remain an important part of punk history?
Jack: No, a lot of people don't know and don't care. People think that punk rock in LA was Black Flag with Henry, and that actually was the end of Black Flag. We had seen them with Keith Morris and shit, and it was like a whole different deal, like with Dez. I remember Gibby from the Butthole Surfers going, "How much did you make at that show?" cause he was shitting. I mean, we were getting paid a crazy amount of money back then. We were getting four to six thousand bucks a show. Back then, that was a fucking lot of money for a punk band.
Ron: But we played countless shows for twenty-five bucks.
Jack: Yeah, but I'm talking about the sold-out huge shows, when people were shitting and going, what the fuck? I mean all the bands on the bill got paid crazy. It was like, hey, here's five hundred bucks. There were baskets full of cash. It was pretty funny.

You've described yourself as an asshole kid with a high IQ? Is that still true, and how do you view your preteen daughter?
Jack: My IQ is steadily lowering everyday. Actually, she's really cool about it. She's been around and seen it all, so she has a pretty straight head about all that stuff. I just took her to her first show a couple of weeks ago, and we were duct taping some chick to a chair, and my daughter was just like sitting there checking it out. I was like, "Don't do this at school" [laughs]. Sometimes when the dad's fucked up, the kids come out a lot straighter. You know how straight parents sometimes get really fucked-up kids? Out of fucked-up parents you get really straight kids.

Do you think parents who grew up around punk rock are any different than the baby-boomer generation parents?
Jack: Yeah, I think my kid's a little more cynical. It's like they look at governments differently, they look at ads differently because I'm constantly on her

about stuff. I mean, I wasn't raised like that. None of that shit even got mentioned at my house.

What happened in the late 1970s that turned your attention to punk rock?

Jack: There were a couple of things I was stoked on, well, like just meeting guys that caused trouble. That's how I met our drummer. I was causing all this shit at school, and this girl said, hey you should meet these guys, they're just like you. So I went over and met these guys.

Ron: Hellraisers!

Jack: We hung out, we talked about music, then we said, hey, we should start a band. So, we ripped her off that day, took a guitar, and started a band that day. I got into it mainly for the trouble and then later on got into the music.

What about you, Ron?

Ron: I don't know what got me into it. I wasn't really into music, ever. I was into surfing and skating, that's it. Then sometime in 1978 the Dickies and Weirdos played a couple blocks from my house, and there were Elvis Costello and Joe Jackson, like we were mentioning. There were all these bands, and I kept going to shows. It seemed like every weekend you were going somewhere. And standing there watching these guys, I thought, I could do that. I worked a job in a parking lot until I could buy a guitar, then I quit. I bought my first guitar and just tried to do what they did. And I was really involved in the skate scene back then, so Skip Olson and I started our first band and toured skate parks and played with Jack and Todd's first band. Then it just came together.

Over the years, people have said that rock'n'roll is sometimes the only way that a poor or working-class kid can stand up and be counted, can be noticed.

Jack: That's nothing we ever thought about. We were clueless about that shit. It was never like, we're going to do this and be a success. It's just what we did. We played music. I was so fucking naïve about music. I was clueless. I thought everybody that got together and made a band that people liked sold a ton of records. I had no other frame of reference. That was just the way it was. It wasn't like,

yeah we're going to get out of the gutter or whatever. It was just like, this is what we do.

Do you think the three records you made with the Joykiller will be remembered as being as powerful as your TSOL records, or will they slip to the back burner?

Jack: I don't know. I get a lot of good stuff from the Joykiller stuff. Especially the *Static* record, which *Flipside* voted record of the year. We had great reviews. At the time, we were doing something different. It was a time for us. It's real cool when people later on say, "Man, *Beneath the Shadows* was a great record, what a groundbreaking record." You guys did this and this, but that's never been what we're looking for. It's never been something we've looked for.

Do you think that anger or hostility is a creative force?
Jack: Yeah, a little bit, but we're antiviolent. I mean, we are so far fucking against it it's not funny. We won't play backdrop music to it. If someone starts fighting, we stop.

Except you'll duct tape someone to a chair? [laughs]
Jack: But it's controlled mayhem [laughs].

Do you think it's because you are older and more sober, you can control the chaos more than before?
Jack: The live shows are still pretty fucking full of chaos. I was telling some guy before, with this group of people, you take fire and a match, and it's always going to make a bad deal. No matter whether it's twenty years ago, it doesn't change those elements, fire and a match are still going to cause an explosion. It's the same thing we have now. It's like you stuck the fire and match together again twenty years later, there's fighting, fucking insanity, all that shit, nothing has changed. It's just that we're a bit older.

What's the least satisfying part about re-forming and playing all these shows the past few years?
Jack: Getting harassed for using the name, that's one. Then, for me, getting yelled shit at, like "Play 'LA Guns,'" guys making rock comments, that pisses me off. The people getting confused about the fact that it was two completely different bands. Mainly, that's the shit. It's not about not getting paid for shows, long trips without money because that's been a factor always, that's never been it. It's the people yelling out the later songs or giving us shit. I remember a girl showing up at a Joykiller show with a *Strange Love* T-shirt on with a big fucking wig trying to burn us. That pissed me off. The rest of the stuff doesn't.

We've always been underdogs. We're getting sued. We're being told we can't use our name.

On a very personal level, how has the way you see your music changed?
Jack: Musically, it's about the same. Basically, what's going on is the attitude is the same. The attitude we had then is the attitude we have now. We've always been libertarians: that's our badge. We're not anti-policemen, but we're anti-police. Our attitude has basically stayed the same: there's no backstage area, everyone's involved, you're not coming to see some rock stars, you're coming to see your friends play, get involved, you can do this too. We've always kept that same attitude no matter what. That's why people go and see shows and say, fuck, nothing has changed. There were reviews on the Warped Tour saying how amazing the gap is between the old punks and the new punks. After seeing us on the Warped Tour, they were amazed to see how far the gap really was.

What constitutes the gap between you and Blink-182?
Jack: I can't say. I can't tell because we're doing it.

It's a studied routine for them, but you're still bringing something fresh to it?
Jack: Right. People were looking at us while we toured and saying, how the fuck do you do it? There's that sense of, well, this comes from people who have told me because I can never tell, but they say sometimes when they look at us, they feel threatened. It's a scary situation, like, what might happen? I might get injured here . . . You know, the fight or flight thing that kicks in at those shows because it's not a safe, nice thing.

Isn't that what drew people to punk rock to begin with?
Jack: That's why I go. I used to joke with the kids, I'd have somebody doing a pulse check, you know that thing in *Silence of the Lambs* when they say, he ate her liver and his pulse didn't go above eighty [laughs]. That's what happens at these shows because unless some kid is going by me on fire, my pulse isn't above sixty-two. We were at this show at the Troubadour, and there was this little girl, the daughter of one of the guys from the Weirdos, who was sitting in front of the stage. There was all this craziness, this guy climbing up the light rack . . .

I heard you were egging kids to jump off the PA speakers.
Of course [laughs]. Every few minutes, I'd reach in and go, pulse check, to the girl, and she'd go there and do it and say, nah, it's still sixty.

Keith Morris
(Circle Jerks, Off!)

Some bands drag on for years, featuring only one original member, desperate to remain potent and pitched forward. Making potboiler punk, they endure the glares of endless new generations of wanna-be's. Keith Morris doesn't opt for that route. Inspired by seeing Iggy and the Stooges in the early 1970s and Los Angeles's first wave of punk, Keith Morris became the first irascible singer for Black Flag, then led the Circle Jerks. Still bickering and bellowing, he recently forged Off!, which makes manic music with stainless-steel nerves. Sprouting from a genre rooted for three decades in Hermosa and Redondo Beach, the band is a scruffy all-star affair culled from Hot Snakes, Red Kross, and Burning Brides. Their barrage feels taut and titanic, brooding and relentless, like a fresh stab at all things lame; in doing so, they pause during concerts only for extended monologues by Morris, who struts the stage like a well-meaning counselor and history teacher.

A portion of this interview was originally published by *Houston Press*.

You desire a gig in Mississippi or Alabama. Why?
I can barely remember the last time any of my other bands played in either of those states. Now, the excuse I keep getting is that they are very depressed states and maybe they are not doing very well financially, or just a whole list of things. But the fact of the matter is that there are colleges and universities down there, and when kids are paying their tuition, they pay into an entertainment fund. So, why can't they scrape up a couple thousand dollars for us to play at the local beer hall and get a party going? How often does a band on tour go to those places? You might drive through there on tour and never stop. You could also include Arkansas in there too. There's a whole area down there. I thought it would be cool to play some of those places. My recollection of playing, I believe it was in Mobile, Alabama, was getting punched in the face trying to protect a couple of kids from getting beat up by drunk rednecks.

Like the Sex Pistols heading to the South during their 1978 tour.

There's another part to that picture too. Malcolm McLaren was managing the band and he is very manipulative. He is media-savvy. He is looking to create some kind of scenario, create a scene, stir up some trouble, and what better way than to send these loudmouth drunken punk rockers that don't look like anything anybody's seen in any of those places to come and play those places. It was confrontational—you got Sid Vicious spitting on people, slashing himself with glass. It was like, let's create some controversy. That's pretty much what that was about.

As a kid, you listened to AM radio. Does Off!'s music link to that?

Some of the stuff we got to hear on the radio when we were kids, there was some pretty wild stuff: the Kinks, the Who, "Louie Louie." The Seeds' "Pushin' Too Hard," that's kind of punk rock. That's kind of aggressive . . . that's kind of antiauthoritative type of music, like, "Don't mess with me. I'm tired of your stuff. Don't hassle me, man. Get off my back. Get out of my face. Let me do my thing. You don't like it? Cool. No big deal. If you like it, well, that's fantastic."

The Circle Jerks covered both the Creation and Creedence Clearwater Revival. Would Off! do that?

When it comes to the Circle Jerks, you can go all the way back . . . to friendlier AM radio–type songs that we were mangling. With Off!, that's not going to happen. There's some of that mentality that runs through the band, but it does not come through our music. Bass player Steve McDonald is a huge fan of girl groups, the Partridge Family, and all that fun kind of stuff, but when it comes to the songwriting it's Dimitri and me. I write the lyrics, he basically just does a bunch of down stroking on the guitar, and we take it from there. I mean everybody is allowed to add bits and pieces, but it's on a musical level, it's not on a lyrical level. The structure is pretty much set . . . and the aggressiveness. That's kind of what Dimitri and I do when we're bashing it out in my living room.

Do you consider Off! less humorous and political than the Circle Jerks?

The Circle Jerks were light, fluffy, and airy. The Circle Jerks were popcorn compared to Off! which is more like sandpaper, glass, and rocks. Throw all that stuff in your mouth and see how it feels and tastes and what happens to your teeth and tongue. There is a lot of the same mentality, but at the same time a lot of it is missing. The CJs were just out to be the life of the party. We wanted to be the guys that played the music for everybody to do their drugs and squirt red dye in the swimming pool and start the orgy. All the kids out front putting paper in the trees, removing people's hub caps and putting rocks in there.

Off! is a soundtrack to . . . ?

Our party leans a little bit closer to Black Flag, like the dark party. I think our thing is a little bit more sinister. Now, I personally try to hold onto as much sarcasm as possible because keeping a shield of humor gets you through a lot of ugly situations, where you can kind of shrug your shoulders and laugh under your breath and get on with it. You can be in some real ugly, evil situation, and if you hold on to your sense of sarcasm, that helps deflect a lot of the crap that gets tossed your way. It's almost a scenario out of *Snow White and the Seven Dwarfs*, like whistle while you work. Maybe that helps speed up the time, so you don't have to pay close attention to the clock, and you don't have to pay that much attention to the boss breathing down your neck.

That sounds akin to chain gang music.

Well, yes and no because it could be chain gang music. How often do we see the chain gang anymore? The last time I saw a chain gang was in a movie called *Cool Hand Luke* with Paul Newman. So, that's more like a group of guys knowing they have to go work their asses off and the best way to get through it is hum and whistle, tell jokes, and try to keep it light and airy.

Was it important for you to have Off! be perceived as a band, not simply as a project?

This turned into a project, but the fact of the matter is I have been in a band for over thirty years of my life and I had to walk away from it, because it became dysfunctional and things became ugly. Really crappy decisions were being made, and I was just frustrated. We were all working towards a common goal, but we couldn't even make that work right. So, in the process that was taking place, sometimes you are presented opportunities, and Dimitri presented me with an opportunity. And I am happy, I am having a blast, I am having a great time. We just got done going touring Europe. I haven't been to Europe since 1985. I don't remember too much of it. This last tour that we did we played festivals. We played a couple of parties, smaller shows in London, and that was totally off the hook, amazing. We were playing these festivals, and everybody loved us. We played a festival in Oslo, Norway. When we did our line-check, we were all looking at each other thinking, and talking to ourselves, this looks bleak. It looks like all the people that were at the festival were done at the other side of the park. And when we play, there's gonna be five hundred people in front of us. And all of a sudden we thought, if we have five hundred people in front us, we're doing really well. We waited for fifteen minutes, then it was time for us to get up on stage and play, and by then it looked like there were ten thousand people, and everybody was going crazy and having a great time. It was beautiful. There was sunshine, a summery kind of day, and we just happened to be there. It was pretty amazing.

I know you believe in karma, so how do you think the good karma of this event came about?
Well, maybe it's the music. Maybe it's just a reward for all of the stuff I have done in the past. Maybe it's a reward for stumbling upon something and not knowing its value, or not knowing its worth, or even paying attention to anything like that, and then all of a sudden, there it is.

It's been fifteen years since Jeffrey Lee Pierce died, your former roommate and the subject of an Off! tune. How would you describe his legacy?
If I were sitting in a room with Jeffrey, which I am, even though he is not sitting here physically, I am sitting here looking at a Gun Club *Juno* European tour poster on my wall, but Jeffrey and I would probably just laugh and shrug all of this off, and go, hey, what it is . . . In the beginning, just to use Black Flag as an example we didn't know what we were doing, what we were creating. We were just doing it. We didn't know what longevity we would have, or what kind of effect it would have, or [if] we were creating a blueprint or some kind of a map. It's like all these bands that go out on tour right now, they're all pretty much taking the route that some of the early bands like Bad Brains, Black Flag, and Circle Jerks, some of those bands, it was just get in the van and go. A lot of those tours, after a show we'd be in the van and call the next city and see if there was a place for us to play, somebody's back yard we could play in, or someone's living room. It is kind of the same way it is now, except now there are booking agents

handling a lot of it. There are bands that still book their own tours, and I have much respect for them.

Getting back to Jeffrey Lee Pierce, he also started a genre of music. When he took everything he . . . well, I see a cook standing over a big pot. There's already some ingredients in the pot, it's already boiling, and it's time to throw in some of the spices. Okay, here's some chopped garlic and here's some chopped onions, and here's some chopped carrots, and I look at Jeffrey as having done the same thing, with the rockabilly, blues, and the country. Hank Williams and the old black guy with the acoustic guitar on an old dirty porch, stomping as he's rocking in a rocking chair. Combining all that stuff, plus in his travels, adding bits and pieces of that to it. I think the dusty south, the dirty, gritty parts of Southeast Asia, the jungle. You toss in some Americana, of course. You kick it up a couple of notches by adding the punk rock flavor, the aggro flavor. That's what you got, and that's what he helped create. That's his genre. Nick Cave was one of his heroes.

Do you think women like Alice Bag and Diane from the Alley Cats, or women in general, have received enough attention for their early role in punk?
There's also Penelope from the Avengers, Dinah Cancer from 45 Grave. I think we could actually generalize that and say, have women in rock have not got their just rewards? Then you would place Grace Slick in there, Suzi Quatro, Janis Joplin, Patti Smith. I don't think women will ever get their equal slice of the cake or pie, or what have you. I don't see that happening. When you think of rock'n'roll, you think of it being more rugged, sweaty, well, I don't know if this is the right word to use, but manly.

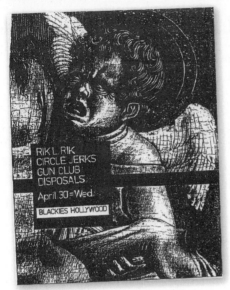

RIK L RIK
CIRCLE JERKS
GUN CLUB
DISPOSALS.
April 30 = Wed.
BLACKIES HOLLYWOOD

People describe Alice Bag as tough or protohardcore. Did she seem that way to you?

I think that these women we have brought up, I think they are all insanely talented. So, on a talent level, they are all right up there with the best of the men, but as for her being a tough gal and part of the hardcore thing, every now and then there are a few that are capable of keeping up with the men. I think that she did a great job, but I think the fact of the matter is, I would have liked to see a larger body of work.

What makes Raymond Pettibon's body of work so enduring to you?

First off, he is a very iconic artist. He is one of *the* artists of our times. I don't know how many others you can cite, but he grew up in it, he was part of it. We hadn't even named the band Black Flag yet, and he played bass at a couple of our rehearsals. He wanted to be a part of it one whatever level he could be part of it. He started contributing artwork. He actually contributed the name Black Flag and the four bars. In my world, he's highly influential. He did artwork for Red Cross, the Minutemen, the Circle Jerks, and Sonic Youth. Dimitri and I went down and hung out with him. He apparently felt and sensed our vibe. He could sense the energy. I guess he could feel it. He wanted to be a part of it, just like at the very beginning.

It circles back to that original vibe?

Well, this would be Dimitri whamming away on guitar in my living room, and he's doing something he is not used to, and all of a sudden he's doing this, and he's playing this song, he's playing these riffs, and it was like being in a time machine. It took me all the way back to being in the Church in Hermosa Beach, which would be 1977–78. So, we went down and we hung out with Raymond, and we played Raymond some of this music. He got it immediately. He knew what we were up to, he knew there was something happening here that took all of us back to this place. For me, it's a really great place, it's not a bad place. There was great stuff that came out of there. The Last and the Alley Cats were right up the road, then there was Red Cross. So, that was a great place to go back to. Raymond obviously knew what we were up to. Like I said, he wanted to be a part of it. And how could you say no to a guy like Raymond Pettibon?

Can you tell me about "Poison City," which I thought might be another one of your narratives about Los Angeles.

When I wrote the lyrics to "Poison City," I was basically lashing out about the event that happened on 9/11 and how our government had glorified it. Now we have another group of people we can go fight with. That's what "Poison City" is about. It's not necessarily about New York and what happened. That could have happened anywhere. We had the Oklahoma bombing, and everybody seems to forget about that. The government said it's these people, and we're going to go chase them in the desert, we're going to go kill them and spend all this money, and there's more and more troops going over there . . .

Fred "Freak" Smith
(Beefeater)

For me, the legacy of Beefeater is summed up most forcefully in their brilliant, genre-blurring LP *House Burning Down*, released on Dischord after the band's demise in 1986. Combining hard funk, tribal stomp, raw jazz, shades of reggae, metallic leanings, and hardcore prowess, it's an unmatched landmark, even now. Yet, the band was unstable (drummers came and went) and their fiery brand of politics set the teeth of both right-wing and left-wing punks on edge. Guitarist Fred Smith, whose name is now officially Freak, was the nimble musical back-bone of the band. After joining Strange Boutique, he also helped pave the path of elegant post-hardcore music in DC as well. Now, he shreds in American Corpse Flower.

This interview was originally published in *Maximumrocknroll*.

Tell me about your musical heritage.
In very early 1983, I had just quit my government job at the Department of HUD. My dad was one of the first black U.S. deputy marshals. My dad was a doo-wop singer in the 1950s with Marvin Gaye and Van McCoy. The band was called the Starlighters and had a hit song called "The Birdland." After they fizzled out, my dad got into law enforcement—the second generation of the Smith clan to do so. My mom was overseas working for the State Department (a gig she earned struggling in the ranks for at least fifteen or so years) while working in the 1960s for a program called Voice of America. They divorced in 1971. As my dad kept stressing me to go into law enforcement as a lifelong career, the music side of me was tearing me apart. So, I finally decided for the latter.

And you started to immerse yourself in punk music?
All this punk rock shit was happening in DC as well as New York, Massachusetts, Michigan, Ohio, and LA. I was so intrigued. It was kind of like the hippie move-ment of the late 1960s but more radical and more in-your-face—"We are sick

of this shit world, and we are now here to fucking change it whether you fucking like it or not" attitude. In this circle of mostly pale, tattered clothing, safety-pinned boys, aside from the few black fans in the audience, *there was us*! Gary Miller, aka Dr. Know of the Bad Brains, John Bubba Dupree from Void, Stuart Casson of Red C and the Meatmen, and the late, great David Byers of the Psychotics, Chucky Sluggo, HR, and myself. Now I am just noting the guitar players, but would never, ever, exclude or forget Shawn Brown from Dag Nasty, their first original singer, and the late Toni Young of Red C.

Through friends & some various acquaintances, more notably a guy named Ray Tony aka "Toast" and Eric Laqdemayo, aka Eric L. from Red C, I heard about Madams Organ and the Atlantis Club. Soon I was auditioning at the old Dischord house for a band that, from the start, proclaimed, "We are not here to make any money. Are you in?" My brother Big Myke said, "Fuck this," and split. I hung around. Beefeater had an amazing but, at any given time, very tumultuous run, with two vegan, militant vegetarians and throughout the two and a half years of our existence, three meat-eating, substance-abusing alcohol-driven drummers, and myself!

What was it like to be a black punk in DC?

Let us all keep in mind that DC is what, 80 percent black, and this punk rock scene was fueled by angst-ridden white kids, a lot of whom I found out had fucking trust funds waiting for them when they became of legal adult age. Shit, I didn't even know what a fucking trust fund was back then. It was very strange to be these "token negroes" playing in front of predominantly all-white audiences, but we did it. As Shawn Brown and myself will attest, there were fucking issues, man. A lot of fucking issues that we had to address when we did shows. When I first heard someone refer to me as the "negro Lemmy," I was floored. I immediately lowered my mic stand down from the height that I set it. When I heard Shawn Brown being referred to as "the negro version of Ian MacKaye," I was floored again. When I told him, he was taken aback but still plugged on. In retrospect, even in this new scene, I was always wondering, would racism ever end?!

Most of us know you as Fred Smith, so tell me about the name change to Freak.

Like many blacks back then, through the 1930s until the early 1960s, a lot of fucking name changing went about due to many horrible scenarios always occurring in the segregated United States of America. I legally changed my name to Freak some odd years ago. My birth name, Frederick E. Smith Jr., is not my real name. My real last name is Ellis. When I found this out in 1980, I was horrified, shocked, saddened, and felt raped by both the world itself for letting me be born as a lie and by my parents, who knew this shit but never told me until I was an adult. So not cool, man. There was some incident with one of my family members in the 1930s in another state, possibly a homicide. I really don't know. If this was the case at the time, I am very sure it was probably in self-defense against not getting lynched. My family keeps it very cryptic, but the truth was, this individual had to get out of town, disappear, and begin a new life. So, in doing so, the name was changed to "Smith." I have never tried to find our true lineage and probably never will. That would be too much of a strain for me right now and would probably just make me very, very fucking angry to find out all the lives I could've known all these years but didn't because of this incident. And a lot of other blacks will tell you I am not alone with this issue. So, changing my name finally gave me peace that I had been seeking for a very long time.

Being a drummer, I have to ask: why did Beefeater have three drummers, one for each recording?

Beefeater had three drummers due to the fact that three drummers went through Beefeater. What I mean to say is basically guys came in and left for various reasons—theirs and ours. Bruce Atchley Taylor, our first, left due to the fact that his life was changing and he wanted not to tour. We were very ready to go out of town during the early stages. Mark Schellhaus, our youngest skinsman, was pretty much asked to leave by Doug and Tomas due to various addictions and attitudes at the time. I never got over that one. It was a band vote, and I was pretty much outvoted and pressured. If he wasn't out of it, the band would've ended, or at least gone on without the two of us. Again, that is a very painful part of the history of the band for me, and I am still not quite over it. Mark and I are still very close, and he took being asked to leave pretty cordially and just did so without much opposition. To this day, Mark is one of the coolest people I know—a very talented fucker like the rest of the other drummers. Again, it was a sad moment for me. Kenny Craun, Mark's replacement, and drummer number three, just came in and took us out through the rest of our days and just went his own way to do other project when the band dissolved in 1986. Most notably with a punk outfit called the Rhythm Pigs, and he also hooked

up with Chuck, Faith No More's first original singer. With bands, chemistry is vital, and for some reason, the boys, Tomas and Doug, were okay with Kenny. This was pretty unusual at the time for Ken was more of a rocker than a punk dude, but he had his style, and they really didn't buck at it much. The timing was funny. Each drummer played on his own individual album, thus leaving his distinctive mark—funny.

Need a Job came out on Olive Tree Records, which a member of Lunchmeat described as "a shady short-lived label, part of the HR (Bad Brains) Dave Byers crew . . . I doubt those tapes even exist." Everyone knows Dischord Records, but tell me about Olive Tree.

Hmm, for me, *Need a Job* is one of my favorites. The band was really getting out of the standard basic hardcore genre and were really starting to mix that genre with funk. On *Plays for Lovers*, the funk was there, but it was being played so fast that those grooves might have gotten lost in translation to some. It was being accepted by a new breed of hardcore punks actually hearing that fast groove, somewhat like the Big Boys were doing in Texas. Though the production for the *Need a Job* recording wasn't exactly what I was hoping for in a finished product, I was still glad the EP came out to show that we were growing as a band. As I remember, the actual Olive Tree label was established by some of the punk/rasta scene in DC. Founding members of that label were Julie Byrd, Kenny Dread, and HR himself. Shady is a harsh word to describe the label, but . . . things sometimes did not happen in a timely and professional manner. Shit got done, but not without drama of some kind. Oh yeah, there are master tapes out there with shit still waiting, I hope, for life to the world. Everyone at Olive Tree just smoked too much pot sometimes. Not saying that liquor and drugs don't affect other aspects of labels and bands and the music scene, I am just stating a known fact, and as musicians we have all pretty much really been there.

When interviewed in *MRR*, the band listed people like the Isley Brothers, John Coltrane, and John Lee Hooker as influences. Is that why the band had such a melting pot sound—pulling from jazz, funk, and world music— because the band wasn't simply listening to Minor Threat records or mimicking 1977?

Fuck yeah, man. Beefeater, throughout its existence, listened to pretty much anything. We all were into our own worlds and brought them to the lab all the time. We took from this and that and just blended it into something. We fucking pulled from anything and everything. It was cool. Nothing was off limits. That is what made it cool. That is what kept things fresh. Yes, we were a hardcore band, in essence, but we had a lot more shit to experiment with, and we made damn sure we did. No restrictions.

I know Tomas was critical of go-go music (the genre of bands like Trouble Funk, who played with Minor Threat) because they often emphasized materialism (once called it "stupid music about dancing and being cool"). Do you feel he misjudged or misunderstood go-go music?

Tomas's judgment of the DC go-go scene was, in fact, his opinion. Whether it was a critical misjudgment of it, dunno. You would have to ask him. I couldn't stand the shit myself. Nonblacks have always loved grooves. It took forever for those to admit it, but they fucking love funk, soul, and grooves. I think at one time in the U.S. it was against the norm to reveal liking such music, but alas, times always change. Go-go to me was just a rip-off of bands that played stadium shows and gave the drummers a spotlight in the middle of the set. Go-go basically took that spotlight drum part and made it an hour-and-a-half-long song. Just basic jam sessions really, only highlighting a beat, *the beat*. Everything else— guitars, keyboards, etc.—were put on the back shelf. The actual song was the beat. I didn't care for it, but tons of fuckers in DC and around the world loved it. How can a hundred Frenchmen be wrong?

Looking back, the band is considered part of the Revolution Summer era, including Rites of Spring, Embrace, Marginal Man, Gray Matter, and others. Did you feel a kind of "movement" was happening, or is our notion of that time really a kind of myth-making?

Probably about a good four years prior to me even joining Beefeater, I, in fact, was becoming, in essence, a fucking real punk rocker. Learning the values and creed of that phenomenon and adapting it to my lifestyle. Revolution Summer was fucking bad-ass and very, very real. I am so proud to say that I was a part of that shit, and it was no myth in any way, shape, or form. I remember us out there doing the Punk Percussion protests at the South African embassy and Reno Park shows and shows benefiting those privately funded organizations that actually help and make change for the good of the city's poor and under-privileged. That was a beautiful and awesome awakening for me in the punk rock world. All of us weren't fuck-up miscreants. We actually cared about real positive change, and we went out there to do it at any cost. Fucking cool, man. Great memories there. And the bands and individuals who were out there with us at that time all have my sincere and undying respect. Again, when I say it was fucking cool, man, it *was* fucking cool. I believe my friend Amy Pickering of Fire Party started the whole concept. Again, way cool.

For many on both the Left and Right, Beefeater was vexing. Obviously, the Right dismissed the vegetarian/environmental/"political correctness" of the band, but even the Left was baffled by the antiabortion stance of some members as well. What was your personal sense of politics at the time?
From day one, Beefeater was Doug and Tomas's vision, and it came with at least a couple of ground rules that the band stood for: vegetarianism/non-alcohol, environmentalism, and total political awareness and civil and human rights. No matter who was in the band at any given time, this message was creed. Now, with that in crystal clarity, Beefeater was comprised of four members struggling in groups of two. On one side, there was militant animals rights/vegan/non-alco-holic activist fucks, and on the other alcohol-drinking, women-fucking, and at the time chemical-experimenting, meat-eating pariahs. As you can only imagine, this chemistry caused, on more than several occasions, problems. With most bands, this is usually considered a marriage, albeit ours was a very fucked-up, dysfunctional one, insanely. But we all definitely had no issues or disagreements regarding a woman's right to choose and gay and lesbian rights. At shows, we were always very vocal about what Beefeater stood for, even though at times you saw beers on a Marshall or near the drums. I know that was hard for Doug and Tomas, but they put up with it. But not for very long. All the drummers and me tried our best to respect them and their messages as much as we could. It was hard considering our lifestyles and various vices at the time.

Supposedly, at your last show, which happened at Fender's (I once read), Gang Green played after Beefeater and were vocal about being anti-PC and anti-Beefeater. Do you feel that other punk bands were pretty hostile to the politics of Beefeater, or feel that the politics overshadowed the music?
Beefeater's last show was not at the Fender's Ballroom in Long Beach, California, in 1986. I really don't know where that came from. As far as Gang Green is

concerned, dissing us at that show after we opened for them and others, that
was just a retaliation for an incident that happened early on that same tour in a
different city in which the show was overbooked. They showed up and weren't
allowed to play, and the promoter asked us to step in and talk to them about it.
Not a good day for them at that time, but on the road shit happens. They said
what they said, and so what? Gang Green is one of the great bands of the early
and existing punk rock scene. I got no beef with those fun, crazy motherfuck-
ers whatsoever. Shit, I used to work at the 9:30 Club in DC, as we all know, and
those guys and me are all right. No issues at all. What was done was done. As
far as bands hating our brand of politics on issues or whatever . . . shit! It just
depended on what bill we were on, whoever that night was doing something
totally stupid, like starting fights for no reason during our pits, racist skins *sieg
heil*-ing us, dudes trying to get girls out of the pits, out of control bouncers, etc.
Any form of bullshit we did not tolerate whatsoever, and we would stop performing at any given second until those issues were addressed by the crowd or
the club. Whether the bands or fans gave us shit, we were able to handle anything. Not always contain it, but it got fucking dealt with as best we could. I
believe our last show was in Washington, DC, in 1986. A sad show, but one that
needed to happen so members could progress and move forward and still grow
individually. Thankfully, everyone did.

**I know Tomas has been critical of the punk scene, once telling a zine, "In a
way they [punks] are society now too and that's a shame. They still buy 7–11
food; they have no impact on the government, or the economy. They still
entertain themselves the same way, they have the same values and futures
as everybody else . . . so there's no anarchy, rebellion there at all." Did you
feel that punk represented an alternative society, or not?**
If here ever was a true punk, Tomas Squip was one of those at the head of
the pack, for real. Tomas really didn't give a shit about living beyond menial
means—food, shelter, lifestyle. He lived at the Dischord House for a while in a
room, shared a bathroom. He slept on the floor with no furniture. His pillow
was a medium-sized rock and he had a blanket to cover himself. He was always
reading and constantly on top of all the news, local and global, and on every
political issue on the grid. That fucker probably doesn't even know it, but he
taught me so much about the world, the system, and us as human beings. He
really wondered why punks were doing the same things as everyone else did—
get fucked up, do stupid things, resulting in altercations with law enforcement,
and not really trying to distinguish themselves from the norm they were rebelling against, other than clothing and music association. He wondered why
people, including myself at the time, didn't try to alter their eating habits to
respect animal rights, to change daily aspects of their lives to respect the earth,

to be aware of things that are said at times that are racist and sexist and homo-phobic. He always thought a lot of punks weren't really trying to make change at all. No rebellion or real anarchy at all. It saddened him all the time. It was very tough for him. He really wondered if anyone, aside from a very small faction of the scene, were any kind of real alternative society at all! I thought it was definitely an alternative society then, and I still think so now. But then again, a lot of things would make an observer looking in totally disagree with me. Like everything else, it basically comes down to what a certain individual is going to do with it—with that punk rock ethic.

After joining Madhouse and Strange Boutique, one of your best stories involves Geordie from Killing Joke. What made that time period special?
I don't know if any of you really know this, but I must be one of a very minute number of the luckiest punk musicians that has actually had a very uplifting, incredible life through the various bands he's been in. Not only did I work at one of the country's top underground, cutting-edge clubs of all time, Nightclub 9:30 in Washington, DC, I have also been in two very special bands that have allowed me to play with all of my peers for each band genre that I was in at the time and to excel at the music genre, whatever it was. In Beefeater, we were honored to play with such bands as Rites of Spring, DOA, NOFX, Agnostic Front, the Dickies, Scream, SSD, Dag Nasty, 7 Seconds, Bad Brains, Big Black, the Necros, HR, etc. As my run with hardcore came to its end in 1986, I was, in about four hours after leaving Beefeater, already enlisted in a now upcoming post-punk

band—one more accessible than the hardcore scene and appealing to a more eclectic adult dance audience

Strange Boutique emerged out of the ashes of Madhouse, fronted by lead vocalist Monica Richards, formerly of DC punk band Hate from Ignorance. As my style was now changing to the heavily Euro pop indie sound, I was getting influences from the likes of the Cocteau Twins, the Damned, Killing Joke, PiL, Punishment of Luxury, the Slits, and Magazine. Unbeknown to me at the time, I would soon be touring with the likes of some of them as well. Fucking incredible, fuck, you couldn't make this shit up: this is a dream, right? Whaddya mean we are heading to England? For real? In fact, on a support gig with Killing Joke in England I was approached by one of my idols, the all-time European guitar great Geordie, during a sound check. He actually got to check me out and see what I was really about. I passed him in the corridor of the club, and he goes, "Mate, you're a pretty good guitar player." I then asked, hey, would you put that down in writing for me?" He quickly responded in that heavy English accent, "No!" [laughing]. Always magical when one of the greats takes even a little time out for the little guy. One of my best days of all time. Will never forget it. Wow.

For me, it makes sense, musically, since people like James Stevenson from Chelsea joined Gene Loves Jezebel, and New Model Army can be linked to the Crass scene. But why did Strange Boutique become such a good fit for you?

Strange Boutique took a real fucking gamble on me, really. Here I was this totally out of control hardcore guitarist, chains dangling from belts and shit, and they just took me in to play this new form of music I was coming into— dark, pop, heavy dance groove shit. After some early experimentation, we soon were labeled goth. Now, at the time I was really growing. Unlike the days of Beefeater, I was now fully exploring new territories—new amps, effects (which I had never even considered ever using before in Beefeater), the now signature classic trademark Ovation acoustic/electric twelve-string, which I learned to also send through the Marshall and JC-120 to run a solo through once in a while with full-on lead distortion. Strange Boutique was my time, and I was definitely ready. Probably to this date, even though my Blaxmyth did make a dent, Strange Boutique was and always will be the best band I have ever been in, period, fucking F.

U-Ron Bondage
(Really Red)

While flying home from Portland last weekend, I flipped through a mid-1990s *Maximumrocknroll* with multiple angry letters to the editor about Mykel Board, the magazine's perennial "straw dog." Today, I read angry letters denouncing my interview with John Paul of Really Red in March, which I prefaced by explaining that punk was a wide umbrella genre with an inclusive community.

If we denounce him with a purge befitting Stalin, then we should throw out our records by the Dickies, Dag Nasty, Bad Brains, and the list goes on. I support the editors. In today's saturated media environment, easily entrenched political slogans and platitudes on CNN and punk blogs act as substitutes for authentic discussion and discourse. The real danger is smug self-satisfaction.

When *Maximumrocknroll* offered to reprint my 2005 interview with U-Ron, I approached him about openly releasing his e-mail to me too, which explains his reaction to the article. I do not seek to fissure the band's relationship with each other. I seek to explore the multiple perspectives (even multiple truths) that occur throughout the history of most punk bands. As a reader of the fanzine since the winter of 1984, I feel more dedicated to its efforts than ever because it is willing to engage, not pretend, and to incite, not recite.

Flex your head. *Maximumrocknroll* and *Left of the Dial* originally printed this.

Letter from U-Ron to *Maximumrocknroll*

You published an amusing interview with John Paul, former bass player of Really Red. He repeatedly described me as a Marxist. As flattering as that is, I suggest that John Paul wouldn't know a Marxist from a pharmacist, and I thought that his description of my political views were quite hilarious.

As a result of his apparent diet of Limbaugh/Beck/FOX lies, it seems that to John Paul anyone is a Marxist who doesn't aspire to unlimited personal greed and who might have ideas about equality justice and democracy that are to the left of Hermann Goering. It seemed that he was implying that he actually thinks

that Obama, Clinton, etc. are some kind of socialists . . . no, he said *Maoists*!!!!
I'm sure most readers of Max RR are too intelligent to fall for that nonsense.

Making it the law that people have to pay corrupt predatory insurance
companies for health "insurance" not health care) is "socialist"? Aren't these
insurance companies the zenith of the capitalist ideal? How about the "socialist" . . . no, "Maoist" act of forking over hundreds of billions to corrupt banks,
corrupt brokerage companies and CEOs to do with as they want and no strings
attached. That's socialism? I think ole JP needs a dictionary. There's yet another
reason why I wrote the lyrics for Really Red. But in all fairness, the guy was a
monster bass player and that is a fact.

But just for the record, let me say this. All of the claptrap and labels, from
JP, Beck, FOX, and everyone else, about socialism, capitalism, left, right, up and
down . . . to me it is all a bunch of bullshit. You still don't need a weatherman
to know which way the wind blows. It is really just a matter of what is decent,
fair, just, and truthful.

It doesn't matter what "ism" you call it. Things are either decent, fair, just,
and true, or they aren't. THAT is the bottom line, to me. Facts are facts and
there are plenty of scholarly books on history out there, from various sources.
There ARE actually some agreed upon historical realities based upon this thing
called *facts*.

To me, it really isn't that complicated to figure out. Killing innocent people
is wrong. People shouldn't do that, and those that do are evil scum. All people
should have food, health care, a place to live, a job, and freedom from violence.
That's it, and that is what people have been either fighting for or fighting against,
forever. I'll go with the "for" side no matter what it is called.

In the U.S., the entire two party system is rotten with corporate corruption
and a serious third, and fourth, party is needed. Not that you asked.

Enough about all that. As I used to yell from the stage at the end of a gig:
Now go make your own band!

Deep South Punk Legends from Ozone City

**From Lightnin' Hopkins and Roy Head to Townes Van Zandt, Steve Earle,
and ZZ Top, Houston has been the home, at one time or another, to a myriad
number of artists. When you started listening to music in Houston, were
you at all aware of the city's rich musical history?**
First off, it is very flattering to be asked to do this interview twenty-five years
after the release of Really Red's first LP. It's even odder that Empty Records
wanted to rerelease it twenty-five years after the fact. I'm pretty stunned. Really
Red never thought that we would be remembered three years after we broke
up. All that said, I have no idea who in the hell would want to read this but at

the risk of being totally boring I'll try and give you the best answers I can. I have to point out that this will be my perspective and recollections. In no way should any of this be taken as reflecting the opinions of Bob, John Paul, or Kelly, the other three former members of Really Red. They might remember things in a whole other way. Maybe no one will care about or remember these people and places but they were all involved in Houston's formative punk scene in one way or another and they do deserve to be mentioned. This is about a scene that is long gone, but it took a lot of brave and unique people

DO "THEY" sometimes Get on Your Nerves? IF SO, come to our party after the REALLY RED and MY DOLLS concert ⟨the concert will be in Rumours Jan 29 at 8 o'clock⟩. You will meet good people → Your favorite music will be played (Oingo Boingo, Stranglers, Dildos from Hell) and the beer is plentiful. Party is at Apt. 11 Q Viking Apartments, 1601 Holleman St.

to make it happen. They deserve credit. I appreciate the chance to give it to them and to tell our story.

I'm Canadian by birth, and my family moved to Houston when I was in the ninth grade. I knew very little about any Texas music at the time. I think I remember having a couple of 45s by the Sir Douglas Quintet, but at the time I thought they were from England, as Huey P. Meaux, their manager, intended. By time I was in the tenth grade I started going to see live music. One of the greatest bands that I ever saw was the 13th Floor Elevators. They were amazing—a bunch of working-class acid heads from East Texas who shirked any trappings of being wannabe rock stars. They were drenched with acid mystique and when they weren't too high to play they were like a damn hurricane. They were playing their own brand of psychedelic punk. They were one of the greatest and strangest bands that I've ever seen. I still love them and still listen to their recordings.

I met Kelly Younger around that time. We formed a band with Andy Feehan, and some other guys, called the Lords. We played these community center teen dances in places like the Bellaire Community Gym. That was the first place we saw the 13th Floor Elevators, actually. Unlike the Elevators, most bands that were around, including the Lords, only played covers. Hit singles and the like. The Lords at least did album cuts of the Velvet Underground, Rolling Stones, Animals, Yardbirds, and Love. We thought we were pretty radical because like the Elevators we refused to wear uniforms and most other groups did. Most bands only played known radio hits and we played album tracks. You have to remember this was before FM radio started playing album cuts. With few exceptions, radio only would play the selected single. There were other interesting bands doing some originals, like Fever Tree and Billy Gibbons's Moving Sidewalks, but not too many at that time. Everything was so restricted and stifled. I remember at one gig some older asshole stepped up and sucker-punched Andy because he had yelled "fuck it" in frustration about something. It was ridiculous.

Later, Andy Feehan and I started hanging out in the psychedelic clubs. You could go there under age because they were not serving alcohol, just lots of weed being smoked. There was the Living Eye, the Catacombs, and the best one was the ridiculously named Love Street Light Circus and Feel Good Machine. It was located in the heart of downtown by the bayou at Allen's Landing. The place was great. We saw the 13th Floor Elevators playing at 2:00 and 3:00 a.m. We saw bands like Bubble Puppy, the immensely underrated Children from San Antonio, the Chessmen of Dallas [the Vaughan brothers] and we got to see Sam "Lightnin" Hopkins a bunch of times. It was an excellent introduction to live noncommercial music. Very little of this stuff had any radio airplay at all. It was a live music scene. The older brother of one of our buddies was Steve Cunningham, who played bass in another really weird Texas band, the Red Crayola. I never saw them play a club, but once I did get to go watch them practice in a gutted store on Tuam Street. We smoked weed and they played stuff that was going to end up on their second LP, *God Bless the Red Krayola*. They also were one of the strangest bands I've ever seen. Really whacked.

The Lords broke up before I finally got kicked out of high school for "subversive political activity" and I left my parents' home. My "subversive political activity," by the way, was nothing more than being very vocally against the damn Vietnam War. They didn't go for that shit. I was on a Houston Independent School district blacklist. They were out to get kids like me and they finally did. It happened to a lot of kids. High school was an Orwellian nightmare. It was really an eye-opener. Once you see the lies exposed it is impossible for anyone to stuff the genie back in the bottle. I'll give you an example. What would you think of the graduated football team, who were now Aggies, being brought back to the high school by the principal and the coaches for the sole purpose of beating the shit out of the little group of antiwar kids? Well, it happened. With coaches and some teachers present they did it during lunch in the school cafeteria and those that got beat up were suspended for fighting! I was chased down the hall and I ran into a full classroom to escape. After high school, I moved into a big house with Kelly and a crew of crazies, and it was a time of lots of live music, experimenting with acid, weed, beer, nothing too different from the rest of the world. Kelly and I met up with John Paul around this time.

After a few years of working shit jobs and staying stoned, Kelly, John Paul, and I ended up living in a series of old houses in the Montrose district. Kelly

got hit by a car, and as a result of the insurance settlement, he bought these huge Orange amps and some guitars and stuff, and we used to get fucked up and try and make original music. We sucked but we had a lot of fun. We would go out to the Attics Dam area and pick shopping bags full of Texas psychedelic mushrooms. It was wild. You just waited until after a good rain and [then] go out to the cow pastures there and pick all you wanted. People would have these mushroom parties. Crazy, crazy times.

By this time the psych clubs were long gone and the local live music scene began to really suck. There were touring bands all of the time but the local rock'n'roll music scene had dried up due to lack of club and radio support. Everyone who was on tour came through Houston in those days. I mean it. But a lot of the Houston clubs had a preference for cover bands only, if you were local. It was fucked up. Austin had the Cosmic Cowboy thing and Houston had cover bands, kicker bars, and pre-disco DJ clubs. It was a bleak time for local rock music.

Apart from music, tell me about Houston during the late 1970s, which you've called a turbulent time.
Houston in the early 1970s, for me, was really a bore. As I said, the local music scene turned to shit and there was not a lot to do. Kelly, JP, and I would go to these boring disco "fake nightclubs" and do a kind of "Clockwork Orange" thing. Basically it was getting loaded, trying to pick up women and just being rude and obnoxious. As a result of acting like jerks we were thrown out of a bunch of these places. We didn't fit in. We didn't want to fit in.

Sometimes we'd get a drummer for a while and try and create some music, but there was no place to play, so it was a lot of directionless jamming at our house. The frustration and boredom were typical of the times, I guess, and it probably was happening all over. The police were always a total pain in the ass. I got arrested so many times for rinky-dink stupid stuff. Just police harassment types of things. You always had to be looking over your shoulder for the cops. It was worse for blacks, Latinos, and gays. At this time, the HPD had been investigated by the federal government for all kinds of questionable uses of lethal force. They were known as the "killer cops" as a result. Houston also had the distinction of being the "murder capital of the nation" at this time.

The city was a big corporate shopping mall on the surface, but underneath it all the frustration and boredom was brewing creativity. It was a mean city. A repressive, fucked-up city. We stayed in the inner city areas like the Montrose and the Heights for the most part because if you ventured out to suburbia it was a real nightmare of strip malls, Cadillac cowboys wearing their spurs just for show, disco clubs, sports bars, mindless suburban rednecks, and the vulgarly rich. It was disgusting. The politics were retarded and smug. Nothing was going on. There was no kind of "street scene" that I can remember except people driving around the strip shopping malls in their cars. The cops didn't want to see you "on the street." You were supposed to be off the street and spending your money in consumer frenzy. If you weren't doing that, then you were suspect. "Hey, why aren't you inside there playing foosball? Where's your car?"

The only thing you could hope for was a cool touring band coming through. My girlfriend and I crawled in the bathroom window of Liberty Hall and got to see the Velvet Underground. There was a short-lived club in the Rice University district called Of Our Own. It was a nonprofit co-op club, a very progressive idea for the time, actually. The MC5 played there for two nights. I wormed my way into hanging out with Rob Tyner and Wayne Kramer the first night. Some buddies and I smoked weed with them until dawn. They talked a lot of radical politics. I was listening, you can be sure. They were a fantastic live band. They made a big, big impression on JP, Kelly, and me. Really Red used to do a cover of their version of "Ramblin' Rose." They were very nice guys, too.

The turbulence, so to speak, was to come at the end of the '70s. It was a result of the mind-numbing boredom and frustration that came from living in what felt like a huge fascist corporate strip mall.

I assume punk roots were centered in the Montrose era, which some called a hippie ghetto in the '70s, where a lot of psychedelia was happening, and by 1980, had become a very open gay district, with bars up and down the main drag, Westheimer. But then again, from what I understand, the best place to see music was Liberty Hall, over in the Third Ward.

After the demise of the 13th Floor Elevators, there was very little that I can recall that had even the remotest resemblance to what would become punk. I'm talking about local bands, Texas bands. The Cosmic Cowboy thing was in full swing in Austin and the disco scene was everywhere. Montrose was a fairly low-rent district and it was full of the remainder of the hippie scene, the artists, the gays, the characters and lower-income people. Herschel Berry had a band that would sometimes play in a tiny little bar. They were called the World. They played Herschel's original rock'n'roll tunes and some good covers too. This was before he put together the Natives with Wiley and my old friend Andy Feehan. Herschel's bands weren't punk, in the sense that we know it now, but they were playing their own stripped-down noncommercial rock'n'roll in a sea of blandness. It was live, it was rock'n'roll, and it was original music. It could have been a start for original music in Houston but no one supported it. A dozen or so of the band's friends would show up, but that was it. He had this one three-chord, Who-influenced song that I loved. The lyrics were, "Me and my friends like to smash cars. So what if that's what we like to do? It's okay cuz we don't know who buys them and we're too young to try and drive them." I liked that one.

You're right about Liberty Hall. It was a place that tried to bring all kinds of music to town. It was the club that took chances and it was also an unpretentious, real Texas music hall. Cold longneck beer, a wooden floor, a fairly big stage, and a friendly crew of employees made it great. They booked all kinds of stuff and there were no racist limitations. They booked the little known Bruce Springsteen and the E Street Band there for a whole week. I saw the New York Dolls there two nights in a row and later on that was where the Ramones played their first Houston shows, also for two nights.

Before that by a few years, Kelly, JP, and I had finally linked up with some other guys and made a cover band called China. To get any gigs you had to do covers, so we played covers of everything from the Dave Clark Five, to the Yardbirds, to Roxy Music, to whatever. It was a horrible mishmash of stuff and China fell apart. Who wanted to just play cover songs at Houlihan's Hamburgers, even if they were good cover songs? Then a year or so later, Kelly, JP, and I linked up with a guy named Curtis Riker. We started learning Curtis's original songs with the intent of doing original music. A guy who had seen China introduced Bob Weber, our drummer, to us. We learned Curtis's songs and some covers, but it wasn't any fun. Everyone but Curtis was secretly very dissatisfied. We played our first gig as Really Red at Ray's Icehouse in Pasadena, outside of Houston. Pasadena at the time was known for two things. One was the drive-in porn theater and the other was the Ku Klux Klan. We played for "all the chili we could eat." I think we bombed at Ray's Icehouse in Pasadena. The four patrons thought we stunk. The chili was good, though.

The first thing that I was aware of on the local Houston scene that had anything to do with punk rock was the advent of the band Legionaire's Disease. The Sex Pistols had come to Texas and gone and one Jerry Anomie, fresh out of prison, had somehow ended up at their show in San Antonio. Well, he was inspired. He came back to Houston and put together, what I remember as Houston's first punk band. They were the Legionaire's Disease band. They were chaos! Superb chaos. Just exactly what Houston needed. Musically, they were nothing very original. Their original stuff was either a version of the Sex Pistols or a version of the Stooges. But what they lacked in musical originality, they more than made up with sheer guts and spectacle. They would literally con their way into playing some sleepy hippie bar or unsuspecting club with the intent of causing a riot.

They would walk out in front of an unsuspecting crowd of beer-guzzling hippies and completely freak everyone out. There was blond and stacked Gwen Duke playing bass in her underwear. There was Norman dressed in a mock Gestapo uniform and holding a completely unplugged guitar. Their real guitarist was way loud and could actually play. By the second song, Jerry would have dropped his pants and begun playing air guitar using his dick for a guitar. He would be totally naked by the third song. He was this skinny little guy with his back covered in a jailhouse tattoo. He would yell things like "it's deprogramming time" and "wake up." He would run into the audience and turn over tables and pour people's beer on them. They were part threat and part farce. It was dangerous, exciting, and hilarious. They were also amazing at self-promotion, too. Jerry could talk bar owners into booking them after they had been banned from any place they had previously played. They were the first Houston punk band that played anywhere in public, as far as I'm concerned. Really Red learned a lot from their attitude and their approach to self-promotion.

Kelly, JP, Bob, and I started seeing Jerry and Legionaire's Disease gigs. It wasn't until we saw Jerry and the Disease having a blast doing punk rock, and actually doing it in Houston, that we realized that we could also get away with playing what we really wanted to be playing. We were so ready to create some chaos of our own. We told Curtis that this was where we were going and he bailed. This was about 1978, I guess. We started making our own songs and practicing our asses off. We got some gigs in shithole bars and didn't do too bad. We gigged with the Disease several times and got along with them just fine. That is when we started to get serious. From then on it was every Tuesday, Thursday, and Sunday nights for practice, booze, and sometimes arguments. We did that religiously the whole time we were together.

This is how you've phrased your experience of that time: "The bands, audiences, publishers, artists, and DJs were cutting their way through uncharted areas, breaking lots of rules as they invented a new counterculture. Being a small part of the lives of the wild, inspiring, and often crazy people that we met along the way was well worth the time, money, and energy spent—not to mention the often frustrating experiences with rip-off promoters, cheap motels, lousy sound systems, unresponsive DJs, and abusive police." Were all these things just the nature of the beast in terms of touring the United States in the early punk days, or were they extremely magnified in Texas?
Well, I don't think that I can improve on that quote, but I can sure expand on it. Back when there were no "punk" clubs or bars to play in at all, and I don't just mean in Houston or Texas, what you did was start from scratch creating your own scene. I mean you had to con down-and-out bars that had no clientele into letting you put on a "rock show." Then you would spend the week plastering up posters and telling everyone you knew about it. The gig would usually be on a shitty night like Sunday or a weeknight and when you played the bar would have a shit fit and kick you out, or at least say "never again." Then you would go to the next shithole and try it again. This is how it was all over the country. This is what DOA did in Vancouver, the Avengers and DKs in Frisco, Black Flag, Circle Jerks,

and X in LA, Big Boys and the Dicks in Austin, Meat Puppets and Hüsker Dü and on all across the country. If you ran out of bars you would rent VFW halls or any warehouse space that could be used for a one-off gig. Anywhere. We played a health food store in Portland, Oregon, once. You would play anywhere that would let you. We were thrown out of and banned from lots of places, as were other bands all across the country. It wasn't like it is now where a punk band has a readymade and waiting club in every town. Oh, no. You didn't have punk booking agencies

to find you places to play. You had to talk people into letting you play a show. You had to twist arms and bullshit people. You had to do it yourself.

It went on like this for a year or so, until some place started warming up to the idea of letting these crappy bands have regular shows. These "crappy" bands were drawing a whole new crowd of people. Then those places became the local punk clubs. A scene started growing around them. Then a band could try and play in some other town. Bands started contacting each other asking where there was to play. The fanzines exploded and every town had some little rag with interesting scene reports and reviews. Dozens upon dozens of little Xeroxed zines full of rants and reviews. When you toured, you slept on people's floors, in fleabag motels, and in your van. You met all kinds of interesting characters as a result and you ended up playing some strange "venues." We played the Tool and Die in San Francisco once. That was a bizarre place. A gutted storefront on the street level that you walked through to a closet. In the closet was a trap door that had a ladder that went straight down to a big cement basement room. That was where you played. There were no windows, no exits, and no air conditioning. You had to carry your gear down and up that ladder. It must have been 110 degrees down there once the place was packed. That place did pack them in, too.

It took a long time, a lot of diligence, and a lot of work to create the punk scene. You had to not only work on your music, but you had to literally create places to play before anyone could even go to a gig to hear you. You had to design your gig flyers and go out and put up them up. You often had to rent a sound system as the little joints didn't have any. You had to do all the work hauling equipment and setting it up because maybe you would only have one friend/roadie to help. You wouldn't make any money because you would keep the cover charge down to nothing. We had plenty of shows where two or three bands split a two or three-dollar cover charge. We did gigs for one-dollar cover charges! It wasn't about making money. Really Red's idea about the money was that we weren't out to make big bucks, but if someone was going to make money off of us, then we would be getting our share. In the early days and up through 1983, most bands were pretty cool about playing for low covers. Of course, this invited certain greedy club owners or asshole promoters to try and take advantage of these bands. They did, too. Rip-offs were common and brazen. Sometimes, it got ugly just trying to get what you were promised. Real ugly.

The scene at that point was totally creative and exciting. There were few rules and people were defining what *their* punk scene was. People dressed in any old thing that they thought was punk. Bands were raw and adventurous and didn't all sound exactly alike. There were all kinds of influences showing up. It was terrific. It was also a constant battle. Club owners, promoters, and cops didn't know what the hell was going on. Audiences were just as confused at times. For a while some people thought that spitting on the bands was what they were expected to do. Later on, throwing bottles and stuff was in fashion. Breaking up shit, like chairs and stuff, would happen in this period. It was the explosion of turbulence that I referred to. It was the audience and bands versus the bar, their staff and cops. It was frustration and boredom with corporate America and the suburban nightmare exploding in desperation. It was dangerous and chaotic. There was that big Latino guy shooting off his gun into the ceiling at the Island before Phil Hicks took over the management from him. There were sadistic bouncers beating the crap out of people because they were panicked and didn't know what was going on. It was exciting all right, but at times it was scary because it was new territory for everyone. Where it was going was anybody's guess.

It started to gel into a real scene once the majority of people realized that if we destroyed the clubs then we would have no where to go. If club owners allowed bouncers to beat up people then no one would show up anymore. Clubs/bars, bands, and audiences started working together to make *our* scene. The Island was the first openly punk club in Houston. You went out three or four nights a week to see fledgling bands to "support the local scene" and to keep it all alive. I must have been at one show or another almost every single weekend for about seven years. It was intense, as we were all getting a bit of control and autonomy over our own lives, and that was exciting. People were being creative in a wild, satisfying way. We were collectively doing what we wanted, how we wanted to do it, and doing it in spite of the lack of attention paid by the media and the dominant corporate culture and in spite of the attention paid by the police. We didn't need either. We were alive! I wouldn't have missed it for the world. It wasn't all violent and scary, either. Sometimes it was downright hilarious. It didn't matter if you screwed up or made an ass of yourself because nobody but the local scene would take notice anyway and the bands and the audience were often hard to differentiate. In a way, the audience had taken over the stage. It was freedom.

In fact, the intro to 90.1 FM's 2003 *History of Houston Punk*, states, "It's 1977. The Houston cops and the Knights of the Brotherhood of the Ku Klux Klan are the same organization!" Is this an accurate portrayal of the Bayou city, later perhaps embodied by the Really Red song "Teaching You the Fear"? Absolutely. It was an "occupied city." Corporate culture, a police army, dumbed-down suburban zombies waving flags and then the oppressed underbelly consisting of blacks, underground artists and writers, Latinos, gays, old hippies, and now punks. Has it changed that much? That sounds like a description of Dick Cheney's America.

Christian Arnheiter, who actually saw the Pistols play in San Antonio, is often claimed to be one of Houston's original punk purveyors, since his band the Hates formed around 1978. He had a radio show on KTRU and used to buy tons of records from the import bin at Cactus. But what characters do you remember who might have formed the genesis of the music scene as bands like the Ramones, the Nerves, and the Pistols played Texas in 1978?

Yeah, Christian was around in the early days. I never heard of him or his band until after Legionaire's Disease happened. The way I remember it, the original Hates played some gigs in few places and then broke up. Before they broke up, they recorded a bunch of songs. After they broke up, Christian pressed the songs and then released them over the next few years. It was a while until he got another lineup of the Hates together and this kept the name out there. He would show up at a lot of gigs, not especially Really Red gigs. We weren't very close. The next versions of the Hates played rarely. Once every eight months or so, at least that is how I remember it. To my knowledge, the Hates did not tour or anything, just play the occasional Houston gig. But then he would write his own show reviews, "scene reports," for *Maximumrocknroll*. I didn't know anyone that was into the Hates. Maybe I just missed the Hates scene. I don't know. He did have the first punk radio show in Houston. It was really short lived, though. It was at KPFT, and I think they canned him after a few shows for swearing or some stupid reason. I don't know what happened there. That was early on, though. He was there at the start of the Houston punk scene, that much I know.

Other notable characters who contributed to the original Houston scene? Wow, let's see . . . I gotta say Phil Hicks, the manager of the Island. Without Phil there would not have been anywhere to play. The Island was Houston's

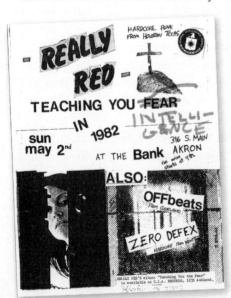

first real punk rock club. It was crazy. I'll never forget it. At first it was pretty violent because of a couple of psycho sadist bouncers, but after Phil got rid of them it was a lot of fun. Later on, Richard Tomcala became the booking guy for Phil and the Island really took off. Richard kept his long hippie hair throughout that whole time and that took some guts. Certain idiots would beat you up if your hair wasn't just right. He was constantly getting shit for it. But he was as much of the punk scene, when all is said and done, as anyone. So much for uniforms, eh? Then along came that guy Joe Star.

He had a place called Joe Star's Omni. We had a terrific New Year's Eve gig there. I saw some great shows by the Dicks there, too.

There was a crew of characters who put out a kind of alternative zine for a while. It wasn't punk exclusively, but it was the first Houston publication to give any coverage to the young punk scene along with other alternative music and fashions. It was called *XLR8*. I can only recall the names of two of those people, Kathy Jolly and Terry Moore.

I should be careful, because I don't want to slight anyone. It was a long time back. Let's see, the Plastic Idols were early on but short lived. They had an early Devo-type sound. Gary Yokie and the Ruse were in there and they were great scene supporters. The strange MC5-meets-Hawkwind outfit known as AK47 would pop up. Starting at the beginning there was Henry Wilddog. He was this great character. He was an ex-Yippie who promoted some real early shows and had a fanzine. Later on, he had a band called the Vast Majority. There was Houston's first predominantly female band, the Mydolls, whom John Peel of the BBC interviewed live on the BBC. There were the new wave popsters, the Judys. J.R. Delgado came along later with Doomsday Massacre, and later he had the Party Owls. The Killerwatz were early on and around for quite a while and the Recipients. There were the high-school kids with bands like the Delinquents and the Parents. And I cannot forget Culturcide! Ho, ho. They really freaked out a lot of people. You just couldn't put them into any category, thankfully.

There were scenesters like Matt Fatt, a guy who lived behind the bar at the Island and sometimes ran the door. He literally lived there, in that heat and squalor. The Island sold liquor as well as beer and wine, but I don't think they ever carded anyone, as the place was always full of underage kids as well as the legal-aged adults. There must have been some kind of payola going on, because the cops never busted the place for minors, but they would just come by and randomly arrest ten or twelve people or just get on stage and say, "Go home, the show is over." They closed a Big Boys and Dicks show, I think, on a Friday night for no particular reason. We were playing the next night so we found some old cop uniform shirts at the Goodwill and wore them that night when we played. We painted big bulls-eye targets on the backs of them, though.

Lots of really colorful characters contributed to the whole scene. There was the handicapped kid known as Crippled Punk. He once fronted a short-lived band and one night he wore a whole jack-o'-lantern pumpkin over his head for the whole set. He had cut a hole in the bottom and it was like a mask or helmet. There was that old Austrian avant-garde filmmaker, Kurt Kren. He was bumming around Texas totally broke and ended up hanging around the punk scene for years. There was Marilyn and Sean at KTRU with the S&M radio show. They played new wave and some punk and promoted gigs on their shows. There was the late Butler Hancock, who brought the big-name touring acts to town. Later on, there was the always-positive Ronnie Gaits who had clubs like Cabaret Voltaire, where there were amazing shows. I know I'm not remembering everyone. My apologies.

Apparently, FM radio was barren. Biscuit once told a DC interviewer, "A three hour show on a Sunday night in Austin, a four hour show on a Thursday night in Houston, is all that there is. And Houston is two million people and an outrageous amount of people go to shows there, but there's like no music on the airwaves." So, how did the people swell around the new music? Was it due to fanzines like _Ultra_, _Wild Dog_, and _Bondage_, record stores, word of mouth, or what exactly?

Like I said, at first it was just the bands getting out there at night and stapling up their flyers. That and word of mouth. I had a dinky little record store that promoted everything I could. Other indie stores like the Sound Exchange let you put up flyers and promoted gigs too. That was about it in the beginning. A bit later on, there were actually several radio programs on KPFT that played real punk and alternative rock and announced gigs. Art Gnuvo, Mr. Lee, and others promoted shows on the air. I had the Funhouse show on KPFT for about four years with a couple different partners, first Bill Steen and then Ralph Armin. By the way, I want to say here and now that there was no conflict of interest there. I never played Really Red on my own radio show. It was probably a stupid move on my part but it wouldn't have been the only one I made. It was a matter of principle at the time. Later on, I turned Funhouse over to the capable hands of Chuck Roast and Austin Caustic who took it to new heights for years. As I previously mentioned, there was KTRU's S&M show too. That was about it for radio in Houston. Of course there were the zines, too. I remember _Wild Dog_ and _XLR8_ and later the fledgling version of the _Public News_ weekly came out and took ads for gigs and would have the odd gig review. Once places like the Island and Joe Star's Omni were established, then people would just gravitate there to see what was going on. They were hangouts. A street scene evolved.

Another big hangout, that didn't have bands at the time, was the old Rudyard's Pub in the Montrose. There, mixed with the emerging punk scene, you would find the hardcore skate gang the Urban Animals and a myriad of incredible characters. I understand that Rudyard's is still there and they have taken over the entire building. The pub was just the downstairs then and above it was where Trish of the Mydolls lived and had her haircutting place. Mydolls practiced there, above the old Rudyard's. There was many a serious party in that building. Wild all-nighters. Start at Rudyard's and see the dawn come up at Trish's. I understand that, Rory, another guy who strongly supported everything in those early days and sometimes worked at the Island, manages the place now. Or did.

Supposedly, according to Scott Telles from the band Vast Majority, the early appearances of Really Red and Legionaire's Disease were at Yippie events, sponsored by the likes of the Direct Action Committee, a University of Houston organization. Is this what helped shaped the band's politics, or were these people just convenient in terms of getting gigs and publicity? For instance, Mark from Mudhoney comments in the new publicity for the rerelease just how political the band was, yet it did not seem nearly as rigid or self-righteous as bands like MDC.

Ah yes, the Yippie events were put on by Henry Wilddog who, like I said, was an early supporter of the Houston punk scene. I can say that even though the Yippie scene was fading and the punk scene was emerging there was a certain anarchist anticapitalist area where they overlapped ideology-wise. He saw that and so did we. I can't speak for Jerry and Legionaire's Disease, but I remember both bands being in full support of what the Yippies were on about at the time. While Legionaire's Disease's politics were sheer chaos and shock, Really Red's politics were somewhat more focused and defined.

Really Red members were never in total agreement all the time on everything, but we had general areas where we were on the same page. However, as I wrote my own lyrics and made most of the flyers, I guess that allowed my politics to dominate the band. We never were out to become rock stars. We had day jobs. We were not making any money to speak of. With expenses of recording, equipment, a van, and traveling, we called it "paying to play," as we always were in the hole and had to kick in money from our day jobs. We loved what we were doing, and what we were doing was trying to make high-energy rock that might be a small catalyst to inspire people to start thinking and to start standing up

for social justice and political change. We tried to practice and not just preach. We did benefit gigs all the time, for everything from the John Brown Anti-Klan Organization to KPFT radio to raising money for an operation for someone's dog. One of the times we were playing Vancouver in Canada, we headlined a benefit concert for the legal defense of the infamous anarchists the Vancouver Five. Great gig with Greg Ingraham, guitarist of Avengers and Subhumans fame, as well as a slew of others. The RCMP paid a visit just as we started into playing "Teaching You the Fear." It couldn't have been more ironic if we had scripted it. If it was a worthy cause then we would usually do it. It was part of the gig. Social conscience. Civic duty, if you will. My politics were way left. We sometimes would have major battles within the band about it. But there always was enough common ground to find an agreement.

We made some really dumb "career moves" as a result of my becoming dogmatic about ideological things. Crass was a big influence on us at this time. I remember two really dumb things that we probably should have done differently. We had few rules but one of them was—no photos of the band in our press releases. The thinking behind this was that photos were too "rock star" and promoted "personality cult" stuff. As a result the press, punk or otherwise, rarely had a picture of us to print. Obviously this didn't help promote Really Red. Most of the photos that we have of the band were taken by someone who had nothing to do with the band and who gave us copies. Of course, all of our friends in other bands that we respected very much were turning out glossy 8 by 10s for the press. Duh.

Another stupid move was at the height of our popularity. The Clash were coming to Texas on their *Combat Rock* tour. Butler Hancock was promoting the Texas part of their tour. He said that the Clash wanted us to open for them in Houston and Austin and if all went well, maybe Dallas and wherever else they were playing in Texas. It was going to be those big arena-type venues. We were for it except we had some reservations about playing those types of huge venues. Then Butler showed me the contract rider from the Clash. They were demanding all this rock star crap for backstage. It was amazing and very disappointing to see. They were demanding china plates, silverware, tablecloths, cognac, and massive amounts of special catered food and drink and who knows what. I thought, what a bunch of petty bourgeois crap! What a load of rock star poseurs! These aren't punks anymore, sez I. We told Butler to tell the mighty Clash to piss off. So? They contacted these New Orleans guys, the Red Rockers, and they flew in and did the whole tour of Texas with the Clash. However, Butler did let us into the show and backstage where we did eat and drink our fill of the Clash's fancy food and booze. There was a line of people getting Joe Strummer's autograph and so I walked up to him like the drunken jackass that I was and said to him, as he was signing an Ellen Foley album that he and Mick had produced,

"What's it all about, Joe? Autographs?" He told me that if he didn't do it then people would get pissed off. I said, "We don't want to be in a punk band and piss anyone off now, do we?" I was a bit of a jerk to old Joe, I suppose. I really liked him. May he rest in peace. So, no one saw Really Red opening for the Clash and we proved what? I don't know. Anonymity?

Do you remember how John Paul Williams ended up playing with Deniz Tek in 1981 for the 100 Fools seven-inch?

Actually, I do remember that, and it is both John Paul and Bob Weber backing Deniz on that and another song that was called "RPM," I think. The background vocals were the Mydolls. Deniz Tek was the guitarist for Australia's Radio Birdman. The guy that engineered most of Really Red's recordings, Andy Bradley, was formerly the sound man for Radio Birdman. Deniz was visiting Andy and he wanted Andy to record him for a Bomp! Records compilation. He needed a backup rhythm section so Andy called up JP and Bob. Andy, along with Culturcide guitar wizard Dan Workman and Rodney Meyers, now own of the legendary SugarHill Recording Studios in Houston. There's a lot of history in that place. Did you know that Deniz Tek is a surgeon? Yup. Like, a doctor-type surgeon.

You owned Real Records, and supposedly another good store was Evolution Records on Bellaire. How did you end up owning and operating your own store, and did you see that as part and parcel of, say, the IWW's making a new world within the old, meaning changing the way people did business, or was it simply a job? The same idea could apply to your label, CIA, which in addition to the Really Red records, put out vinyl by the Mydolls, Culturcide, Introverts, and Doomsday Massacre.

I started Real Records with a $2,500 loan from a friend and a partner who kicked in the same. Of course, I couldn't have done it without the total support of my ex-wife. The object was to eke out a living, promote good alternative music, and sow the seeds of discontent. Not too original of an idea, really. I had very high ideals about what could happen. My partner had other ideas and decided to become a heroin addict. He looted me blind. I got rid of him. I floundered for a few years trying to dig myself out of debt. I came up with the idiotic idea to deal cocaine to help get myself out of debt. How brilliant! I became strung out on coke. I later went bankrupt and was stuck with a drug habit. It took a few years to kick that. A disaster. I ended up working for my competition, the Sound Exchange. They were gracious enough to hire me back, as I had been the original store manager before I opened my place.

The CIA Records label was never mine. It wasn't really anybody's. Really Red was paying for everything ourselves. We were the label, as far as who paid for our recordings and pressings etc. CIA Records was an address and a phone number and Bob's closet full of records. So when our friends were going to put out a record we would invite them to use the CIA name. They would pay for their own recordings, pressing, artwork, and freight and we would add them to the "CIA roster" and give them contacts and help them distribute their records. If their records sold they got all the money. Same for Really Red and we never broke even. The idea was that it would be more likely for distributors and radio stations to pick up something from some label that they already knew than from yet another unknown band and label. It worked fairly well. It was a kind of distribution co-op more than it was a real label.

I have pictures of you standing outside the Island with Klaus Flouride from the Dead Kennedys, but how did you end up on the *Let Them Eat Jellybeans* comp? It seems as if Jello might have chosen the Dicks, who were later on Alternative Tentacles, but Really Red alone represented the whole South, and thus exposed you to a worldwide interest in emerging hardcore music. That came about because on our first tour to the West Coast we played some shows in San Francisco. Biafra saw us at the Mabuhay Gardens. He liked us. A month or so after the tour, he called me up and asked if we would be on the compilation. We sent him the tapes of the *Teaching You the Fear* album that we were working on and he picked the song "Prostitution." I would have picked something else but we wanted to be on the record so "Prostitution" it was. The picture of Klaus and me was taken in front of the Island. We were fortunate enough to share the bill with the Dead Kennedys on a couple of occasions. Really Red got to share bills with a lot of great bands besides the DKs. We toured some West Coast dates with the truly awesome DOA around 1981. I've seen them so many times and they never have done a bum gig! We toured the West Coast and Texas with DOA and also with Articles of Faith and we played shows with MDC, the Effigies, Negative Approach, the Stranglers, 999, the Dicks, John Cale, Circle Jerks, SPK, the Lewd, Mark Arm's first outfit Mr. Epp and the Calculations, Bad Brains, Big Boys, the Fastbacks, Die Kreuzen, and many, many others. But my favorites were always DOA and the Dicks.

The song on the comp that really announced the band was "Prostitution," a personal fave of mine. Did this song directly relate to your feelings, later expressed in the promo for the new reissue, that "Really Red never had any dream of becoming stars nor was our intention ever to 'get signed' by a major label.... Our aim was to be somewhat of a catalyst (however small) for thought, outrage, fun, action, and ultimate *change* and to have a great time provoking it." Are you suggesting that many indie bands prostitute their ideas, images, and music, still today, for the sake of contracts and an

illusionary audience? Therefore, no lessons have been learned?

I'm flattered you like it. I don't dislike it. I just would have picked something else for the compilation at the time, but for some reason Biafra wanted that tune. I guess that we all are prostitutes to one degree or another. I guess it comes down to what one's motivation really is. I wrote those lyrics about those people who the corporate rock industry had made into untouchable gods, who at the same time were churning out meaningless dribble that was supposed to be some heavy thing, because it was they who were putting it out. All form and no content; all personality cult and

no real substance. Phony, hollow rebels driving around in limousines making money for huge corporations . . . but still wearing their blue jeans and "street clothes" for sales credibility. Later on, you'd see mohawks and leather jackets doing the same thing in the 1990s.

Yeah, there's also a lot of it around today as Clear Channel buys up the airwaves and spews out slick, manufactured, sexy, alternative rebelliousness that is censured from singing any antiwar lyrics. Don't kid yourself; the likes of bad boy rebels such as Eminem and Marilyn Manson are on a leash. They can go just so far. The very term "alternative" has been prostituted. I mean, how could Nirvana have been any kind of "alternative" anything? They were the number one record on a huge corporate label with videos shown on corporate TV as they played huge venues and they were still referred to as "alternative" rock? They are still called "alternative rock." What were they an alternative to? I'll tell you what—lesser-known independent groups who were as good or better—that's what. Is alternative music a hairstyle or maybe a leather jacket? Is it just playing fast, using swear words, dressing in drag, or shaking your hair around? I don't think so. If you want to be a Nirvana or Eminem or whatever, that is all fine, but for cryin' out loud at least have the guts to call it what it is, mainstream corporate rock selling a rebellious youth culture image for a big corporate profit. Some of it can be entertaining to listen to, of course, but the only thing it is an "alternative to" is independent noncorporate music. To me, the term "alternative" music was coined for music made by artists that were an alternative to corporate rock. The term is meaningless now and it is no accident.

It seems that unlike Austin, and even Dallas, the Houston punk community is relatively unknown. Yes, bands like the Mydolls, whose member Linda you were once married to, were on the *Cottage Cheese* compilation and AK-47 had some notoriety, but bands like the Egos, Urban Guerillas, Plastic Idols, Recipients, Spys, and the Tix are mostly unknown. Has there always been a historical bias towards the other cities, or was Houston truly second-rate?
Maybe Houston's scene was just *really* underground? [Laughs] Maybe other cities get more support from people with money? Maybe Houston lacks the ability to promote itself? I am not too sure what the problem is. I know that there always have been talented smart people kicking around there. I know that the general mass media across the country seems to ignore the Houston music scene and focuses on Austin. That's why people move to Austin to "be discovered." I was never impressed with anything that came out of Dallas except the Hugh Beaumont Experience. They were wonderful. The Mydolls accomplished everything that they accomplished on their own merit. Yes, my ex-wife was in that band, but aside from a few gigs that we did together, they were independent from Really Red and didn't "ride on our coat tails" in the least. They were out there doing their own thing.

John Paul writes in *Break My Face*, "Really Red was a band committed to freedom of expression, political statement, some misguided opinions, and a lot of volatility . . . Ronnie didn't want to 'sing' anybody else's lyrics so we went along with that as long as we agreed on the content. After all, Ronnie sang, and we played. . . . One thing is for sure: Really Red had integrity and a lot of faults and through that friction came fire." John Paul seems to be suggesting that the other members perhaps didn't share your insight or beliefs. Was there volatility and confrontation when it came to subject matter?
Like I was saying, sometimes there were disagreements. Sometimes there were shouting matches. A lot of times it was about the band's direction or political ideology. Sometimes it was about sorting out current events. Sometimes it was about stupid stuff like who didn't help pack up the gear. Hell, being in a band is like being married to three other people all at the same time. Three times the ups and downs. Three times the haggling and compromising. There always was enough common ground between us to eventually get to an agreement.

Ian from Minor Threat once casually dismissed Really Red as being in their "cow punk" phase by the time they made it to Houston, and your "New Strings" seven-inch does play its part visually, but what led to the change in direction?
I don't know what Ian or you mean by that. Ian never saw us play, to my knowledge. We never consciously changed our direction with the exception of "Just

the Facts, Ma'am," that long industrial piece that we did on the *Rest in Pain* LP. We did a thrashed up country riff on *Teaching You the Fear* called "Bar-B-Cue." That was an early song. That was the closest thing to "country" that we did except occasionally covering Cash's "Folsom Prison" and briefly Johnny Horton's "Battle of New Orleans," but we also did a jacked up version of Petula Clark's "Downtown." We put the phrase "cow punk" on our T-shirts early on because we were from Houston, Texas! Later on it was a term that fit groups like the Hickoids, Grinding Teeth, and Blood on the Saddle much better than it did us, I guess. We never really moved in that direction although we liked it. We loved Merle Haggard, Carl Perkins, and George Jones as much as Flipper, Joy Division, DOA, or anything else.

The photo on the "New Strings for Old Puppets" seven-inch was a bit of sarcasm actually. At the same time, we had a photo of me with my pants down pretending to buttfuck a stuffed calf that we got from somewhere. That was going to be used for some record sleeve or flyer but never was. We tried to keep from being pigeonholed with our music. Hell, we were working on a thrash version of Kurt Weill's "Mack the Knife" at one point.

The only phase we had was the Really Red one. We had our influence, that's for sure, but we tried to create our own niche because ultimately we were doing it for our own pleasure. We were doing songs like "Balance of Terror" and "I Refuse to Sing" while we were sporting cow punk T-shirts and bandanas. It's all an illusion, my friend [laughs].

John Paul went on to say, like the Minutemen, "Really Red as a group worked hard. We practiced every Tuesday, Wednesday, and Sunday afternoon without fail. If you were hung over, pissed off, not feeling good or whatever, there were no good excuses. You showed up, and you played. We were a band that jammed for hours on end. We played stuff we didn't even know what it was. We just jammed. Through the jam we came up with interesting riffs." Yet you've written, "But I do feel that we turned out some good music, for our limited abilities and the somewhat restrictive musical genre we chose." It sounds like you were trying to stretch the envelope, and did, especially when compared to bands like DRI.

J.P. was totally right on. There's no disagreement there. We worked really hard, and we partied really hard, and usually at the same time. I'm very proud of our stuff and I am extremely proud to have been in a group with these three guys. We had our differences and we don't even talk these days *but* listen to those bastards. Killer bass all over the place, frantic freaked-out guitar shit that steps way outside the clichés of punk, and full tilt drum assaults that pushed everything over the top! Like I said, we tried to make our punk rock *our* punk rock. Sometimes we failed and a lot of times we succeeded. We didn't want to be a cliché or a stereotype. What I meant by, our limited abilities and the somewhat restrictive musical genre that we chose, is simply this. No one will mistake Really Red for, say, the Mahavishnu Orchestra, and punk rock isn't a technically complicated genre when it comes to music in general and I wasn't going to give the likes of Tom Jones or Pavarotti any competition on vocals but . . . who gives a fuck, eh? My only regret is that I wished we had gotten down better-produced recordings. But then would that have been in keeping with the spirit of DIY punk rock? Raw is good.

Many people are aware of the Bad Brains incident in Austin when they stayed with the Big Boys, but let's not go there. What were your impressions of the band, since you did have a chance to play with them? How would you compare their music and politics to bands like DOA, the Lewd, Articles of Faith, and many others you shared the stage with?

I thought the band was ferociously good. Technically amazing, too. It was obvious to me that they could have been playing other types of more complicated music prior to being Bad Brains. I didn't like HR much at all on stage or off. He was into that weird Rastafarian religion and he seemed a little fanatical about it. He was very cold and aloof backstage. I don't think he liked "reds." Later I heard about the incident in Austin at Tim's, and it didn't come as a big surprise. I don't know enough about the Bad Brains' politics to comment.

I think the politics of Joey and DOA were and are brilliant and a total inspiration. I have great admiration for that Shithead guy! He's never sold out. Check out his book *I, Shithead: A Life in Punk*. I just saw him a month ago on the twenty-fifth anniversary tour or something. They were like a runaway freight train *still*! Amazing. Articles of Faith were terrific guys and a terrific band. Very progressive politically too. Very intellectual people. Very well read. I just learned that Vic Bondi also lives in the Seattle area now, as I do. The Lewd's politics seemed to be closer to Legionaire's Disease's pure hedonism. It would be impossible to give you my take on the politics of all the groups we played with, and even if I could, who gives a shit what I think about someone else's politics?

All I know is that people had better wake up and get rid of this cabal of corporate fascists who have taken over the country. They are destroying it more each day. This is not even Republicans' business as usual. We've had a rigged election and a bloodless coup. We've had a terrorist attack that somehow the national defense allowed to happen. There were a lot of things that happened on 9/11 that are not being explained and that stink. We've had the invasion of Afghanistan, but Pakistan and the Saudis still have U.S. support. We've had 100 percent total lies to justify the invasion of Iraq and a coup in Haiti. The combined death toll of innocent civilians is up over twenty-five or thirty thousand now. They have antagonized the whole Arab and Muslim world and they blindly support any genocidal thing that Israel does to the Palestinians. They are

hacking away at our civil rights at home and trying to bankrupt the federal government so that they can privatize everything to be run for profit. The Cheney regime is full of insane liars and they have to be sent packing. People better start getting the facts. For starters, I recommend *Democracy Now!* with Amy Goodman on Pacifica Radio or streaming on the Internet. They are one of the very few TV and radio sources of uncensored, real news. Also, foreign news sources like Canadian, and British. The real info is out there if you look.

How did the Really Red cover of "Downtown" finally end up on a seven-inch with unreleased songs by the Hates and Legionaire's Disease?
Well, we used to have a rotating selection of cover songs in our repertoire. We would always have a couple to toss into the set when we felt like it. They were a variety of things: a Sham 69 song, a Stooges song, a Clash song, a New York Dolls song, an MC5 one, and our versions of nonpunk stuff, like things by Johnny Horton, Johnny Cash, or Petula Clark's "Downtown." When Bob was going through tapes that Andy Bradley had, he came across a recording that we had done of our version of "Downtown." We might have recorded it around the time of the *Teaching You the Fear* LP, and it probably should have been originally included on it. I actually like it a lot. Someone approached us about any unreleased material and we gave them that one for a 45 EP pressing.

One fan site gal wrote, "I like U-Ron's advice of not letting anyone grind me down. He's a wise man. I know this isn't the U-Ron life dedication site or like U-Ron fan club, but shit, he knows what's up dammit! However, he told

me once that if you're really passionate about what you do, you're bound to step on someone's toes sooner or later." Lastly, whose toes do you think you've stepped on the way to, well, fulfilling your passions? And, looking back over these past two decades, what are your passions, and how have they changed?

That's two huge questions. I don't know if I can even answer them. There are probably a lot of people's toes that I stepped on getting myself strung out on coke. That was a fucking nightmare that lasted about six years, more than half of which were post–Really Red. I let a lot of people down with that shit, but I let myself down the most. That was a total perversion of passion. Also I'm sure that in the struggle to make Really Red what we were I probably acted like a jerk to a lot of people along the way. Regretfully the list is probably long.

My passion now is to try and understand what being alive is. That's a big old Zen one: the investigation of consciousness, the ancient "understanding myself" bit, the inner personal work. I am passionate about my lady, too. The other thing that I'm still very passionate about is doing what I can to promote freedom and justice—the outer impersonal work. Of course, both of these passions take a lot of learning and that is endless. I'm passionate about my kilt and about a little hell-raising now and again.

Vic Bondi
(Articles of Faith, Alloy)

Having grown up in Rockford, Illinois, a mere seventy miles west of the Windy City, I know the small crowd of punks from the northern prairie state area deeply admired bands like sing-along Naked Raygun and ferociously fast and nimble Articles of Faith, especially since AoF wasn't afraid to wield heavy-duty political sentiments that were avidly debated in the pages of *Maximumrocknroll*. Plus, work like *In This Life* also revealed a deep poetic sensibility. His post-AoF musical trajectory, from Jones Very and Alloy to Report Suspicious Activity and Dead Ending, has percolated with intelligence and integrity as well.

This was originally published in *Maximumrocknroll* and *Trust*.

Both you and the Kinmans from the Dils grew up in military families, yet you espoused ardent leftism that definitely questioned those military value systems. Do you think you would have been so political if your father had not been in the service?
Probably not, but not for the reasons you might imagine. My politics aren't a direct reaction to growing up military. Instead, what growing up in a military family teaches you is a visceral and intuitive suspicion of authority.

My father was a captain in the Navy, and a fairly daunting figure. At one point he was the executive officer of NAS Corry Field in Pensacola, with a

command of about twenty thousand sailors. And he was as much the captain at home as he was on base—strict, authoritarian, and in charge. Except that every two years or so, we'd have to uproot the family, lose all our friends, and move on to another military post.

Not to overly psychologize, but that kind of itinerancy is traumatic when you're a kid. I moved twenty-two times before I was eighteen. And what you learn from it is that no matter how powerful an authority your father might seem to be, there are more powerful authorities capable of dramatically affecting your life, whether you like it or not. That experience breeds a healthy skepticism, and makes you constantly consider the difference between how authority is represented and what it is actually capable of doing. That's the experience that led me left.

Was it hard to reconcile your father with what you have described as an era in which "the 1960s had blown the doors open, Nixon had gone down, and we had lost a colonial war. I thought we'd have a future of reason, peace and prosperity."
Well, my father wanted a future of peace and prosperity, too. Remember that he was in the military during the Cold War, when nuclear war was a real and viable threat. My father could hardly hope for a future of ignorance, war, and poverty. Besides, my father was; and is, something of a progressive. He grew up when GIs had fought the Nazis, so joining the military could easily be interpreted as a progressive act. He supported the Civil Rights Movement when it counted, and has always embraced diversity and tolerance.

That said, he was a Nixon Republican and voted for Reagan, and for a variety of reasons, some of them political, we had a very difficult relationship in the early 1980s. But his attitudes have evolved significantly, and the Bush years caused him to break with a lot of the more regressive attitudes he held at one point—he very much despises Bush and what that administration did to the country and the world. So my father's political opinions and mine—especially today—are less divergent than you might expect.

People who join the military aren't monolithic in their outlook. There are probably soldiers in war zones who become so corrupted and warped by their experience that they emerge full-blown nihilists. But I don't find it difficult to believe that some people joining the military today are, in fact, joining it with idealistic motives—whatever the actual practices of the military as an institution. Members of my family are in the service. They're not fascists.

Some of the political leaders of the last ten years—people like Dick Cheney and Karl Rove—are fascistic in the sense that they have a contemptuous and cynical attitude towards humanity, and that outlook predisposes them to commit the military to adventures such as the morass we are in today in

Asia. Many of them do fundamentally believe that people are innately ignorant (and need to be managed); that war is inevitable (and needs to be proactively engaged); and that poverty is a sign of moral weakness (and therefore the poor need to be isolated and contained). To the extent that members of the military share this toxic philosophy I'd say they are trending fascist, but there are more people outside of the military today who have this witches' brew of outmoded concepts as part of their outlook. These attitudes are becoming more prevalent as our elite push larger and larger groups of people out of the middle class and into poverty—the vicious circle is that people who are the victims of this philosophy become adherents of it, in a vain attempt to manage circumstances that seem beyond their control.

You get a lot of this, even today, in punk rock music and in music subcultures. To some extent, I've always hoped that the music I do can act as a corrective to these attitudes. But I don't know that my father and people like him are the ones I am actually fighting.

An ex-Marine, Mike Sukow, helped finance *What We Want Is Free* and fund shows. Were there other vets that opposed the same traditions you wanted to tear down and support AoF's efforts to use "music to attack the broader conventions of society"?

No, not that I remember. Mike wasn't really a vet; he was an AWOL serviceman. There may have been plenty of punks who were vets for all I knew. I can't remember any who were in punk bands, although there might have been. Most of the vets in those days listened to classic rock. I guess current vets listen to punk; it makes me wince every time I read that GIs play the Ramones or Black Flag during operations in Iraq or Afghanistan.

Like many punks, from Shawn Stern to Biscuit of the Big Boys, you listened to black music growing up, including Marvin Gaye, the O'Jays, Stevie Wonder, and Sly Stone, yet many people continuously describe punk music as a purely white phenomenon. Are there strong links between punk and black cultures (besides Bad Brains, the Clash, etc.) that are routinely ignored or underrepresented, especially if we consider AoF part of a rock tradition that is multiethnic (like Chuck Berry!)?

Well, sure—and it's more than just a rock tradition, especially if you define rock in terms of its musical conventions. People have been singing about their oppression for a very long time, both on the plantations of the antebellum South, and on the factory floors of Victorian England. On the new record we have a tune, "Hammer Song," that begins with a work chant from a Texas prison in 1939. We put it there deliberately, because we were trying to explicitly tie what we do to that tradition.

The biggest single evolution in my thinking over the years has been about how music plays a role in that tradition of resistance. When I was originally in Articles of Faith, I wanted to destroy those traditions—everything . . . I was in my Robespierrean mode, and wanted what we did to define year zero. It's a conceit of youth to assume that you can declare revolution and the world will follow. I'm not young anymore.

If your muse tends to the political, as mine does, then you sooner or later realize you're part of a broader tradition of resistance, and that it will take endurance and generations and stamina. Which is where I'm at now.

As I write this, I'm listening to Sly Stone's "Family Affair," and I think part of what is interesting in your question is how much I love this music and how little it is actually manifest in my music. I simply don't have the voice or chops to be a soul singer, and never bothered to try. So in form, the style of hardcore I've done has almost nothing in common with black musical forms like soul or hip-hop. But the spirit is there. That blues in Sly Stone's voice. I understand that.

In fact, would AoF have existed, at least in the form we know, without you seeing the Bad Brains?
Probably not, given the inspiration they provided. But give the band some credit: we don't sound like the Bad Brains. Dave and Virus and the guys have chops and imagination. I figure we would have found that sound sooner or later.

You went to school in Dekalb, where you formed Direct Drive, barely a half hour from where I grew up in Rockford. There wasn't much of a punk sub-culture there, apart from the Subverts nearby, but was there much underground student radicalism, or any links to Beloit or Madison, that stirred your politics?
No—I wasn't dialed into those student movements directly. They were waning by the time I was in college. The history department at Northern was fairly radical, and that did influence me greatly. The Sixties revisionists made a real impact on me, especially William Appleman Williams. I had started school as an architecture student, but those history classes grabbed me, and I ended up switching majors.

"I wanted to be Joe Strummer," you told one zine, but you never said why. The politics portion might be obvious, but what about musically? In the liner notes to *AoF Complete*, you state you weren't as interested in "reggae, jazz, and funk" as much as the rest of the band. Were you a fan of the Clash's later fusion styles?

No, not really. I think those records are hit and miss. The big Clash record for me was *Give 'Em Enough Rope*. It was one of the first punk records to make it to Pensacola. From the moment I heard that snare shot on "Safe European Home," I was hooked. I learned how to play guitar listening to that record. I learned every riff and chord. The jazz and reggae stuff—that's Dave and Virus and Joe. I didn't get into jazz until after AoF. I was listening to a lot of Miles and Coltrane when I was in Jones Very.

I wanted to be Joe Strummer because he was just the coolest. As a teenager, he was my Elvis. I was lucky enough to meet him a few times and his private persona held up to his public persona. He was engaged and alive. He died too young.

More than once, you've described the irony of the skinhead cliques that were actually the sons of Evanston elites in Chicago, yet have also described the Washington, DC scene as "almost gang-like. And the kids there were suburban brats. But they didn't dress up and act like they were something they weren't." To outsiders, punks often seem to symbolize gang-threats, from the clone style of the Ramones, to the actual gangs at the Fleetwood, to the roving hardcore kids of DC. Do you think that this clannish/tribal behavior was an act of self-preservation, or often family-like—punks helping punks alienated from parents and schools, or were they really thugs?

Well, again, this many decades in, I tend to view those social mores as temporal. Teenagers hang out together. So do young adults. We're social animals, and that clannishness is probably hard-wired into our biology as a selected evolutionary trait.

What's fascinating is how it dissipates as you get older. There just aren't roving gangs of seniors. And the older you get, the weaker you get, so you'd assume that at a visceral level, older people would be more gang-like than kids. But it's not the case.

As you get older, you probably become more aware of the limits and downsides of that natural clannishness. It's a visceral component of conformity, small-mindedness, gossip, racism, and nationalism. Most people drop it from their behavioral set, or sublimate it productively into small-group relationships like families and work teams. Assuming that pack behavior is biological doesn't mean we're bound to it. Quite the opposite.

You've spoken at length about Hüsker Dü, from Bob's recording techniques to their drug habits to their personal ups and downs. In some ways, did they become the Black Flag of the Midwest, shaping touring networks, the sound of records, and the lore? You admitted, "I don't think there is a real DIY ethic without them, Toxic Reasons and DKs too."

I don't know that they were just the Black Flag of the Midwest. Like Flag, their constant touring and support of other bands was national in scope. They were certainly key to the scene in the Midwest though. They were really the first guys out of the box.

Looking back, were you aware of any ambivalence regarding the sexuality of Bob and Grant? Having worked with both Gary Floyd and Biscuit, I have become much more aware of homophobia in hardcore, which Dave Dictor suggests is the result of the younger kids being part of "crews" that really didn't have links to 1970s punk.

I don't know what it is like now. If hardcore kids today are homophobic, I'm not at all surprised. I was pretty homophobic when I was a teenager. In some ways it's a natural, if abhorrent, effect of the complexity of sexuality, and the overwhelming force that sexuality plays in the lives of young people. Sex is kind of scary when it is the subject of every other waking thought. It was for me. You try and box it in, and attach it to conventional objects.

Homosexual desire is all the more difficult because of the overwhelming force society places on heterosexual convention. So boys in particular try and fence this stuff in, or laugh it off—I'm sure "that's so gay" is still a mainstay of the conversation of boys.

Since hardcore was, and probably still is, a very homosocial subculture, this denial and panic can become pretty acute. We all know someone who is intensely homophobic precisely because he is so attracted to the same gender. In a more open society this would be less of an issue, which is why we have to work for a more open society.

I don't even remember when Bob told me he was gay. But it was pretty important to me in terms of helping me get past my own anxieties about sexuality. Bob put to rest a lot of stereotypes I was walking around with. Hopefully that is happening a lot more these days.

As a teenager, I denied how intensely drugs and alcohol were woven into the fabric of the hardcore movement. Until I heard stories about Hüsker Dü, MDC, and many others, I didn't realize the cost. No doubt people like Sid Vicious and Johnny Thunders symbolized this, but do you feel that the toll on hardcore punks is much greater than we realize? For instance, even Pete Hines in Alloy . . .

Well, Pete was an alcoholic, and if you're keeping score, booze has ruined a lot more musicians than drugs. I don't know that hardcore is any different here than jazz or rock. There's a lot of theories out there about how creative people self-medicate, or are drawn to dope because of their brain chemistry. I just finished a book, *Pandora's Seed,* where the author argued that creative people are similar to schizophrenics, and therefore likely to use drugs. I've definitely experienced people whose physical tendencies made them addicts. Pete was a physical alcoholic—you could actually see the way booze would transform him. And I know depressives who are physically unable to function without their meds.

Still, I'm not sure I buy the connection between drugs and creativity. The convention is that genius and madness are proximate, and therefore creation and hallucination [are] linked. I saw a lot of guys try and cop to a lifestyle image via drugs, and it didn't have a lot of direct connection to their creativity. In the case of a lot of people I knew, like Grant Hart, it destroyed it. Bob became a better musician after he gave dope up. And Ian and Biafra have never touched the stuff. So I don't know how important it is for real creativity.

In Texas, three of the major clubs in three cities—Raul's, Tacoland, and the Island—were Hispanic-owned. You were able to use a performance space owned by Guatemalans (the Centro-America Social Club?). In LA, there was the Vex. There seems to be a link between marginalized groups— Hispanics and punks that were able to work together. How important was it for AoF to play outside the bar/club scene of Tuts, COD, and Metro, which you played as well?

It was crucial for AoF. But I'm not sure it was for the scene. The Chicago bar scene was open to punk: OZ, O'Banion's, Exit, Club COD, Lucky Number, Tuts, Metro—there were a lot of places to play, and AoF played all those bars. But most of those places were over-age, and if you wanted to play for and with the kids, you had to put on your own all-ages shows. So we did it. But the scene didn't need it. When AoF broke up, the shows stopped. So, clearly the DIY scene wasn't that important for the other bands, who kept playing the bars.

I do think you're romanticizing the inclusiveness of the scene. There's a pretty healthy Hispanic hardcore scene in Chicago today, but there wasn't in 1984. The Guatemalans didn't hang around for the shows. Which is not to say that they couldn't—they just didn't. We paid them, and that was about the limit of their interest in what we were doing.

Your critiques of John Kezdy have been detailed and forthright (he's "temperamentally and aesthetically a conservative . . . defending the status quo"), and in recent years the politics of Leonard (the Dickies), Dave Smalley (Dag Nasty, Down by Law), and John Paul (Really Red) have caused much ire in the left-wing side of punk.

How should we cope with such differences, which were felt even early on, like your *MaximumRnR* interview with Ian MacKaye and Dave Dictor? Is there a common ground between the Mentors and Meatmen and Crucifix and False Prophets?

No, there isn't. Other than musical convention, there wasn't a lot of common ground back then. Conservatives like Tesco Vee *hated* AoF. He probably still does. God knows there are more than a few of those guys who still hate me. It's actually more uncommon that you get along with someone from that end of the spectrum—Dave Smalley, for instance.

There was always a heavy right-wing movement in punk. The Sex Pistols were ambiguous enough in their politics that their fanbase went both ways. Even today I'm astonished that people misinterpret me. When AoF played in Germany, we had one show where some guy kept throwing up the *seig heil* as we were playing "Remain in Memory." So he was interpreting the line "Remember me!" in a way I had never intended.

Punk and hardcore are not intrinsically expressions of political resistance. So it's a mistake to try and lump all the bands from then into that category. More

often, those positions evolve over time, which is why I like Fugazi a lot more than Minor Threat. You've got people like me, Biafra, and Dave Dictor who have been pretty consistent in their perspective over the years—but none of us were born that way, and none of us are dogmatists.

I think one of the saddest things I experienced was touring with Born Against in Germany. They were dogmatic and severely judgmental, part of that punk fundamentalist direction MRR took in the late '80s. They just couldn't accept that we drank, or ate meat. They imputed all sorts of "sell-out" motives to us because we wouldn't toe their ideological line. It's pretty hard to take that anywhere—you end up in a puritan cult and check your compassion and reason at the door.

I certainly understand the perspective that says that compromises with the status quo end up compromising your commitments—he who fucks nuns joins the church. But you can become a monster the other way, too: when your politics become so dogmatic that you become intolerant of the broader human-ity—the *evolving* humanity—of people, you've lost the whole reason to resist the status quo, because that's ultimately what the status quo does.

In *AoF Complete*, you discuss the issue of resistance—the electrifying romantic defiance of G7 rioters, Attica prisoners, and even Woody Guthrie. Many people have described punk as folk music: music by and for the people, about the topical issues of the day. You seem to feel that AoF was part of the continuum. Did the other members of the band see it similarly, or were they more interested in aesthetics? I know Dave was a heavy metal fan, but Virus and Bill were more ideological.

I'm not sure how the guys view the band's place in that continuum of resist-ance. I will say that when we got together for the new record and rehearsals for Riot Fest, it immediately clicked for us. There's an unconscious sync that we have at a musical—and political—level. We picked up immediately where we left off. It feels pretty good.

We'll have to see how the reunion plays out, but I wouldn't be disap-pointed if we kept the band as a recording project for the next few years. It feels great to play with them again.

Does your work with Tom Morello, and your own cover of "Fortunate Son," pay homage to this ideal more than, say, the last AoF record, which seemed steeped in abstract poetry?

I'm reluctant to overthink it. I've been playing music for over thirty years, in four different bands and as a solo act. The stuff with Tom fits into that. With all the differences between what I've done, it still feels like a fairly cohesive body of work.

Two of your more adamant declarations are worth exploring. "The record industry deserves to die." But isn't the record industry partly responsible for delivering bands like Elvis Costello, the Ramones, and the Clash, into your life? Is there no room for an industry that can be remade for the new era?

As far as I'm concerned, the deeply capitalist record industry does deserve to die. For every Elvis, Ramones, and Clash, there's a Night Ranger, Britney Spears, or Lady Gaga. The dimensions and goals of this industry are inhuman and designed to exploit the talent and industry of some people for the overarching benefit of some other people, who in my experience lack imagination and passion.

The exciting thing about digital technology is that it has shattered the monopoly on distribution and creation that the music industry used to have. It opens a whole new space to folk music: people who can make music in their basement, and put it on the web for people to consume. Already this is happening. People are finding each other and the sounds that appeal to them without intermediaries and middlemen. It's very exciting, and produces a lot more interesting music than the old record industry, which is desperately clinging to the last vestiges of the celebrity industry à la *American Idol*). Last.fm has more interesting music than radio. And most of the bands there are unsigned.

If the record industry dies, will Alternative Tentacles go with it? I know you've argued, "Independent labels can be as rapacious and greedy as major labels. Jade Tree never did right by me."

Well, yes, AT is struggling, like a lot of independents. They had to cut back when the recession hit. But I find it interesting that people are more than ready to pay for the music they hear on independent labels. A lot of people understand that these labels have a direct relationship to the bands, and the money they pay for a download goes more directly to the bands.

Truth of the matter is that no one really needs a label anymore. You can do it yourself. AoF and RSA worked with AT more out of solidarity for the broader goals of the label than need—that, and I'm kind of lazy. I haven't updated my own website in about four years.

"You need to look no further than Christian radio stations to realize the complete bankruptcy of embracing the hardcore sound without the hardcore ethic." In this Internet-teeming, easy-download era, can the ethic remain the same as in the hardcore years? For instance, how can we maintain them when, as Devo recently argued, music itself has been culturally devalued and nobody wants to really pay for it?

All content has been culturally devalued—but that's because it was overvalued. Writing, making music, and storytelling certainly sometimes rise to the level of art and have the ability to evolve and transform attitudes and lives, but I don't feel they are really equivalent to science or technology. There's no rock'n'roll without electricity. And electricity can do a lot more than power amps. So let's keep this in perspective.

Digital technology is now democratizing the creation and dissemination of art and entertainment, and that's a good thing. We overpaid and overvalued it in the past—in part because it was so directly tied to an industrial process that enforced scarcity and elevated prices.

Talent and creativity are almost ubiquitous. Everyone has a story. The more people are able to frame and structure that story, the more they understand themselves and their place in the world. The fact that certain lucky individuals can't make obscene amounts of money telling their story anymore doesn't bother me in the slightest. Their stories and their lives were never that much more worthwhile and important than the rest of us.

I know a lot of people, like Bob or Kristen Hirsh, who've managed to have a pretty good life playing music with modest returns. They would play music even if they got paid less. It's what they love. I've never made a living at music, and I'm still doing it. For thirty years. Because I value it, regardless of the broader culture.

If the record industry disappears tomorrow, it's no cause for worry. People will tell stories. They will share them digitally and in person—hell, the live concert business has never been more profitable. People want to get together and share their lives and their passion for life.

Digital technology has the potential to really deliver on hardcore, precisely because hardcore was never specifically about the musical genre. It was about a host of great ideas, expressed in the music: drive, passion, anger, intelligence, and hope. Some of that is unique to youth, and some of it you can grow with. But all of it is generally translatable to other musical genres and forms of expression. We listened to more Johnny Cash in the van on tour than anyone else. He was hardcore before there was hardcore. And that attitude will outlast and survive the specific musical genre of hardcore that I was and am associated with.

Lisa Fancher
(Frontier Records)

Longtime punk fan, writer, and label owner Fancher is one of the most under-the-radar, important punk women in history. Although she never sang bellicose lyrics for a tumult'n'frenzy band or garnered attention in the fashion-punk pages of *Flipside*, her hard efforts to release albums by iconic bands like TSOL, Suicidal Tendencies, Circle Jerks, and Adolescents remain seminally important to documenting the Southern California hardcore explosion. People may disagree about her business policies or even later tastes, but they cannot argue with the merit of Frontier, a label that created a kind of maximum tour de force in the early 1980s.
    Originally printed in *Left of the Dial*.

Your label history is a bit cloudy at the beginning. You borrowed some money—was it $200?—to begin the label, beginning with a band whose record and chance at success evaporated right away. What really happened?

Actually, I didn't borrow any money. That was the weird thing. But let me start from the beginning. Besides working in a shitty suburban record store called Licorice Pizza, I spent post–high school life working at Bomp! Records (all props go to Greg and Suzy Shaw, who were my saviors). Working for an indie label meant I knew all the various steps to putting out records, and even distribution, but it didn't occur to me to do it myself initially because Greg was so on top of the local scene as evidenced by the Weirdos, Zeros, Devo . . . I got paid very sporadically because *they* got paid very sporadically, so sometimes I would get a paycheck for $1,500! Of course that might have been for two and a half months, don't be too impressed! Besides my crummy fanzine, *Biff!Bang!Pow!* I also wrote for the *LA Herald-Examiner* and made a few bucks reviewing cool touring/local bands or picking on clay pigeons like Styx and Pat Benatar. (My boss was Ken Tucker, who's now the "TV guy" at *Entertainment Weekly*.)

In short, I was floating around with no particular aim or purpose in life other than buying records and going to shows. When I interviewed the Flyboys for the *Herald-Examiner*, they said they had no label so I thought: What the heck, I could do that. Of course I ran it by Greg to make sure I had his blessing. He wasn't that fired up about the punk scene by '79, so I decided to take the band in the studio. We recorded in the middle of the night at Leon Russell's Shelter studio in the San Fernando Valley. The engineer was Jim Mankey (Sparks, Concrete Blonde) and the producer was Scott Goddard, who had a couple songwriting credits on Dickies' earliest songs (Johnette Napolitano answered the phone at Shelter!). Since I was paying Jim and Scott under the table, the rate was fine, and it was a seven-song EP. When it was mixed, it didn't sound so great, but that wasn't the point—I was Cecilia B. DeMille! The Flyboys record was started in mid-1979, and I finally released it in March of 1980. Naturally the band broke up before it came out. If I had a lick of sense, I would have just chalked it up to experience and moved on. Since I had zero chance of being accepted into college and subsequently getting a "real" job, I just decided to stick with it. So, I didn't borrow money from anyone. I used my various paychecks, if and when they came in!

First, what drew you so specifically to the Orange County hardcore scene? Was it simply because it was underdocumented at the time, or because the music was so dynamite and damaged? Fewer women ended up as part of the scene, correct?

I regularly drove down to Huntington Beach in the late 1970s to see bands, especially British bands like the Damned and Magazine, play at the Cuckoo's Nest. In LA, you usually get a bunch of people standing around with their arms crossed, like "impress me." Down there, people went apeshit, so it was way more fun, other than the hour plus drive back and forth to my house in the valley. I think I was telling Andy Schwartz at *NY Rocker* about how the punk scene had mutated, and he had me write a story about it—"The New Beaches," which I wrote months before but was published in September of 1980. By then there was a fully fledged OC scene, and it sounded completely different than the first wave of LA punk bands. I think the Adolescents embodied what was going on the best: great melodies, mighty guitar playing, not overtly political or "art school," not influenced by British punk bands. I liked to think of OC punk as a backlash against that fuckin' asshole Ronald Reagan: the suburbs' furious sons and daughters rising up. In retrospect, it was just the younger kids interpreting punk and making it their own.

I was pretty unique in that, since my earliest days. I was a record collector and writer. I basically never thought about anything except rock'n'roll! Maybe I should have joined a band, but that, honestly, didn't interest me as much as documenting the local scene. In the original LA scene, there were lots of girls in bands (even all-girl bands), but you're right, the nascent OC hardcore scene was virtually female-free. I never thought of the reason why. Ask an academic, which I am most definitely not!

Were you at all concerned about the violence that had plagued the scene starting as far back as the Bags' art gallery show onwards to the infamous Elks Lodge incident?

Of course I was concerned. Violence is always deplorable and unnecessary. You have to separate the actual fighting, which oftentimes was considerable, from the slam pit. To the outsider, that might *seem* like violence, but it was a completely visceral reaction to the music coming from the stage—a few bruises here and there, no problem. Fighting was not prevalent in the X/Weirdos/Screamers era. The beach punk hardcore scene was young and a high-testosterone scene, alas there were kids that were morons and came to shows with the goal of landing punches. A lot of this centered about the Huntington Beach crowd, but I also witnessed gnarly fights in Long Beach, San Pedro, Hollywood, and the SF valley. The most common was a pack of punk rockers chasing after a long-hair, but they certainly liked to fight with each other too, make no mistake! These morons were also responsible for shutting down the Whisky (throwing bottles at the police) and causing many other venues to ban punk rock or specific bands like Black Flag.

Elks Lodge was a whole 'nother matter. I was at that show, and the police went berserk on the crowd for no reason! I'm far from a conspiracy freak, but it genuinely seemed like the LAPD was trying to eradicate punk rock. They showed up at the most obscure venues and always used excessive force on the crowd, not to mention threats and intimidation on the club owners and pro-moters. I remember the night that *The Decline of Western Civilization* opened on Hollywood Boulevard. We were standing in a long line, and dozens of police showed up in SWAT gear! They closed the boulevard and lined up across the street in formation, waiting for some action. When nothing happened, they goose stepped up to the line and started shoving us. Still no action . . . I was close to the end of the line, and there's nothing quite as panic-inducing as an LA police officer with a riot shield shoving his baton into your back, let me tell you! I guess I should count my blessings that they didn't shoot me, I guess.

Did you ever worry that by promoting bands like the Adolescents and China White, you were in some ways part and parcel of what was becoming a very violent scene that drew less from older city hipsters and more from the suburban skate scenes? Keith Morris says that he would routinely stop shows when fights occurred, thus trying to somehow avoid the conundrum.
To me, the bands were not responsible for the fans' behavior. They were never up there instigating kids to fight, and if they did, I would have had nothing to do with them to begin with. They just played their sets and had no control over the small percentage of boneheads that ruined some shows. Tony Cadena and Mark Martin would definitely stop shows if there was a fight, but from on stage it's often hard to differentiate an enthusiastic slam pit from a punch out. When the dance floor clears and the crowd stampedes for the exits, then you got trouble! The very first time I saw TSOL at Devonshire Downs in Northridge, the crowd literally pulled Jack into the audience and beat the shit out of him. Mike Roche brained someone with his bass to get him to let go of Jack! Maybe it was the clown make-up and dress Jack was wearing? Anyhow, no one was immune to the violence, not even those who were on stage.

Yes, the Adolescents did have a song that bemoaned violence, but they also sang "When we become one/the violence never ends" on "Wrecking Crew," which, in addition to being on the Frontier record, ended up on the very popular BYO compilation *Somebody Got Their Head Kicked In.* It's a great Rezillos song, but the title says enough.
I would never, ever interpret any lyrical intent from anyone I've ever worked with. Probably what I think isn't even true at all! "Wrecking Crew" could be a fantasy, could be poking fun at violent types they've known. I'll pass the floor to the Adolescents!

Looking back through *We Got the Neutron Bomb*, you are noticeably missing, even though Frontier was a major player. Could you discuss why Brendan Mullen overlooked you?
Ahhh, do we have to go there? Brendan and I are friends. I just spoke to him on the phone yesterday. We had an unfortunate screaming match in his backyard as I was waiting to be interviewed by the Experience Music Project people, around 1999 maybe, who had set up their cameras in his rehearsal studio. He

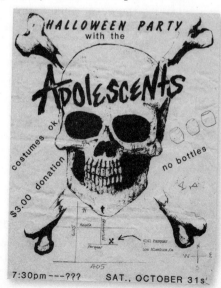

was telling me that I was the enemy, that I was fake, and that I only liked pop music. Of course I like pop music. I love pop music! I like all music that doesn't suck! Anyhow, I think I called him a pseudointellectual twat and rip-off and struggled for a slur against Scottish people. It was ugly, and we scared the holy hell out of those nice people from Seattle. So, a couple years later, I hear he's doing this book with Marc Spitz, who had originally contacted me about an interview for the book. I'm an excellent holder of grudges (too excellent), so I said I wouldn't do an interview until he apologized. He did finally apologize and everything is happy face now. Unfortunately, it was very late in the interview process, so I think most of my quotes had probably been said by someone else. Cliff Roman's the guy who really should be pissed; he wasn't even interviewed, though he founded the Weirdos and wrote the song "Neutron Bomb"!

One of the least-discussed aspects of Frontier records is the incredible label art, whether we talk about the painting from the Circle Jerks "Group Sex," the bold minimalism of the Adolescents self-titled record, or the legendary photographs that fill the Suicidal Tendencies album. Like the early UK punk bands, did you have an aesthetic in mind, or did you let the designers work freely?

Thanks for noticing that, I get no respect! Being a psycho record collector, album cover art is *really* important to me, almost as important as the music in many ways. Besides being lucky enough to work at Bomp! and learn the record releasing game firsthand (Greg and Suzy were very patient with my personal calls to pressing plants and printers), I tapped their graphic artist, Diane Zincavage, to do my first twelve album covers, posters, and print ads. We worked really well together, the band or I usually had a basic idea, and Diane would always come up with something a million times better than I ever hoped for. For instance, the concept of the Adolescents album cover was "we want it to look like generic supermarket packaging," so she gave us the boring Ralph's font but added the eye-popping magenta-on-blue color scheme that said *buy me, now*. She patiently hand-painted the Circle Jerks photo and wrote all their lyrics in the style of their logo, which they had before they ever met me. I also was lucky enough to know the most talented punk photographers in town—Edward Colver and Glen E. Friedman! Glen brought Suicidal to me (several times, I turned them down) and even better—he documented their fans' homemade shirts, which I think were a huge aspect of their aesthetic, and shot the classic album photo of them strung up on a jungle gym.

Jack from TSOL once told me, "If you look back at our early contracts, they're signed in blood. It was like, hey, watch this. We'd throw contracts down the toilet, and say we didn't care. We didn't understand anything

about the business, we never had a lawyer, we didn't ask about publishing, we had nothing, they took everything."

I don't know, or care, if Jack's referring to me. I gave bands a contract based on our original conversations, if they didn't take it to a lawyer and didn't want to sign it, it was entirely their choice. I was hardly a shark in a three-piece suit. I lived at home with my parents and paid for their records myself. I insisted that contracts be signed before we started a record, and they were. A one-off for a band is a pretty good deal, however you slice it. Most labels tie them up for years. Knowing I was a person with a day job who did not have much to offer them besides making that record, I didn't push my luck. The reason I copublished is because I didn't know if I would recover my original investment *and* because it was a one-off record. It worked out okay for both of us in the end, but y'know, if Jack regrets it, what can I do? I have to say that a lot of the bands I worked with are still around and still popular, and I think a little, if not a lot, of that has to do with the fact that I kept the records in print all these years.

Did bands like TSOL only sell about two thousand records a year, sometimes a thousand within the first few weeks, even though they were playing up to three thousand people at the Olympic?

Not sure what you're asking here. Did they play to many more people than ever bought their records? Definitely. *Dance with Me* did very well, but it was nowhere near the local icon that *Group Sex* or Adolescents' blue album was. It was, dare I say it, more sophisticated and goth than the Posh Boy EP, and that threw some of their original fans off.

If possible, I'd like you to respond to more of Robbie's comments, all freely found on the web, just to set the "history" straight: "When I saw how my artifacts were arranged (in the *Forming* exhibit), I almost pulled everything out. They finally pacified me by changing one or two descriptions on the wall, one of which claimed that Lisa Fancher discovered the OC scene. In the late '90s, Fancher made this ridiculous attempt to follow up her stealing artists from my label by then getting me written out of the punk histories. Just pathetic."

Huh? I was lucky to be included in *Forming*, and I dropped off a good amount of Frontier archive materials, and only a portion of it was used. I had *no* idea what the captions would be for my stuff, let alone anyone else's. I was following the OC scene from the beginning, but I did not "discover" it. I never stole Robbie's bands. I never tried to write him out of punk history. He's nuts.

"*Group Sex* took off like a rocket, of course, especially with 'Wild in the Streets' getting airplay. Of course, it was not on *Group Sex*, but it made

them. Then TSOL carried on with the allegations of nonpayment of royalties within a month of their record being released and used that as their rationale for having secretly recorded for Frontier while they were supposed to record a second EP for me."

Those were not allegations! Any local fanzine, from *Flipside* on down, had many interviews with bands saying Robbie never paid them. Please. It was the one consistent thing you could get bands to agree on! TSOL weren't "secretly" recording for me. They told Robbie to fuck off. So did the Jerks, so did the Adolescents. How many masters has he had to return to his artists for nonpayment of royalties? Social Distortion and Agent Orange spring to mind. I'm sure there's more. How many Frontier-originated masters have I had to return? Zero.

Interviewer: "Didn't Lisa Fancher pimp out her good releases to Epitaph a few years ago, only to now reclaim them?" Robbie: "She sold one then licensed the rest and, as you say, has now reclaimed those others."

I did sell the *Dance with Me* record to Brett when he made me an offer I couldn't refuse. Presumably it was to keep it away from Bryan Holland, who he was having a considerable feud with when they left Epitaph for Sony. I did license the two Jerks records, the Adolescents, Suicidal, and Christian Death to Epitaph from 1996–99 after two earlier distribution deals left my company in tatters. Epitaph didn't work out for me either. I walked into it with eyes open. It seemed like the right thing to do. Oh well! It was a licensing deal. It ended, and I got my records back, eventually, except for *Wild in the Streets*, which belongs to the Jerks. Those other records are going to be on Frontier and Frontier only from here on out.

"And so incredibly, I actually put Greg and Lisa Fancher together and she got *Group Sex* and I put my money into the Crowd's *A World Apart* album. The Jerks for their part refused to finish the other tracks they had already recorded for me, except for *Wild in the Streets*, which went on *ROTR*. It was only on the second album that they rerecorded 'Wild in the Streets.' Worse was to come, when I went to England for Christmas 1980, behind my back Lisa offered this $10,000 deal to the Adolescents (it really wasn't, she was counting all the costs!) and I felt stole them from under my nose. She then followed by poaching TSOL from me. Incredible, and I had put her into the punk business."

Oh for gawd's sake . . . You almost have to pick every word in this paragraph apart to separate the falsehoods! I met Greg Shaw when I was still in high school. I wrote for *Bomp!* magazine (remember that fabulous Runaways cover article?) in the mid-1970s, then I went to work in Greg and Suzy's store in 1977, then I worked in the mail-order division from '78 to '81. *Group Sex* came to me because I called Lucky Lehrer in mid-1980, I heard they had a finished master and were looking for someone to put it out. We made a deal, I put it out. As for the Adolescents, I got a call from Frank Agnew when I was working at Bomp! They wanted to make an album and did not want to work with Robbie again after the way he treated them while recording "Amoeba." Their manager at the time, Eddie from Eddie and Subtitles, took off with the advance—$1,500. I then had to save up another $1,500 before I could take them in the studio. $10,000 advance?! That's the wildest story I've heard from him yet. They made that record in *three days*. Frank and Tony were also my unofficial A&R men and pointed TSOL (and China White and Christian Death) my way. TSOL didn't want to work with Robbie again after the EP. Truly, if Robbie had been respectful of his artists and paid them, none of them would have come to me. There was no need to poach his bands. They were done working with him. If I didn't have a label, they would have gone *anywhere* else—he (or I) was not the only game in town. As anybody can see, the albums I did with previous Posh Boy artists were one-offs. Did they leave Frontier and return to his label? No. These were also nonexclusive deals. They could have recorded different songs for Posh Boy the same month or year they recorded for me! How sad that after all these years he still dwells on *me* ruining his life instead of even considering that his own behavior produced the consequences he blames me for.

Commentary on Robbie Fields from a Few Noted Persons

John Roecker

Hello, my name is John Roecker and I was the curator for the *Forming* show at Track 16 a hundred years ago. I just need to make one thing clear: I did not know Lisa Fancher at the time of the show, only knew of her. And what I knew of Ms. Fancher was this woman that put out the classic punk albums of the Orange County scene. You could not touch her or her label, and I myself was an observer, a fan at the time. I put in the description—Lisa Fancher, owner of Frontier Records, put out the most important records by the most important bands from Orange County. Now, to me, this seemed to be an accurate quote and came from how I felt. Well, when Mr. Fields saw this he blew into a rage and demanded I take this down, which I had to do. The idea that Lisa herself wrote this is insane. It was my quote and I still (as the majority of the world) agree with this statement. Thank you.

Greg Shaw

Robbie arrived late on the LA scene. Nobody had ever seen him before he appeared as the, usually drunk, door man at the Masque in, what, 1977? I had been involved in punk rock for many years before that, but if anyone could be said to have their "ear to the ground" it was Lisa, who I met when she was in high school publishing a sort of glam magazine, at least as early as 1973. Even then her taste in music was impeccable. Any band she told me about invariable turned out to be important somewhere down the line. She was the one who told me about the OC scene first, bands like TSOL, Agent Orange, the Adolescents, the Circle Jerks, etc. You should probably talk with these bands about the events concerned, since I wasn't a party, but I can certainly confirm that Lisa was not in any position to offer large sums of money to bands or to wheel and deal in those days—she was working for Bomp! helping out in the mail room, and believe me we didn't pay very much!

Like many people, myself included, historic events tend to become cloudy in memory, and to take on a self-serving cast. I know I didn't "invent" punk rock, for instance, but enough people have told me that I did, that I sometimes don't mind hearing it.

Robbie was very astute at signing bands (that is, he signed everyone he could), although he didn't have any money either. At the time, I couldn't even afford to make albums, so I would sign bands for one single at a time. Most of us were in the same boat. So, I can perfectly understand someone like the Jerks doing a track for a Robbie compilation, then leaping at Lisa's (quite generous and risky on her part, except for her faith in the band) readiness to do a full album with them. But my clear memory is that in those early days of punk, when none of us had any money, the spirit was predominantly one of coopera-tion between bands and labels. There were enough great bands for every label, and more. My recollection is that Lisa discovered and recorded most of her bands long before they passed to people like Robbie. But there are individual cases of course. However, I have never known, and could not believe, Lisa to be capable of any unethical behavior.

Also, both Lisa and Robbie were frequent visitors to the Bomp! offices, and while I could sense some jealousy on Robbie's part, I recall no controversy about any band having been stolen (by either of them) from another label. I should also add that Robbie was always honorable (though shifty in his own lovable way) in any business we did together, such as the Nuns album.

For what it's worth, I'd like to add this two cents to the discussion.

Tony Cadena

TSOL and China White were turned on to Lisa by me. I used to go see both bands quite regularly and had their demos. I clearly remember telling Lisa about both bands. Frank may have also done the same.

As for Christian Death, I knew them through the Pomona people—Toxic Shock (now Toxic Ranch in Arizona, back then in Pomona, CA, where Rozz, George, and James were from)—but I never told Lisa about them because I

thought they were too corny. I think it may have been Rikk's involvement that got Lisa's interest.

The blue record was recorded in Sun Valley over a weekend. We ate food from a taco truck for the most part, and Lisa treated me better than I deserved. I remember we all stayed at a little hotel in one room. It was the first time in my life I had actually stayed in one.

Robbie Fields was given a one-off song. We were very aware of his reputation and would never give him anything more than a song. Actually, that wasn't for Robbie, it was for Rodney. We thought Robbie was just the point man for a compilation record. We realized later that he was more than just the contact person, but we felt we owed a lot to Rodney for supporting the band when no one else did, so we followed through. At the time, Rodney was calling us to facilitate the meetings, including having us talk to Robbie, and at one point Kim Fowley.

Robbie and his engineer were absolutely dreadful to work with. They sent us out to grab some food once they got the tracks they needed, and then locked us out of the studio! So, there we were in West Hollywood, food for the chicken hawks, until they were finished mixing. We felt pretty humiliated by the whole experience. I think we ran into Tar at the burger place, and he gave us a ride over to the Starwood in his cab.

Although Robbie tried desperately to get us to lay down more songs when we were there—live—we had said no. We knew some of the Simpletones, Rik L. Rik, the Crowd, Red Cross, and they all suggested we wait for someone else.

Any other story, such as his leaving town and that Lisa swiped us from him, is just Robbie having a wet one.

Lisa researched us independently of Robbie, having traveled to see us at a couple OC parties and the Hong Kong Café (where she approached us about a record). Frank loved Lisa because she knew the Quick. I talked to the Flyboys and the Circle Jerks about Lisa, and they said she was cool: bottom line, straight up.

The advance was $1,000. Eddie spent it. He then proceeded to invoice us the entire amount for drugs he said we spent the advance on and stuck the invoices in our mailboxes for our parents to read! What a guy. It said stuff like, "Quaaludes, $100, Black Beauties, $350." So, my mother had no idea what this all meant. She thought we spent it on black hookers!

"Wrecking Crew," quite simply, is about tearing down the existing social order of 1979–1980. Nothing more or less. Teen angst, high school style. We were very much against punk-on-punk violence.

Steve and I wrote that song on the telephone. He brought the idea to the table, and we wrote it up in about twenty minutes. The song is more an anthem to survival (suicide is no way out, running away from home doesn't solve the problem) and joining a more tribal and basic primal pattern (join our primitive way of fun).

"The violence never ends" simply refers to the mindless smashing of things, not of hurting people. To get an accurate idea of what we meant, think more along the lines of *Peter Pan*, not along the lines of the *Lord of the Flies*.

Keep in mind that we were all a pretty wimpy bunch of guys, and the original lineup of the band in 1979–1980 still went to church on Sunday mornings. John, in fact, went to parochial school. Frank had a five-inch tail of hair that he bobby pinned under a baseball cap so his dad wouldn't know he was slightly off center, so there you go.

The title of the BYO thing was a BYO thing. Those songs of ours were from a demo recorded two years before the other bands on the record, and Frank submitted them. I would have never agreed to it at the time (though I'm quite fond of the Stern Bros., I didn't think our stuff fit on their compilation).

Dave Dictor
(MDC)

I first cornered Dave Dictor at a coffee shop gig in Eugene, Oregon, when the band reunited the original lineup of the band, serving up incisive, pithy, reenergized versions of their dizzying earliest material. I videotaped Dictor at length that night discussing the band's tumultuous past, which became a key portion of my documentary *Chronicles from the Zero Hour*. Later, we discussed matters further on the phone, attempting to begin a larger, nuanced band history project. MDC's blitzing blend of rage and humor bridged the world of late punk and early hardcore, and their wide-encompassing issues, from homophobia and "radioactive chocolate" to marijuana decriminalization and racist police forces, remains ever-potent and controversial. Meanwhile, their career continues, like a stone that gathers no moss.

This interview is previously unpublished.

I saw an archive photo of the iconic club Raul's in Austin, Texas, with "No War No KKK No Fascist USA" spray-painted on it. Did the band graffiti on tour too?

It's from our song, "Born to Die." There's a picture from *Spin* magazine from 1983 when we spray-painted on a wall, and they took a picture of it. In between all the post–classic rock stuff they had, "New bands that are coming along," and blurbs on us or bands like the Misfits or Bad Brains. It wouldn't be a whole article, but it would be in the beginning section.

They ran a picture of the four of us with the "No War No KKK No Fascist USA."
We were just planning a shot, and we brought up a can of spray paint with us.
They said, why don't you stand up against the wall, and we said hold it, and
we sprayed that line there, so it was kind of a thing we had done on purpose
a bunch of different times. There we were, and we realized we were getting a
national audience, so we sprayed.

**One theory is: graffiti creates do-it-yourself media. Is that how you saw it,
or perhaps as more criminal?**
We didn't think of it as criminal, though I was arrested in New York City for
spray-painting Millions of Dead Cops on a subway wall, and I went through the
Tombs. It took me three days to go from different precincts to different precincts. Eventually, I ended up in a place called the Tombs, where basically you
start out chained together with all the other prisoners, and you work your way
up, and you finally get out to court. There I was literally on the bench with all
these momma rapers and sister rapers, these people with blood all over them,
pretty harsh people, and there I was for graffiti. In fact, while I was in jail, all
those guys there were like, "Graffiti? I want your baloney sandwich." So, I'd just
give them my bologna sandwich.

Was that during the Rock Against Reagan tour?
It was Memorial Day, 1983. MDC went on tours in 1982 and 1983, where we'd go
across country, and we had friends in New York City, the guys from Cause for
Alarm and the people from Reagan Youth. We would stay in their apartments
for a month or two and actually recorded the "Multi-Death Corporation" single
with Papa Jerry, who's in the *American Hardcore* movie. We'd stay until the point
we were quasi-considered a New York band. We weren't really a New York band,
but we just hung there so much. One year we stayed there three months. The
next year we went back and stayed there about four months. That's how we
got this part-time New York City band reputation at the time. Right after that
period, punk started dividing up, and one of the divisions was definitely where
there was kind of a left wing and right wing in punk rock. In 1982, there really
wasn't. It was just all of us going crazy, declaring our independence, being part
of the hardcore music revolution, and then it broke down. We started realizing, we don't have that much in common with . . . Well, we like the Bad Brains
politically, but what they say about gay people didn't rub us right, then the
scene started breaking apart.

Did you feel hardcore punk was less tolerant of gays?
It definitely wasn't tolerant of gays on the whole. There were individual scenes
that were more political and cooler; of course, Austin, Texas, was probably as

good and friendly of a scene and not as homophobic. We were very connected to the 1970s punk rock scene, which was more like a freak revolution than say, what started happening in the early 1980s, when a lot of younger kids got involved, like Minor Threat, SSD, and 7 Seconds. That was more like young guys in the crew that didn't have a background in which they were into the Dead Boys or New York Dolls or into all that. That was one of the first big divisions that we began to notice: people had different backgrounds. The original hard-core pioneers—Ian MacKaye, Kevin Seconds, most of those people per se—were not homophobic because they were kind of like leaders in this musical move-ment, but the fans they attracted, and then the second generation hardcore that came 1983–85 (the first wave was '81), I would say were. As hardcore got bigger and bigger, it became more about random lost young people, and it became about less focused people. There was a time when every scene had about two to three hundred punks, and that was the whole scene [laughs]. They used to go to every gig, and it was really together. Then bands started getting really popular. All of sudden, there was thousands of people everywhere. They started having shows at the Olympic Auditorium with five and seven thousand people for regular punk rock shows. A lot of those people didn't have the spirit of 1981, if you know what I'm saying. It was the next generation, and they didn't have the empathy or connection to the Dead Boys and stuff that was pre-1980, which was definitely a lot more open-minded about sexuality than what came out of 1982–84. Yes, the hardcore scene was rather homophobic. Let's get that out in the air. There were very few out singers that were gay, and the ones that were, like Gary Floyd, well, you could ask him about it. He got a lot of shit. Once the Dicks broke up, even though they were pretty popular, they'd go and perform

places, and people were rough and crazy. More and more people like LA gangs got involved. It just became less comfortable and less fun. There are still not a lot of gay people in hardcore or punk rock in general. I mean, there are a few but not a lot.

Why did it attract gangs?
The music was outsider music, and gangs felt outsiderish. I felt like a lot of the punk rock and hardcore things were, I don't want to say gangs, but they were crews. The straight-edge crew out of Boston and the straight-edge crew out of

DC were these crews of people. There was a certain amount of conformity, and they were kind of athletic guys with hooded sweatshirts, and it became like this, well, crew is the word they used. It was somewhat gang-oriented, but then in LA it was such a monster. The gangs really started moving in. There were just subsets of people in San Francisco, and the skinheads came out of it. They were there for a while. It took a year or two, then all of a sudden, they felt they were white Aryans, or a certain amount of them felt that they were white Aryans. They were a gang, or they were tough nuts, and they stood against communism, all that stuff, while they were eating in soup kitchens and on food stamps themselves.

Do you attribute any gang activity to bands like Suicidal Tendencies or the Fuck-Ups?

I don't know a lot about the Suicidal Tendencies things, other than they were into punk rock music. They were kids that hung out at the beach in Venice, and then all of a sudden gangs kind of came up around them, and they kind of rode the tidal wave of that. I didn't live that LA thing, but offhand, from what I know, that could be true. I don't think Bob Noxious really like headed up the skins. He was just an individual singing his thing, and his thing was that, "I feel like an outsider," and there was a certain amount of "white boy in the Mission, against the world, against the politically correct world" thing, but I don't think he was trying to lead any kind of gang. I kind of know Bob. He lived off the fame of it a little. Well, it was a crew in its own way. I used to live a block up from the Fuck-Ups storefront. I just don't think they planned it out like a gang, it was more like their bunch of people.

In Berkeley, you had Special Forces led by a black man, and DH Peligro from the Dead Kennedys was black, so did you feel that punk and hardcore were multicultural?

Yeah, I think especially in the San Francisco scene, especially in certain scenes, people were open. People liked the idea that Darren Peligro was black and liked the guy Orlando, who was black. There were people who definitely didn't want it to be a lilywhite musical revolution; they wanted people of all kinds of different backgrounds, colors, and ethnicities, or whatever the right word is. The majority really wanted that. There really was only a small minority that just didn't want them. In fact, some of the first skinhead gangs in San Francisco had black guys in them. And then they kind of went white Aryan resistance, then they got into trouble with those guys. They were young guys just trying to . . . Well, gangs are like families, people looking for people to look out for each other. At its best, you know. At its worst, it can be this mean-spirited, us-versus-them, beat anyone up you want to for power and kicks. In many scenes, there

was a conscious effort to overcome racism, but since it was a post-rock'n'roll phenomenon, and it kind of came out of the suburbs, it did have a 97 percent white start. To this day, bands in the Profane Existence world are very politically conscious, like Aus-Rotten and Witchhunt, those kinds of bands, but the scene is 97.8 percent white. It's just the way it works out. As far as the culture, that's who likes this music.

MDC seemed to have a black musical influence. You covered "Spanish Castle Magic" by Hendrix and used jazz-like riffs.
I think that's very true. I mean from the very start, you know, one of our first songs was "No War No KKK No Fascist USA," so right off the bat we were a political band that was out there. We weren't singing about straight-edge and we weren't singing about, "If I could only have a Pepsi or I am about to explode." Not to put anyone down, but that just wasn't our thing. Right away our songs were "John Wayne Is a Nazi," "Corporate Deathburger," "I Hate Work," and "Church and State." Everything had a theme that was political. We were older; we had that 1970s punk rock background in us. We were twenty-four by the time 1981 came around. So, we weren't like sixteen and seventeen. We kind of had been on our own for six or seven years. Nobody was living at home with their parents. We had a certain amount of political sophistication. When the shit went down with the Bad Brains, the Bad Brains were also about our age. They

were used to dealing with, you know, Teen Idles and the like in the DC scene, and all those people were like five to seven years younger than them. So, due to a certain amount of respect for their age, just social maturity, they could get away with saying some outrageous homophobic things and nobody would challenge them on it. But when they did it with us, I'm looking HR in the eye and going, "We're the same age, and your homophobia is creepy and doesn't ring a bell at all." I'm not going sit there and go, wow, you're a great musician and you write some great songs, so everything that comes out of your mouth is so cool or plausible. I will call you on what I find is not plausible. So, right off the bat, that element was there. The Bad Brains were older, we were a little older, and some of the bands were a little older, say Randy Biscuit from the Big Boys was a little older, and the Dicks were a little older. Whereas bands like SSD, and a lot of the young bands that were coming out, were definitely seventeen, eighteen years old in that 1981–83 period. Joey Shithead in DOA was older. And the Black Flag guys were a little older, which wasn't true of the DC or Boston scene in particular, and many scenes that followed after them.

When you got to Europe and saw the politics of Europe, how did that gel with your homegrown, radical American spirit?
It totally fit. In America, people were amazed by our music, but people didn't know what to make out of our politics. It was coming from such a different place than so many other kinds of bands. When we got to Europe, we really found a home because the political culture in Europe is more sophisticated. The continent has been through two world wars and the Cold War. People are a lot more up on what is going on. There's more political sophistication. We saw the squat movement, the whole idea, "We don't want to work within this system that is going to squeeze our individuality and work us to the grave. We want to create an alternative society," which could be considered the squat movement of Christiania in Copenhagen, and all the big squat houses in Germany and Holland where we came up and played, and in Italy as well. It was like we found a new home. Right off the bat, our music struck a chord with those people. In some ways, I wouldn't say Europe discovered us, but Europe heralded us more than America, if you hear what I am saying.

Is that why you feel compelled to do the *Peace/War* compilation?
I wanted to be behind the world community, and that was the intent of that, like, "we're all these bands, and we're fighting for an antinuclear, peaceful world." Hence, the *Peace* compilation, with fifty-five bands, thirty from outside the United States, and everyone just tried to integrate it and use it as a tool to get to know each other and make scenes happen for each other. I was very happy and proud that I got to go to places like Spain and Italy, new places where we

were very much introducing American hardcore, under the umbrella of we're all punk rock, and this is our version of it.

Did it ever surprise you that, maybe beside ABC No Rio or Gilman, the European idea of squat spaces or alternative spaces never really took hold much in America?
There were definitely people trying to do that. One of the big things it really comes down to is, squatting people's property in Europe is more of a civil offense than a criminal offense. As long as you're in a building that you don't own or are not renting in America, you are trespassing, and you can be arrested for trespassing. The way that the interpretations of the laws are, if you are trespassing in a building, people will call the police and say, look, this my building, this is the deed that shows I own it. There's these forty kids living there. I want them out of there, and the police will go and get you out of there. They take their nightsticks in and beat the hell out of you and get you out of there. Europe has this thing in many countries, not all of them, where it is a civil matter, and the owner of the building can go to the police and authorities and say, hey, forty people moved into my building. They won't immediately send the police down there to beat you up and throw you out. They have to get a court order, the government has to tell them to do it. To a certain degree it's changed, but in 1980, that was very much the situation, so the squat moment was able to breathe and grow in Europe before it could in America. There are some squats in America, but it's more like you move into an abandoned building and you keep a very low profile, and hopefully nobody notices that you are there. And you stay there for year or two, and in some cases in New York City if they've liked what you've done with the building, because a lot of times it was just drug addicts living in the building, and you've made it safe and added to that neighborhood, the city will buy it and then sell it to the squatters at a certain price. There's a place called C-Squat in New York City where that happened. In general, again, I think this has to do with the political sophistication. Americans, in general, when they squatted, were just looking for a cheap place to stay; they didn't have this ideology wrapped around trying to create an alternative universe.

They weren't community-building per se?
I've been to about forty to fifty squats over the last ten years here in the United States. I would say, by and large, that people want free or cheaper place to live. That's 85 percent of the political motivation. They're not building a better thing, an alternative universe. Sadly, in Europe, a lot of the squats have gone legal, and a lot of the new squatters want a cheap place to live. It's kind of strange for some of the places that used to have bands like MDC, the new people that move into

the squats don't want all the loud music and don't want people to get drunk in front of the house they live in and they don't want garbage all over and they stop having musical shows.

It gets phased out?

They become a lot more kind of, for a lack of better words, a yuppie entity. A progressive, populist spark for real change? No, they want a cheap place to live.

How did you meet up with Michelle Shocked and cut the song "Fogtown"?

We met in San Francisco. A lot of people kind of just drifted out there. She actually was a woman I was dating and was kind of the manager of MDC's brother's girlfriend. And she came out to visit her boyfriend, Michelle did, who was Tammy's boyfriend, who was staying with MDC. Ron was working at a skateboard shop, and we had an apartment in a warehouse practice space, and the brother came out, and his girlfriend came out, and the girlfriend was Michelle Shocked, and she had this little guitar and would play songs together with us, MDC in general, but with me in particular. Most of the songs I wrote were written on an acoustic guitar first, everything from "Chicken Squawk" to "My Family Is a Little Weird" to "I Hate Work." A lot of that was done very folky style, very in the Bob Dylan's children mode of Woody Guthrie/Bob Dylan/punk rock/ hardcore, a political musical expression. We just hung out together, and she'd play me songs. We'd do "Chicken Squawk" together, then we started doing this song called "Fogtown" together, then we recorded it for her first album. She was just a gal with a guitar, and she went to the Kerrville folk festival back

in Texas after staying with us in California, and they taped the session, and it's the famous Texas Campfire Takes. You hear crickets in the background, and it's really taped with a Sony Walkman. They put that out, and England discovered her first. She went to England and played all these big shows, then she got back to the U.S. and got a little deal with Polydor, then the rest was kind of history. Of course, she did one album with Polydor, and they weren't paying her, and this and that. She sued for her music back, and it took a long time, but she got it. She's been an independent artist ever since. We just saw each other down in LA about eight months ago, and she jumped up on stage, and we played a couple of songs together during the Citizen Fish/MDC tour in Hollywood.

In the 1990s, when the band shifted and you worked with all kinds of people as members, did you feel the band was still as viable as in the 1980s?
The 1980s was a fresh, beautiful time. You really had to live in that 1981–82 era. I'm not sure where you were or how old you are. It was very special. Being in that Austin, Texas, scene with Randy Turner and Gary Floyd and all the bands that were part of it, like the Offenders, Boy Problems, and the Next, is just a really special, special feeling. It's like you got this cool thing going that just you and a certain amount of other people know about, and then it explodes, and you're riding the wave of it. Literally, in 1981, when we were in the Austin scene, our only friends in the scene mostly were the Dicks and the Big Boys. There were a few other bands, but it was very new wavey and very competitive, but it was a lot of fun, and everybody was vying for position. Then we sent our "John Wayne Is a Nazi" single out. Tim Yohannan got it, Jello Biafra got it, and they took us out. They called me up, and I asked Biafra for a show, and Black Flag came through, and I asked them if they could hook us up with a show in LA because we hooked them up with a show in Austin, and they did. They gave us a great show at the Cuckoo's Nest, and the Dead Kennedys gave us a great show at Mabuhay Gardens. The whole thing just exploded. Like I was saying, there was like five to seven thousand people at these LA shows at the Olympic Auditorium, thousands of kids. It was just an incredible feeling. We played this Rock Against Racism event in New York City and San Francisco in 1983, free events put on by the Yippies. There were ten thousand people showing up. It just exploded from only two hundred people that even knew who the Sex Pistols were in your hometown, or better yet knew who Black Flag and the Dead Kennedys were in your hometown, to all of a sudden tens of thousands coming from everywhere. It was so special, it's hard to put into words. I guess to say something about it would be to say it was like being at Woodstock, then compare it to classic rock in the mid-to-late 1970s. The feeling was definitely was gone when these bands just kept going on and on, and nobody seemed really to believe it anymore. It wasn't the Summer of Love, it was . . .

The Me Generation.

It became a rock business, a rock commodity, and arena rock—like if we can get twenty thousand people to pay fifteen bucks each, we start dividing up the money, like when Madonna sells out Madison Square Garden, it's a multi-money event. Believe it or not, I remember Madonna back in 1979, '80, and '81, and she was playing in clubs in New York City. I never saw her, but I knew of her existence, and I knew Prince was doing "Little Red Corvette" in New York City. Musically, besides the hardcore scene, it was a wonderful era. After 1977, the whole classic rock thing kind of like contracted, and all of a sudden it was new wave and Talking Heads, Devo, and all this different stuff came out between 1977 and '82. It was just a very, very exciting time. I got to be part of that, not part of Talking Heads per se, but MDC living in Austin with the Dicks and Big Boys and watching that piece of culture explode, and it was thrilling.

Of course, like I said before, you start realizing, "Yeah, there's this punk revolution going on, there's this music revolution going on, but we don't have that much in common with everybody." The Misfits really don't get along with the Bad Brains, who don't really get along with the metal ends of the scene, who don't get along with . . . It's not all one big happy family. People started going their own ways. MDC, and I'm sure a million other bands, made gigantic sacrifices to live together. We moved to San Francisco and we lived in a warehouse room for about a year and a half, together, and that was a room about fifteen feet wide by about thirty feet long. It was in a place called the Vats. It was covered in rubber. It was a beer vat. That's exactly what it was. I used to have to get into it by crawling through this hole that was like a beer vat, I don't know how to explain it. It was like getting in a submarine hatch door. And we lived like that for a year and a half—getting food stamps, eating at soup kitchens, and we were like twenty-five, twenty-six, twenty-seven, and we were living like we were sixteen, seventeen, eighteen. Like we were the Pinocchio kids that ran away from home to live in Candyland, or wherever.

After a few years, it started taking its toll on everybody, not just MDC. Other people said, "I want to start making it financially." People started busting their moves to try and move up a notch. Bob Mould left Hüsker Dü, sold out to a big label. Little by little, that whole snowball happened. When you are young, it is very fresh and exciting; later, it becomes less so. Ron Posner left the band in 1984, though he came back to us five years ago. He just said, "I don't want to do this anymore. I'm just burned out on it." That happened to a lot of people, and then you start trying to recapture the magic of those first four people you were doing the music with. In the case of MDC, in the course of ten years, we had five to six guitar players, between 1984 and 1994. There was Gordon Frasier, Eric Calhoun, Ron came back, and there was Bill from Fang who joined us, then there was Chris Wilder from Sticky who joined us, so there were five different guitar payers. With us, we'd have people join us, do a tour or two, and then just . . . Well, a lot of people figured out it's tough to be in a band. It's like you're married to these people, and you've got to get along with them, and everyone's got their drug habits, everyone's got their weird personalities, everyone at certain points wants to be with their girlfriend and have a baby, and a lot of that different stuff happens. It became watered down and less special for us. It was still special for me to perform, but it wasn't the exciting feeling of 1981, when we drove out in two little cars to play with the Dead Kennedys at Mabuhay Gardens and then play with Black Flag at the Cuckoo's Nest on a two-city tour.

Two-city tour for 1,500 miles?
We went 2,200 miles from Texas to San Francisco. It took us two weeks, we played two different weekends, and we hung out in San Francisco and just checked it all out. Our eyes were wide open; it was a wide-open experience to see all those people and realize the world was bigger than Texas. What I am trying to say is that it is kind of a natural thing that changes were happening.

Do you think the punk movement was able to spread their politics beyond the punk community?
Well, I mean limitedly so, you know. Not in the way that Bruce Springsteen playing a benefit for Barack Obama, where it might be televised on national TV to thirty million people, or ten million people, or whatever. We tried in our own way: we did Rock Against Racism, early on, in 1982. In 1983, it became Rock Against Reagan, and we tried to work with the Yippies, and it was always on a very underground level. It was never with Bill Graham Presents or any of that. But we tried in our own world. In 1983, we actually played with the Dead Kennedys and a band called Permanent Wave in San Francisco at Dolores Park for ten thousand people, and Whoopi Goldberg was the MC.

Did she talk to you at all?
I didn't seek her out. I didn't know who she was, but she was funny, and I liked her, and I cheered. She was always a very witty person. She's the type of person who can jump on a microphone and say funny things, and that right away made me like her. We tried, but we had a lot going against us. Punk rockers in the early 1980s were like the lepers of the music scene. Most music magazines wouldn't even acknowledge us. Bands like the Dead Kennedys, even with thousands of people going to their shows, would not get any recognition from the main music press. To *BAM* magazine and *Rolling Stone*, it was like we didn't exist. Even when they do these lists of the "100 Greatest Punk Rock Bands Ever," 87 percent of it is built on that 1977–81 thing, and just barely mentions, if it does at all, even the biggest bands, like Fugazi. Now, they acknowledge Rancid and

Green Day, but it's almost like according to them, punk started in 1977 and died 1982, or it died in 1980, then was reborn in 1990 when Green Day played Woodstock, or 1996, whatever year that was. For twelve years, like Russian politics under Stalin, all these bands were erased out of the scene. Black Flag never really existed, and Fear never really existed, and DOA never really existed. As musicology goes, when you think about the effect that a band like Black Flag had, or Minor Threat, leading into Fugazi, had, there's still little credit given to them per square inch.

Do you feel close to bands like DOA and Crucifix?
DOA came through Austin early on, and they were very friendly, very nice. We hit it off with them right off the bat. Crucifix were a band in San Francisco. We were kind of friends of friends, and we always got along. They were, even back then, more of a hair band, and we were a little more hardcore punk, which means our music was louder, harder, faster, and their thing was a little more like the British punk thing. But we got along, and we actually did some tours together. We did some playing together in LA, and we did some playing together in San Francisco, and even in Europe. We always liked Crucifix. In that case, with those two bands, yes. In 1982, we totally felt like we were there with everybody. We would drive a thousand miles to play with Black Flag, we'd drive a thousand miles to play with anybody. We felt we really had a lot in common with everything. It wasn't until 1984–86, then we started realizing, those bands in Boston hate us, and we're too political for them. To them, we're all just commie fags, blah blah blah. We started having fallouts with Agnostic Front. Different things started breaking out, then the hatecore scene came out of New York City. It wasn't really us. We never really considered ourselves hatecore. That movement was very popular, the Cro-Mags and CBGBs from like 1984 to 1994. Sick of It All came out of that scene, and lots of other bands. It was a whole kind of different thing.

It didn't really seem to gel much with the early hardcore scene, like Heart Attack or Cause for Alarm . . .
But it came out of the same batch of people. Part of that scene grew into a different head space, where all of sudden, it became what it became: Hatecore.

MDC always seemed to retain a sense of the humorous, like "My Family Is a Little Weird," akin to the Ramones: pure speed and humor.
The tongue in the cheek always seemed to be there. There was always sarcasm going on in MDC, even when we sang "No War, No KKK, No Fascist USA" It was heartfelt, and it was serious, but then we felt the need to turn it around and take the piss out of it, a little. So, it didn't come across like we were the angry commies. That's just who we were. There was a silly misfitsness to us, a silly,

"we don't fit in" thing, and we gotta make jokes about it. That's just kinda who we were.

But that seems to be lost on things like the band flyers. Almost no one does an MDC flyer without a skull on a tank . . .

Even the skull tank, in its own perverse way, has got its own humor. It's like American power, a tank that's really a skull that is killing people. And even though that's not funny if you're a Guatemalan farmer getting killed by a right-wing death squad, the visualization of that is going for a sick, ironic, cynical sense of humor. Less so is the Klan cop pointing a gun at you. But then we also have skateboard Jesus, which is taking the piss out of something: Jesus is up on the cross, and he's skating for your sins.

Who designed the record art for MDC?

Through the years, it was different people and band members. The Klan cop was kinda all of us, a lot of the police imagery, and then the skull tank. "Multi-Death Corporation," was a song I wrote with Ron, and I didn't realize how it was going to catch such fire at the time. It was just trying to be a serious political song, then Al came up with the Millions of Damn Christians album cover idea. In the Wax Museum in San Francisco, we took out certain wax figures, and we put on these clothes, and we took pictures of us being the apostles from the famous Last Supper shot. Different people along the way came up with different ideas and tried to find things. The last one, sad to say, many people didn't get. I'm kind of a media, news driven person, so for the *Magnus Dominance Corpus* album, which went over a lot of people's heads, the picture is of strung-up dead contractors in Iraq.

On the bridge in Fallujah.

I was at a gig selling the album, and I showed it to thirty people and said, do you know where this picture is from? Twenty-seven of them didn't know where the picture was from. Ten percent knew that it was a picture of Iraq, of dead contractors being strung up. I just realized that people don't follow shit as much as I follow shit. There you go.

Did you get your own sense of politics from media and newspapers, whatnot, or did you get it from music as well?

I had it in me already. One of my first conscious memories outside of family life was when JFK was shot. I was seven years old at the time when the president was shot. I grew up Catholic in New York City and it was kind of a big deal, and right away I knew that things were not right. When I was in seventh grade, Martin Luther King was shot, then a month later Bobby Kennedy was shot. You just knew that things were terribly wrong, and there was the Vietnam War going on. You'd turn on the TV and there were people fighting with the police everywhere. You're brought up in this fairytale America where we won World War II, we saved the world from the Nazis, but it doesn't seem like everyone is all that happy. So, I had that political bent, that curiousness, like, why aren't people happy? Why are we in Vietnam? Slowly but surely, you find out that this World War II hero, Ho Chi Minh, is fighting in his own country, to fight the French, then you realize American dominance is based on oil, power, and this vague notion of stopping dominoes from falling and engulfing the world. You fill up with this cynical view of the world. That was me from early on.

Then there were things, like Bob Dylan music, that supported that skepticism, but definitely the politics came and then the music on top of it. I found myself moving to Texas when the farm workers were being found dead and labor leaders were being killed. They weren't sure who they were being killed by, the Klu Klux Klan or an army of anti–union growers vigilante groups. It was sexist in the late 1970s too. It was a really strange world, Texas in the late 1970s. The University of Texas didn't even get integrated until 1973. There weren't even women in the law school until like 1968–69. They were very late on many different things. Maybe these dates are not exact, but it was way behind. Of course, the South just got integrated through the late 1960s. I had a landlord that talked to me about "field niggers" all the time and talked about the football players at the University of Texas, "That one's a good boy. In the old days, he was a field nigger." I had never heard that term. I started realizing that the world I was living in had a deep racism, some serious problems, and some real issues gong on. It wasn't like, we won World War I and World War II, and we're all going to be equal. It's a very prejudiced world, and one where we have to fight and we wanna make music to affect people, that's where our "No War, No KKK, No Fascist USA" came from, and "John Wayne Is a Nazi"—from watching him charge up some Porkchop Hill and look good for dying in some war killing Asians. It was being shoved down our throat. It's made to be popular culture, but it's not beautiful, it's not fabulous, and it's not what I think should be said for people to believe in.

What heroes keep you sane, keep you going?

Believe it or not, I have even been working for the Obama campaign up here in Portland. As mainstream as that is, I think it would go a long way for an African American to become president of the United States. I am hoping for this quantum leap, the hundredth monkey effect to kind of go on, where people can really believe in a world that is solar-run, has more understanding, and is concerned about the environment. That's what I am doing on this personal level for myself. Of course, there are lots of different heroes out there, there's women, like the Gulabi gang women of India, I was just reading about them, and when I was in Austria I had some friends doing benefits for them. They are standing up to patriarchy: they're outcast women who go around with these big sticks and whenever these corrupt police mess with women, they all stick together. It's almost like a gang. They take these big sticks, and in many parts of India, the police won't challenge them, because they are so popular. They'll come into a village, and every woman will pick up a stick. They just kind of freak out. Those are heroes. Those people who are on those Greenpeace boats harassing Japanese whalers are heroes. There are lots of different types of heroes, and I'm kind of glad to be making music that is sharing a similar consciousness to those heroes. That's what we're doing, right? We are part of the continuum of change, people fighting. Emma Goldman in the early 1900s, the people who fought against child labor, we are in the continuum of that, people on various levels of or various energies, some more hardworking than others, but people doing whatever people can do to the benefit of the good is a part of it. Walking around and collecting signatures for Barack Obama, to me, that's got slices of the heroes of Emma Goldman. I know I could go, oh, the Democrats, bought out by the corporations, blah blah, blah, will things really change, but I think it is a continuum, and it's going to take liberal Democrats to lead eventually to a better universe.

Perhaps punks made wrong decisions back in the 1980s: perhaps supporting and getting signatures for a Democrat *was* a better choice than letting Reagan back in. In the long run, we were stuck with some horrendous Republicans.

There were horrendous Democrats too. We used to call Dianne Feinstein "Swinestein" because she stuck those police on us really nastily in San Francisco in 1984. When I still see her on TV, I can't help but mumble "Swinestein." I don't care if she is voting down some conservative judge, or whatever. That personally affected my life. I watched people who got their jaws broken by the police based on her style of leadership. It's not all good; it's somewhat good, if you know what I'm saying. So, I'm not Mr. Democrat. I see a possibility for an awareness and change, and it makes me put some energy out for it.

Thomas Barnett
(Strike Anywhere)

Thomas Barnett, a deeply well-spoken member of Strike Anywhere, a seminal modern hardcore band, evokes righteous fury in boundless well-crafted lyrics. Discussing issues with him is like being tethered to *A People's History of the United States*, the *New York Times*, and the *Trouser Press Record Guide* at the same time. His breadth of humanitarian concerns, capacity for lifelong learning, and intriguing theories keep me under his spell for hours on end. Kindhearted, easygoing, and sincere, he embodies an earnest side of punk, before irony and post-hardcore took over the reins. This interview, completed by Barnett via e-mail in a touring van during the recess of night, ran in *Left of the Dial*.

How has black culture, apart from tragically inspiring the racist police beating narrative in songs like "Sunset on 32nd," left its mark on the band?
I think about this often, and have had an ongoing conversation on this subject with many older punks, hardcore kids, conscious rastas in Richmond and DC, and other members of the African Diaspora, about the roots of punk and the parallels and differences between hardcore/punk and revolutionary black music in the Western world. There are also definite echoes between the working-class, anti-elitist sonic minimalism (and the accompanying shock value) in punk rock and the foundations of hip-hop: Latino and black working-class folks throwing a party, and experimenting with making new songs and sounds with a church PA, a turntable, and some records. I won't try and further academize my perspective on this. There isn't a punk rocker alive now who couldn't find an eerie affinity between the shrill anti-authoritarian rhyming rage in their favorite punk song and the frustrated, simmering patience of countless reggae numbers. It's just there.

Some people have sworn by the "East London" theory. This is the one I'm sure you've heard where the early British punk rock bands and their embryonic, furiously self-reinventing tribes of friends and followers (back then even

©SAMHOLDENPHOTOGRAPHY.COM

more fractured, heterogeneous, and, for that matter, androgynous, certainly hungrier and homeless—orphaned from rock'n'roll already) are looking for pubs to play in, and the only sympathetic ears who'll take them in are the West Indian–owned reggae clubs in the East End. Perhaps, if this is accurate to some degree, this is where the cross-pollination of ideas, and in a smaller way, sounds, first went down.

You could look at it as a window getting opened for the disaffected, self-destructing white punks and artists, and the elements of postcolonial black politics, human rights issues, and the awareness of a binary world system came crashing down through the music into their minds. The often paradoxical and personal politics of punk can be traced back to this artistic intersection, but perhaps this was just one highly public space in history where this same collision of white restlessness and countercultural reaction opened up to the waiting truths, methods, and life-affirming ideas of revolutionary black culture. Not to be too abstract, but I think maybe that the Highlander Folk Schools,

the multiracial training ground for the leadership of the Civil Rights Movement, could also be perceived similarly.

The regional punk world of Richmond/Washington, DC, when I was first going to shows and experiencing the tail end of the second generation of the counterculture, had some cross pollination with the politics and sounds of reggae. It helped to balance things a bit during that time of patriotic skinheads and drunk thrash punks, that HR would live in Richmond and do his Human Rights band between Bad Brains breakups. One of his guitar players was my manager at a pizza place where I worked, and we played in a band together for a short time. This wasn't a playing shows, having a name kind of band, this was more of a getting drunk and writing some cool, unfocused reggae and hardcore songs once a week kind of band. It didn't seem to provoke any self-awareness at the time that the band was made up of half Caucasian punk kids and half African American rastas. That seemed to be a pretty normal thing for the time. In fact, I thought it was kinda what punk rock was in a way. I got a lot of cool mix tapes out of it, and some great friends and good memories from one of my first times singing. It's strange to think of this laundry list of black influences on my experiences with punk rock, but the connections, at least to me, are still vital and transparent.

In both cities, there were punk/reggae bands that pioneered new spaces and held consciousness-raising benefit shows where noise experimental art rock punks would play before Rasta dub poets, and then, say, Fidelity Jones, Scream, Corrosion of Conformity, or Burma Jam would bring the show to a boil. When I was busy dropping out of high school, I went down to the New Horizons Reggae club on Broad Street in Richmond with some friends to see this new band on Dischord. It was Fugazi. I think it was their ninth show or something—you know, the ones where Guy just danced around soulfully. Anyway, these and other examples cemented my belief in a punk and hardcore culture that was in communication with the struggles and the aesthetics of black resistance.

During a period of travel between the end of my first band, Inquisition, and the beginning of Strike Anywhere, I lived for a little while in Bimini, a small island on the Western edge of the Bahamas. I was living with a friend and helping to fix up an old library there. Several new friends I had made on the island were busy transforming an old cinderblock '70s disco shack on the outskirts of the cricket field into a reggae club. They enlisted my help, and I ended up learning a whole lot really fast out there, setting up a sound system and throwing parties for the Alice and Baileytown Massive. This was way before *Da Ali G Show*, by the way. There was a lot of music happening with revolutionary messages that burned with respect for the natural world, and hope for all humanity. So, of course, I ended up writing some songs from the experience.

I think that in these most modern postmillennial music "eras," which seem to be stumbling all over each other, with the bands who represent the mainstream face of punk competing to render this whole culture into a nonthreatening cartoon, the closeness and affinity between black and white revolutionary arts and the contradictions in punk's lurching present are sadly obscured and isolated. I wish I could manifest solutions and find the glue that could make these connections clearer and nourishing again, but it will take small, patient steps to out race the marketing whirlwind that drag substance and continuity from the content of music in order to neutralize its power, and make it an obedient, palatable product. I know that many are making these small steps, both in the conscious hip-hop communities and the hardcore punk ones, and I hope that we can pull something new and unified together from the ruins of the separate rooms we've trapped ourselves in.

Matt worked in Northern Virginia designing spy gadgets and riot control devices for a company that worked in total self-interest "to the exclusion of everyone else, even future generations, even their own children." As America becomes entrenched in Iraq, and now even Liberia, soldiers are being hounded by very low-tech devices used by very driven people, homemade bombs being tossed off bridges, or firing handguns while soldiers buy Cokes at the university. It is what is called an "asymmetrical war," very much akin to guerilla warfare. In a way, is that how a politically motivated punk rock band operates, but in a nonviolent way, by using common-as-mud low-tech guitars and drums to somehow disable or let the system disarticulate/disassemble itself?

Matthew Sherwood says, "We wish." Naw, but sure, the potential is there. The guerrilla war against co-optation is definitely on in earnest now, and many groups use different approaches to creatively undermine the numbing and dumbing-down of the corporate music industry. Including that very industry itself. The collateral waste of the music machine leaves less to transform and take back than in your right-on war metaphor, so I think most of these cultural battles still have to take place in the "Don Quixote" paradigm. Only in *Left of the Dial* can I use that much-maligned word with confidence! All right. I think that independent music, admittedly with its/our own regrettable hierarchies and compromises, is taking account of its strengths and failures against the corporate behemoth right about now, and some new ideas and greater unity are spoiling to become our most efficient technologies. Also, the ridiculous free music/Internet "outrage" in the major label world has, in my analysis anyway, further showed the public that that retrograde "holding music and culture hostage for your money and brand loyalty" shit is obsolete and exposed for yet another false choice that people can now circumvent to the further ruin of the outmoded systems of competition and separation that once defined music's obedience to the market.

Now, the distance between the artist's humanity and responsibility has been shortened from the sounds they make, and the public can, if they have the fertile moment, reveal the middleman for all its waste and bureaucracy. We are also offered the choice to participate in the livelihood of the creators in maybe a more honest way, insofar as we know we don't have to pay for music in order to have it affect us, and we can choose to reward the groups we love with our money for their time and for their survival. This opening of consciousness may pave the way for a soon coming revolution in the way music is perceived by the "average" consumer. Whoever that is.

You have also mentioned the inner, sleeping cop that makes us stay on the treadmill of habit and isolation, unable to really communicate and pry open our own emotions. Some people may just call it the white, privileged, overeducated syndrome: the gripe syndrome. How does one go from simply being a culture critic rocker that leans towards "earthy, elemental, sacramental" rituals to getting inside and reshaping the nature of work, play, and consumption?

Our original demos were burned CDs, which we recorded in Sherwood's basement. We had Kinko's stickers on cardboard sleeves with the collage lyric sheet folded inside. We sat on Matt's porch and hand assembled each one of these before a show or a tour. We toured the Southeast with this document. We then, like many bands before us and after, cemented relationships with like-minded, enthusiastic souls in the underground community who wanted to help us continue to create music and the media upon which it lives. No Idea Records, Red Leader, Scene Police in Germany, and even our single on Fat Wreck Chords were all born from this ethic in this environment of honesty and friendship.

As you've alluded to, there is already a machinery in place to connect the music with the message, and we've been happy to have been able to rerelease our trusty burned demo CD onto a seven-inch in Germany, made by the good people at Scene Police, proceeds from which go to fund the litigation in the defense of the still imprisoned activists from the G8 protests and police riots in Genoa, Italy, in June of 2001. We have supported benefit CDs with our songs for our entire four-year existence, giving money to animal rights groups, victims of police brutality, Food Not Bombs, and antiglobalization activist groups. Also, when possible, a percentage of the money from our Richmond shows goes to the Coalition for the Living Wage. We have hosted speakers at a lot of our shows along the East Coast, in San Diego, and in Europe as well. These friends and inspirational people will engage with the local community and connect people at the show with local area demos and organizations, with geographically specific detail and persuasion. On November 8, 2002, we took the opportunity to have a show in our hometown on the day before the Richmond Antiwar March. We had speakers and activists from our community encourage all the folks at the show to attend, and a whole heaping of punk and hardcore kids, some bringing their parents and siblings, was added to the mix on Richmond's streets the next day. I am sure that some of these folks were already clued in to the march and had their plans to go, but I think that we helped to provide a forum for that speech, and this informed others as to the march's existence.

Our current and three-year-old relationship with Tim and Darren of Jade Tree is, what we all believe, a much bigger and brighter thing than just a scramble for resources and promotion, influence, and fair royalties. Although denying the importance of these factors would be dishonest and, I think, feed into the college punk ghetto mentality of elitism and narcissism, which can keep punk bands from meaning anything to anyone other than punks of privilege who claim and enforce poverty on bands, often killing the growth and continuity of the ideas. Without introspection, humor, or humanity, certain eras of our culture will fetishize punk and hardcore bands and treat the bands' personal survival as a fiction or an afterthought. We've all seen this happen and probably participated in it on some level in the guise of ethics and accountability.

For our part, we try to remain as honest as we can about our goals and our needs. We also have always made our music, as mentioned above, free for people who have access to the Internet. It's a natural thing to bring the self-awareness and self-criticism into the cold ritual of the commerce that allows us to travel and record records. In conversation, and even in between songs, we strive, but not contrive, for our message, and in reflection, our personalities, to focus on demystifying the rock myths, the consumer complacency, and the separation between the music and its deeper roots in community. I try to sense when these conversations are appropriate and don't leave a young punker blinking at you. This is a growth process, and we often learn more about the ideas in our songs from the people who honor us with their attention and connection, than we teach.

Exit English was more "labor intensive. Eric's drums took twice as long, vocals took twice as long, and there was an extraordinary amount of pre and post production tracking." How far can the band go before the

production becomes excessive, even if the band wants more individual color and attention to each song? Granted, the Sex Pistols, Jam, and the Clash all recorded in major studios.

All of our post and pre production work was done at Matt Smith's fine basement studio, UltraSound, which is outside of Baltimore. We added some raucous group shouts and some harmonies to the lead vocals there, as well as acoustic guitars and some secret hand percussion. The difference between our *Change Is a Sound* Salad Days recording and our *Exit English* sessions had less to do with actual time and labor spent but with how much more prepared and focused we were on the songs. We used our time differently, but we feel that the result still retains the naturalness and rawness that drives the songs. When I listen to it, I think that there is even more open rage and emotion present vocally in this record. The crucial times we are living in definitely informed the songwriting and the lyrics on *Exit English* in some ways more so than any of our previous records. This may have to do with such personal issues as having fifteen years' worth of lyrics, photographs, and travel journals stolen from my car while I was working the month before we had to record.

Luckily, I had 90 percent of the final words for the songs by this time, but it still made me feel, as you'd imagine, a bit vulnerable and despondent. My bandmates' encouragement helped me immensely, and we all pulled out the last bits of songwriting together at the eleventh hour. That's why we feel that this record has more urgency, character, and collective spirit to it. Hopefully, that's just the nature of artistic evolution; the intensity of personal experience as it reflects itself into our punk rock records.

Salad Days is a special place for us, beyond the cold assembly lines of many other studios. Recording there is a furnace for ideas, which challenges and refines the songs that the group brings. I am certain that the other bands that have also crafted their records there feel this as well. Salad Days is also a garage behind a small house on the outskirts of DC. We live in Brian and Minu's basement for the weeks we record and mix there. We've managed to schedule our time in the springs of both 2001 and 2003, so we help out with all of the gardening and get to play with their two dogs, Pedro and Nalla. We also help out with their home renovations projects as well, sometimes priming drywall and painting rooms on the nights after tracking. It is an exceptional environment, removed from any rock'n'roll pretension, excess, or self-indulgence. Brian and Minu's roots in hardcore and punk in DC are reflected in the groups they welcome into their lives, and the intensity of the community and compassion present in their house. During my final weekend singing in the garage, Salad Days, I woke up at six in the morning to take the Metro into the city and walk for four hours in the rain, supporting the Syrentha Savio Endowment, a breast cancer awareness group (Shirts for a Cure) started by our friend Mark Beemer.

I reckon that I'm sharing all of this with you to emphasize the unique and independent quality of our recording community. Also, the tone of the pulled quotes referenced in the question above doesn't quite describe the atmosphere and philosophy behind all of our Salad Days recordings. We love a lot of different approaches to making records, and I am sure we will try something different for future projects, but we are personally all quite happy with *Exit English*, and put every bit of our five, six including Brian McTernan's, hearts in it.

I often feel that the younger generation of punk and hardcore kids fetishize the past, yet really want nothing to do with it, other than collect records. It's almost like a cultural amnesia, or enforced ageism, that makes them believe in the often-misleading power and potency of youth that glorifies the past without understanding or coping with it.

We recently had a hometown show during the hurricane that blacked out Virginia and North Carolina and deprived millions of drinkable water and refrigeration. Isabel also knocked down tens of thousands of trees, including many of the proud two-hundred-year-old oaks that line Richmond's streets and shade her parks. At this show, our generator powered record release for *Exit English*, a number of older, second-generation punks appeared. My only theory is that the shut down city was a catalyst for the adventurous souls to come out, and perhaps there was nothing to do at home without power. Anyway, some older (I mean like thirty-seven-year-olds) and I finally had the "transgenerational Richmond counterculture symposium" while standing out under the brilliant stars in the middle of downtown. "We're finally gonna see your band, Thomas!" "Thanks, y'all." Some kind of analysis developed where the elders suggested that we (Me, Sherwood, and many many still active others like possibly yourself who constitute the "third generation") were the keepers of the history. Our particular historical punk experiences took place post–Revolution Summer Dischord, late '80s second-wave New York straight-edge, and the dawn of crossover thrash hardcore. The second-generation punks see us as the last group to have windows on both ends of the continuum. Before the year that punk broke (1993) and the whole underground, its methods and means, was changed forever by pulses of reaction or co-optation. I took it to mean that we were given the choices of both kinds of consciousness, the furious innocence or the paralysis of self-awareness. However, I'm not saying that anything has been lost; in fact, I remember a lot more of an investment in DIY punk art, music, and writing once it got laid out for folks in the '90s, for it proliferated into micro counterculture, at least in the cities where I was connected (Philadelphia, NYC, DC, Baltimore, Virginia Beach, and RVA). Whereas before, and I just could've been younger and less focused (read: drunk), but it seemed like punk and hardcore was still national as far as trends, music, and ideas. Punk houses in the working-class neighborhoods on the edges of the college campuses consisted the fullness of my explorations at the time.

You've said that the mainstream promotes bands that play styles of music that "don't have any roots hybridized and diluted styles that are perfect for our attention-deficit, consumer culture. Digestible but prefab." You prefer to link Strike Anywhere to the dynamics of folk music. Could you illuminate what exactly you mean?

My love for music (and I also think for culture) has a hard time finding nourishment without its sense of history, or continuity. I don't mind it being an imaginative history, and I especially enjoy a perspective freshly reclothed in the tactics of the new (like, the band International Noise Conspiracy as one example), but I (and I suspect many, many unwashed others) feel a bit cheated by bands in the popular mainstream at present. When I listen to songs I love, I often get a rush of visceral truth, belonging, and connectedness, at once intensely personal and quieting to the petty ego as well. That's my simple perspective on it: what music gives me, and what I need from it. I get filled with disbelief, and then some kind of sympathy, when the music machine builds up yet another "new" sound, packaged to statistically represent the illusion of cool and suburban rebellion. The weak musical and visual snarls and poses that these bands perpetrate only, in my analysis, the dead end of passivity and collective confusion that drive the newest generations away from finding the welcoming, challenging, and ever-evolving underground of independent music. That's the stuff of substance that drags you in and doesn't let you let go until you've added to it. That's the true

counterculture that all of us (and probably all of you reading this) have this irrational and unquantifiable attachment to.

I wonder if the punk-looking pop groups on the billboards and bus benches, beer commercials, and hosting teen dance parties for MTV feel cheated as well. I'm not saying that they would feel some specter of guilt for "selling out." I don't think that many of them have even been under the surface of the rock industry long enough to have felt empowered by it. I wish they would stop letting themselves be exploited by their handlers, marketers, producers, and managers, and say something for themselves. They are bound to have something to add, something real, some original songs, some honest stories. We all do, and it's just a thorny path to finding the folks, the culture that defends and demands that courage and honesty. That's what we, down here in punk's many levels and branches, have at the roots. Those are the roots of storytelling, and collective catharsis, celebrating the anger and vulnerability that sharpen minds and strengthen hearts. That's what folk music means to me.

I remember reading an interview with Tad in *Flipside* in the early '90s where he said, "Punk rock is just urban folk music." I agree with that and raise him all of the subversive and independent arts, especially conscious underground hip-hop, garage bands, and dance punk hootenannies. Some of the hardcore electronic shit, too.

Parallel to this, but infinitely related to the storytelling and community-level reaction I find most appealing and lasting about punk rock, is an interest and influence from folk music pioneers. Each of my bandmates has a love for folk or folk-influenced artists, such as Billy Bragg, Woody Guthrie, Pete Seeger, Phil Ochs, the Reivers, Joan Baez, Leadbelly, and the Boss. I also spent a good couple of years organizing and agitating for the IWW with some good friends and comrades in Richmond. This was in between punk bands, the space in one's life I am learning, where a lot of things can get done! We were organizing little syndicalist folk jamborees on streetcorners, porches, bars, backyards, and basement laundromats.

We would sing a lot of International Workers' hymns, songs of struggle and hope from the above-mentioned artists and others, including "Solidarity" by the Angelic Upstarts. That was my jam. This was all accomplished with a bit of creative postering, and word of mouth, culminating in an acoustic set by Red Tom Williams, my IWW delegate, with guest appearances by the entire gathered twenty-five or so. These were rousing good times, and I even managed to get speakers from progressive unions to tell their stories to the Richmond punk and hardcore scene between sets at Hot Water Music and Avail shows. Right around the time Matt Sherwood moved back to Richmond, I lost Red Tom into one of the storms of his life. He fell deep into alcoholism, left his family, and jumped a train for points west. I still try and ask train-riding people I meet on tours about his whereabouts. Much of the writing done during this period has made its way into Strike Anywhere songs, and much more will come from it as well I suspect.

The band's, or at least your, local music roots go back to parties in the late 1980s in two-hundred-year-old barns, with graffiti and extension cords. Even as Strike Anywhere sells nine thousand records here and there, more even, and the studio becomes more comfortable, and the tours becoming

wider and longer, how does one ignore MTV2, sales pitches, open markets, and the press while retaining the original joy?

Garth (our bass player) just stabbed the keyboard with a plastic fork. I guess that is his perspective on how we will retain our original joy. Mine is similar, but wordier, unfortunately—for you!

Our touring in Australia (and the interest that continues in Asia: Taiwan, Japan. Hopefully despite our rejection stamps, we will get to play for those fine folks) all manifested due to word of mouth, e-mail correspondence, and the healthy downloading of our music from our website and others. Only while on tour in Australia did we find partners in Japan (Big Mouth) and Australia (Shock) to license our records to for domestic sale and distribution. So, understandably, we are stoked about this. Kids not having to pay import prices for our Jade Tree records—it's a good thing. I guess we can hope to continue to make plans for touring that make sense to us, honoring our roots and the friends and fans we've made in every city and nation we've been privileged to visit. Beyond that, the other details of your question don't ever cross our paths. I doubt that all of the co-optation and more mainstream options will ever feel right or sensible to us. None of our international adventures, friends we've made, and knowledge we've gained and implemented into our punk rock band's life span would be with us if we were at the "professional" distance that the mainstream structure demands.

The studio, honestly, in some ways feels less comfortable, but when you make the means and the process yours, and work with trusted friends, building a larger community and having experiences, which make it more than music—it helps a great deal.

We enjoy the opportunity to engage with and learn from conscientious, soulful journalists like the many in the independent world we've been in contact with for the birth announcement of *Exit English*. The amount of heart and research that we've seen in the underground punk press is inspiring and shows an awful lot of talent and belief worldwide. We are constantly stunned and appreciative of Jessica's (Hopper) creativity, tenacity, and intellect. We are also fans of her writing and research, the place she holds in the independent media, and the force of will she extends out with her countercultural interests and critiques. She and David Lewis organize and direct our time in relating to writers and for that we are always grateful and infinitely more prepared than if we had to juggle hunting down journalists in the hours after our jobs at home between tours. Those moments where we pop our heads out of punk and appear nervous and restless in the bright wash of larger media instruments are very carefully thought about and executed. It's a case-by-case deal, and we are still learning when to hold 'em and fold 'em, for what ends and what influence our time and minds (and images) are given.

A large march against the War in Iraq in Richmond energized for the band, whose lyrics often deal with underdogs, people of color, and poverty. The war went on unabated, and some of the most striking forms of rebellion were the soldiers who had the nerve to speak out against Bush and the military plans. How does one connect the music, the message, with the people in the middle of the action, the soldiers, including working-class, poor, and minority members?

Interestingly, I have heard from more than a dozen folks who are currently in military service who listen to our music and have solidarity with our songs. A lot of American soldiers in Europe that come out to our shows, and, I'm assuming, also many other punk bands with similar stances and messages. I am always into talking with these folks about their choices and I always learn from them. The military is still an appealing option (from the outside) for Americans who feel like they don't have a clear path to skills training, health care, and survival. Army recruiters have permanent tables at the public high schools in the poorer neighborhoods in and around Richmond. To me, it exemplifies the lack of options and ideas in America for the producing classes. Capitalized upon, of course, by the recruiting industry. I always hear stories from the folks in the service at our shows which run the gamut from a controlled disdainful "biding my time, getting out as soon as possible," to a more heartbreaking "why did I ever do this, I feel trapped and participating in something murderous and damning."

No amount of progressive, middle-class, lefty I-told-you-so's will help or comfort these folks, and I despise people in the activist and punk communities who aggrandize themselves with such cheap superiority and impersonal judgments against those who were corralled into that life. I hope that some part of punk catharsis and empowerment can reach out to the disenfranchised soldiers in the labyrinth of violence and misinformation that we all knew that Bush's War in Iraq would become. Perhaps the same coalition of punk rock millionaires who are right now organizing the Punk Against Bush tour and media assault for the election year could sponsor a "relief compilation" to somehow disseminate among the soldiers who are voicing their objections. The quotes from men and women locked into their tours in Iraq are, as you've suggested, the best and most cutting protest against the propaganda and spin for the war that most Americans get from media. There is nothing more important, in my mind, than for a robust and inclusive Peace movement to stand in solidarity with these brave people.

Certainly, traveling helps "honor and educate" the band, from talking with Muslims in Budapest to finding a forum with Australian zines. What can be done via music; for instance, the artist Francesco Clemente once printed small Hanuman art books featuring writers like Patti Smith and William

Burroughs, hand-stitched in a village in Asia as a means of providing fair wages for product that he could turn around and sell in bookstores. But what can a band do to forge some kind of cultural or even economic link, say, like Clemente did, or a coffee buyer could?

At the moment, we are organizing a cassette release of all of our music complete with new and old artwork, lyrical explanations and translations, and also a benefit record for Chechen refugees, all released through Old School Kids Records in Moscow, Russia. The cassette releases will bring our records into the poorer Eastern European countries, as well as into the interior of Russia and the Caucasus, where cassettes are still the most accessible media for music, and for most the only affordable option. This is the most far-reaching work we've done using our music to connect ideas with action, aesthetics with internationalism. I hope to also continue the pitch down our hemisphere, into Central and South America, with cassette releases, licensing where possible, and lending our music to help people around the world in as local a way as possible. Darren from Jade Tree also donated a few of the Tree's punk/hardcore groups' songs to a Colombian compilation, which features bands from all over South and Central America, and for some reason Poland as well.

Admittedly, these are still very music-related, and still rely on some aspects of counterculture to exist and work for people. I am interested in contributing to the local economies of economically depressed communities and making direct connections with oppressed groups outside of industrial nations. Hopefully, our music will continue to move laterally across languages and cultures, exchanging our ideas and stories with others outside of the standard punk circuits.

You described *Exit English* as a "salvo against the passed down violence of meat eating traditions" and is partly shaped by "the near-forgotten ghosts of slave insurrectors, women's bread riots (Civil War, Richmond), nonconformists and passionate dissenters." Could you provide some clue as to how to navigate the difficult choices of whether to support pro–gay marriage, antiwar Howard Dean, an establishment Democrat who may have a chance to outwit Bush?

Register Green, vote Democrat. Then, once the Democrats are fucking up our country, dancing in the footpaths of a corporate choreography, and whatever else, we should all vote Green, stocking our local governments with Greens, or other progressive Independents, then sockin' it to 'em with a Green presidency. Do I think that the system would allow for such fairness? Hell, no. Not in its current state. Not unless a vital cultural upheaval reforms and popularizes the media, and politics itself changes, starting with massive limits on campaign contributions. And the government starts actually working for the people, not protecting wealth and ensuring obedience by separating people from their inherent power. On some levels of "punk political philosophy" whatever the fuck that is, or is worth, I feel pretty darn suspicious of the quality of American democracy. Our historical roots show a couple [of] cool post-Enlightenment humane ideas coupled with the political ambitions and machinations of wealthy elites. Birthed by corruption, not valor, unfortunately.

But, I also reserve the optimism and integrity to know and fight for defining the problem as a regressive inheritance of social parasitism passed along from power to power. I'm secure enough in my humanity not to fall into the "human nature is to dominate and corrupt itself" weakness. To borrow from Michael Harrington, I believe that we are building ways around the propaganda of the elites, and the ability of the rest of us to gather information and act for the greater good is lurching along on its evolutionary path. We have a big-ass, well-divided nation, with both historical accidents and deliberate manipulations weaving a cloth of separation and distrust between people who have all the common ground in the world—and the entire world to gain by their unity and courage. Getting past these dark, fear-fed times, and exposing Bush for the hollow yet dangerous puppet of wealth and corporate will that he is, could potentially shock the nation into a pendulum swing. How far it can push, and what it can change, will require a lot of unity and coordination on the part of the Left and the punks, and the political working class, and the apathetic middle class, the youth, and everyone in between. As difficult and daunting as this sounds, I believe that it's a rational future to fight for and advocate.

The album title *Exit English* seems very symbolic. Is language itself the culprit, representing modes of power and binary opposition, thus inherently unstable and lacking in real truth? Therefore, is it suspicious? How do we leave language behind?

Right, right, something like language is the equivalent to the dawn of agriculturalism in human development, draining dimension and equity from the realms of thought and interaction, establishing weighted patterns of dominance and myopia, predicting a contamination of history by humanity's complete divorce from seeing itself as part of nature. This also, in some kind of proto-Marxist theory, also equals the beginnings of labor specialization, class systems, poverty, and exploitation of humans by each other. Earth Mother gets stomped by Sky

Gods, the invention of tribalism, trading, war, and time. All of this due to what we call language now but can be perceived more accurately as a web of lowest common denominator evolutionary missteps, pulling our multileveled (New-Agey people would probably use the word "telepathy" here, but I'm not trying to go that route. Hell, we need to be merciful to the few people who are still reading this longest interview ever!) consciousness from a million shades of sense and meaning down into the black and white of our current ways to talk to each other. This is a good theory to chew on and it helps to explain the endless conflict and frustration that we engage in as a species and call our "nature." It's a bit over simplified, but, fuck, I'm driving through Texas at 2:00 a.m., amazed that I can even put this together at the moment. It's the interesting idea that our hunter-gatherer ancestors were connected by a more holistic battery of sensory languages, possibly even living in their bright subconscious in parallel to what we now call the "waking" mind. Perhaps, as evolutionary psychologists have suggested, the invention of time was a viral idea, suffocating and codifying the richer tapestry of consciousness, which our ancestors possessed. Our large brains, and the oft-cited 10 percent of them which we only use, could also have had their growth aborted by this invention of a fractured and imprisoned conscious language.

Many myths and religious texts can be read like this, metaphors ablaze for the fall from grace, expulsion from Eden, Cain and Abel. I read somewhere once that language itself could be viewed as a patriarchal tool, wrenching a balance of senses used in previous communication arts our species had, carving a narrow path of expression to cripple and contain our biggest thoughts. With each successive language introduced, instead of progressing in further detail and achievement, a circumcision of meaning and interruption of creativity occurs by demanding absolutes from ideas larger than words. I definitely can feel this, and I hope that some fierce subtext of this punk rock shit can express revolutionary evolutionary anthropological feminist theory properly, but all of us are too busy rocking out, working ridiculous hours at soul-numbing jobs, surfing websites and chat rooms, and collecting records to really get a proper footing with these ideas—the real tools of our liberation.

But, as a postscript, I would definitely and proudly attach these ideas as one of the proper meanings to the title of our second full-length record.

What does the band see as the most immediate, specific threats right now to the collective underground—musically, politically, and personally?
Musically: marketing to genre, and any isolation of musical styles from the whole. People like to feel that a bunch of bands are inaugurating the new sound, and that that sound is the property of that particular scene or half generation. This, in my view, enfeebles the unity and creative continuity that music teaches

people about culture and the interconnectedness of perspective. It also makes people snobby and ahistorical. We don't have time for that kind of vanity now.

Politically: Much the same as above, but I'd include the recommendation that bands take a wider view and focus on common threads right now. Punk doesn't need to mimic the failures of the Left: picking fights over theory and aesthetics, narcissistic teachers' lounge shit that has consumed, contained, and cancelled too many good ideas. Those that wait for synthesis and practice outside the cloisters of intellectual autoerotic asphyxiation. Punk also needs to acknowledge the importance of all of its branches and eras, its legacies resplendent with contradiction and self-reflection, and now needs to find harmony and admit wholeness. This will give a fuller fabric and make it at once more explainable and nourishing to the post-millennium kids.

Personally: Balance an intellectual life with the obligations and discipline of growing a punk band. Give back as much as possible to those who have supported you. Enjoy the journey always and focus on goals just enough to correct the steerage every now and then. Extend good will out to other groups, even if you aren't in exact agreement on goals or ideals. Remember that it's only gonna boil down to these things in the end: the honesty and depth of the songs, how long they will last in somebody's life, and the openness and good times [they] had at shows. These memories are the things that affect folks the most, and the things that will be carried on the furthest by ourselves and the people who connect.

Credits

About the author

David Ensminger is a Humanities, Folklore, and English Instructor at Lee College in Baytown, TX. As a writer covering music, art, and contemporary issues, he has authored *Visual Vitriol: The Street Art and Subcultures of the Punk and Hardcore Generations*, coauthored *Mojo Hand: The Life and Music of Lightnin' Hopkins*, and contributed to *Popmatters* (where he publishes a monthly column), *Maximumrocknroll*, *Houston*  *Press*, *Art in Print*, *The Journal of Popular Music Studies*, *Artcore*, *Postmodern Culture*, *Trust*, and others. He is also a longtime drummer, including a stint in the Texas Biscuit Bombs with Biscuit of the Big Boys, and a digital archivist of punk and vernacular culture. Find more at http://visualvitriol.wordpress.com.

ABOUT PM PRESS

PM Press was founded at the end of 2007 by a small collection of folks with decades of publishing, media, and organizing experience. PM Press co-conspirators have published and distributed hundreds of books, pamphlets, CDs, and DVDs. Members of PM have founded enduring book fairs, spearheaded victorious tenant organizing campaigns, and worked closely with bookstores, academic conferences, and even rock bands to deliver political and challenging ideas to all walks of life. We're old enough to know what we're doing and young enough to know what's at stake.

We seek to create radical and stimulating fiction and non-fiction books, pamphlets, T-shirts, visual and audio materials to entertain, educate and inspire you. We aim to distribute these through every available channel with every available technology — whether that means you are seeing anarchist classics at our bookfair stalls; reading our latest vegan cookbook at the café; downloading geeky fiction e-books; or digging new music and timely videos from our website.

PM Press is always on the lookout for talented and skilled volunteers, artists, activists and writers to work with. If you have a great idea for a project or can contribute in some way, please get in touch.

PM Press, PO Box 23912, Oakland, CA 94623, www.pmpress.org

FRIENDS OF PM PRESS

These are indisputably momentous times — the financial system is melting down globally and the Empire is stumbling. Now more than ever there is a vital need for radical ideas.

Friends of PM allows you to directly help impact, amplify, and revitalize the discourse and actions of radical writers, filmmakers, and artists. It provides us with a stable foundation from which we can build upon our early successes and provides a much-needed subsidy for the materials that can't necessarily pay their own way. You can help make that happen — and receive every new title automatically delivered to your door once a month — by joining as a Friend of PM Press. And, we'll throw in a free T-shirt when you sign up.

Here are your options:

• **$25 a month** Get all books and pamphlets plus 50% discount on all webstore purchases

• **$25 a month** Get all CDs and DVDs plus 50% discount on all webstore purchases

• **$40 a month** Get all PM Press releases plus 50% discount on all webstore purchases

• **$100 a month Superstar** — Everything plus PM merchandise, free downloads, and 50% discount on all webstore purchases

For those who can't afford $25 or more a month, we're introducing Sustainer Rates at $15, $10 and $5. Sustainers get a free PM Press T-shirt and a 50% discount on all purchases from our website.

Your Visa or Mastercard will be billed once a month, until you tell us to stop. Or until our efforts succeed in bringing the revolution around. Or the financial meltdown of Capital makes plastic redundant. Whichever comes first.

Spray Paint the Walls:
The Story of Black Flag

Stevie Chick

ISBN: 978-1-60486-418-2
$19.95   432 Pages

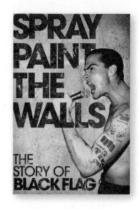

Black Flag were the pioneers of American Hardcore, and this is their blood-spattered story. Formed in Hermosa Beach, California in 1978, for eight brutal years they made and played brilliant, ugly, no-holds-barred music on a self-appointed touring circuit of America's clubs, squats, and community halls. *Spray Paint the Walls* tells Black Flag's story from the inside, drawing on exclusive interviews with the group's members, their contemporaries, and the bands they inspired. Featuring over 30 photos of the band from Glen E. Friedman, Edward Colver, and others.

"Neither Greg Ginn nor Henry Rollins sat for interviews but their voices are included from earlier interviews, and more importantly Chuck Dukowski spoke to Chick—a first I believe. The story, laid out from the band's earliest practices in 1976 to its end ten years later, makes a far more dramatic book than the usual shelf-fillers with their stretch to make the empty stories of various chart-toppers sound exciting and crucial and against the odds."
— Joe Carducci, formerly of SST Records

Barred for Life: How Black Flag's Iconic Logo became Punk Rock's Secret Handshake

Stewart Dean Ebersole with additional photographs by Jared Castaldi

ISBN: 978-1-60486-394-9
$24.95   328 Pages

"The Bars represent me finding my people. We were like a tribe. Together we are strong whereas before we felt weak and ostracized."

Barred for Life is a photo documentary cataloging the legacy of Punk Rock pioneers Black Flag, through stories, interviews, and photographs of diehard fans who wear their iconic logo, The Bars, conspicuously tattooed upon their skin. Author Stewart Ebersole provides a personal narrative describing what made the existence of Punk Rock such an important facet of his and many other people's lives, and the role that Black Flag's actions and music played in soundtracking the ups and downs of living as cultural outsiders.

"The Bars say 'I'm not one of them,' and it also lets the right people know that I am one of them."

"Barred for Life is a book with heart. It also avoids the trap that similar single-subject photo books fall into. There's actually a narrative arc, thanks to a series of interviews with former band members interspersed throughout, telling the story of the band and its fans."
— BlackBook

The Story of Crass

George Berger

ISBN: 978-1-60486-037-5
$20.00   304 pages

Crass was the anarcho-punk face of a revolutionary
movement founded by radical thinkers and artists Penny
Rimbaud, Gee Vaucher, and Steve Ignorant. When punk ruled
the waves, Crass waived the rules and took it further, putting
out their own records, films, and magazines and setting up
a series of situationist pranks that were dutifully covered by
the world's press. Not just another iconoclastic band, Crass
was a musical, social, and political phenomenon. Commune
dwellers who were rarely photographed and remained contemptuous of conventional
pop stardom, their members explored and finally exhausted the possibilities of punk-led
anarchy. They have at last collaborated on telling the whole Crass story, giving access to
many never-before-seen photos and interviews.

*"Lucid in recounting their dealings with freaks, coppers, and punks, the band's voices
predominate, and that's for the best."*
— *The Guardian UK*

*"Thoroughly researched… chockful of fascinating revelations… it is, surprisingly, the first real
history of the pioneers of anarcho-punk."*
— *Classic Rock*

Sober Living for the Revolution: Hardcore Punk, Straight Edge, and Radical Politics

Edited by Gabriel Kuhn

ISBN: 978-1-60486-051-1
$22.95 304 pages

Straight edge has persisted as a drug-free, hardcore punk
subculture for 25 years. Its political legacy, however, remains
ambiguous—often associated with self-righteous macho
posturing and conservative puritanism. While certain
elements of straight edge culture feed into such perceptions,
the movement's political history is far more complex. Since straight edge's origins in
Washington, D.C. in the early 1980s, it has been linked to radical thought and action by
countless individuals, bands, and entire scenes worldwide. *Sober Living for the Revolution*
traces this history. It includes contributions—in the form of in-depth interviews, essays,
and manifestos—by numerous artists and activists connected to straight edge, from Ian
MacKaye (Minor Threat/Fugazi) and Mark Andersen (Dance of Days/Positive Force
DC) to Dennis Lyxzén (Refused/The (International) Noise Conspiracy) and Andy Hurley
(Racetraitor/Fall Out Boy), from bands such as ManLiftingBanner and Point of No Return
to feminist and queer initiatives, from radical collectives like CrimethInc. and Alpine
Anarchist Productions to the Emancypunx project and many others dedicated as much to
sober living as to the fight for a better world.